The Recompete Guide

© 2013 Rebidding Solutions Ltd.

All rights reserved. No part of this book may be reproduced or transmitted in any form or by any means, electronic, mechanical, photocopying, recording, scanning or otherwise, without prior written permission of the author or the publisher.

Nigel Thacker

Rebidding Solutions Ltd.
www.rebidding.co.uk

Published by:
CAI/SISCo
6 West Third Street
Frederick, Maryland 21701 USA
www.caisisco.com

Limit of Liability: While the author and the publisher have used their best efforts in preparing this book, they make no representations or warranties with respect to the accuracy or completeness of the contents of this book. Neither the author nor the publisher shall have any liability to any person or entity with respect to any loss or damage caused or alleged to be caused directly or indirectly by the instructions contained in this book.

First Edition: August 2013

ISBN 978-0-9893708-2-0

Printed in the United States of America.

Design & Production: Avenue Design, Inc.
Editing: Susan Shealer
Indexing: Donna Drialo

The Recompete Guide
60 Ideas for Recompete Success

Nigel Thacker

The **Roadmap To BD Success** Series

A Unified Guide To Government Business Development
by CAI/SISCo and its Independent Authors

Table of Contents

	Foreword ix	
	About This Book ix	
	About The Author ix	
	About Rebidding Solutions Ltd ix	
	About the Roadmap To BD Success Series x	
	About CAI/SISCo xii	
SECTION I	**Introduction and Idea 1: The Contract Lifecycle** 1	
	Actions Based on Experience of What Works 2	
	How Is the Guide Organized? 2	
	Using the Guide 4	
Idea 1:	**The Contract Lifecycle** 4	
	Why Look at Your Contract in Terms of a Lifecycle? 5	
	Review Your Own Contract Lifecycle 8	
	Write Down Your Own Contract Lifecycle and Plan for What You Will Do at Each Stage 10	
SECTION II	**Mobilize, Day One, and Transform** 11	
	Why Is This Part of the Contract Lifecycle Important? 12	
Idea 2:	**Capture Information on Why You Won the Contract** 13	
	Questions to Ask 15	
	Collate Information from Your Review 16	
	Use at the Recompete 17	
	Customer Flexibility 17	
	Manage and Maintain Your Profitability 18	
Idea 3:	**The Promises Register** 19	
	What Is a Promises Register? 19	
	Key Steps to Creating a Promises Register 20	
	Using the Promises Register 21	

i

	Early Fine Tuning	21
	Health Warning!	22
	Ongoing Proof of Delivery	22
	Later in the Contract	22
	At the Recompete	22
Idea 4:	**Capture and Record Previous Performance**	**23**
	Finding Information on Previous Performance	24
	Relating Previous Performance to Present (and Future) Performance	24
Idea 5:	**Set Up a Recompete File**	**26**
	What to Keep in the Recompete File	27
	Keeping the Recompete File Up to Date	27
	Other Useful Libraries of Recompete Information	28
Idea 6:	**Day One Impact Measures**	**29**
	Examples of Day One Impact Measures	30
	What's Different from Normal Communication Done on Any New Contract?	30
	Key Steps for Day One Impact Measures	31
SECTION III	**Target Operating Model**	**33**
Idea 7:	**Conduct a Target Operating Model Review**	**34**
	What Is the Target Operating Model (TOM) Review?	34
	Why Is This Important for the Recompete?	35
	When Should the TOM Review Be Run?	35
	Who Should Be Involved?	35
	What Is Involved?	35
	Key Steps in the TOM Review	36
	How Long Should the TOM Review Take?	38
	Involving the Customer	39
	Final Sign-Off of the Target Operating Model	39
SECTION IV	**Stabilize**	**41**
	What Is the Stabilize Stage?	41
Idea 8:	**Create a Contract Plan**	**42**
	What Does a Contract Plan Look Like?	45
	Objections and Limits to Your Contract Plan	46
	Key Steps to Creating Your Contract Plan	50
Idea 9:	**Help the Customer Manage Risk**	**58**
	Understanding the Customer's Risks	59

	Key Steps for Risk Management	60
	Caveats	61
	Managing Your Own Risks	61
	The RAID Register	62
	Overview of Risks, Assumptions, Issues, and Dependencies	62
	Summary	65
Idea 10:	**Align to the Customer**	**66**
SECTION V	**Improve**	**69**
	What Is the Improve Stage?	69
	Measuring Performance	71
	Introduction to Measuring Performance	71
	Why Is Performance Measurement Important?	71
	Types of Performance Measurement	72
	Development of Contract Measurement	73
	Different Customer Stakeholders Have Different Priorities	74
Idea 11:	**Measure the Things that Make a Real Difference to the Customer**	**74**
	Finally	83
Idea 12:	**Balance Consistent Measurement with New, Relevant Measures**	**83**
Idea 13:	**Benchmark Your Measures**	**85**
Idea 14:	**Measure End User Satisfaction**	**88**
	Added Value, Continuous Improvement, and Innovation	97
	Common Themes	98
	Targeting	99
	Putting Targeting into Action	104
Idea 15:	**Add Value for the Customer**	**105**
	Bottom Up Added Value	106
	Ad Hoc Added Value	107
	Reviewing the Contract for Value to the Customer	108
	Adding Value Through Your Company or Contract Capabilities	111
	More Points on Added Value	112
Idea 16:	**Deliver Continuous Improvement**	**113**
	Focus on Areas that Are Important to Your Customer	114
	Link Your Performance Measurement Regime to Your Continuous Improvement Effort	114
	Clearly Set Out Your Continuous Improvement Process	115
	Link Your Improvements to Your Process	115

Idea 17: Innovate **116**
    Searching for Innovations 119
    Testing and Implementing Innovations. 119

Idea 18: Publish an Annual Review of the Contract **120**
    What to Put Into Your Annual Review. 122
    Quality of the Document 123
    Involving the Customer. 123
    Other Stakeholders 123

Idea 19: Keep Your Contract Up to Date **124**
    Supply Side Changes. 126
    Customer Changes 126
    Market or Social Changes. 126
    Actions to Keep Your Contract Up to Date 128

Idea 20: Resolve Any Problems Quickly and Completely **132**

Idea 21: Know and Use All Available Contract Change Routes **134**
    Understand, Use, or Create Mechanisms for Change 136
    Approach to Formalizing Changes 136
    Collate and Keep All Changes on File 137
    Link Your Changes to Your Process 137

Idea 22: Constantly Build Customer Relationships and Trust **138**
    Build a Wide Set of Relationships 140
    Set Up Regular Meetings 142
    Keep a Record of Who's Who and Your Interactions with Them 142
    Everyone on Your Contract Has Some Relationships
        with Customer Contacts. 143
    Earn Trust. 144

SECTION VI   Mid Term Review **145**

Idea 23: Conduct a Mid Term Review **145**
    When Should the Review Take Place? 147
    Bring in an External Team to Conduct the Review 147
    The Size and Extent of the Review Depends on the
        Size and Complexity of the Contract 148
    Content of the Review 148
    Output of the Review 150
    Presenting the Review. 151
    Follow Up 152

Table of Contents

SECTION VII **Prepare for the Recompete** 153
    What is the Prepare for the Recompete Stage? 153

Idea 24: **Start Your Recompete Preparations Early** 155
    Understand Your Customer's Procurement Timetable 156

Idea 25: **Proactively Manage Contract Extensions** 160
    Don't Delay Your Recompete Preparations on the
        Expectation of an Extension 161
    Use Extensions to Put in Place Changes Which
        Will Help Your Recompete 161
    A Note on Price 162

Idea 26: **Get the Right Recompete Team in Place** 163
    Include People from the Contract Team 165
    Bring in Team Members from Outside the Contract 166
    Put the Right Recompete Team Leader in Place 166
    Manage the Tensions within the Recompete Team
        and with the Contract Team 166

Idea 27: **Prepare the Contract Team** 168
    Keep Contract Teams Up to Date with Recompetes in Your Company ... 169

Idea 28: **Prepare and Implement a Recompete Strategy** 170
    What Does the Recompete Strategy Encompass? 171
    What Actions Should Be Included in the Recompete Strategy? 172

Idea 29: **Run a Contract Review** 173
    Sources of Information 179
    Collating and Using the Information Gathered
        from the Contract Review 179

Idea 30: **Run a Recompete Preparation Workshop** 180
    How Long Should the Review Take? 181
    Suggested Agenda 182
    Output from the Workshop and Next Actions 191

Idea 31: **Reinvigorate Your Customer Relationships** 192

Idea 32: **Understand Stakeholder Views of Your Contract and Your Company** 195
    What Do Your Key Stakeholders Really Think of You? 195

Idea 33: **Understand the Customer's Next Contract** 197

Idea 34: **Analyze How Vulnerable Your Contract Is** 205
    Wider Use of Contract Vulnerability Assessments 208

Idea 35: Understand Who Will Be Involved in the Recompete 209
    Discovering the Process and Who Will Be Involved 211
    Draw Up a List of Who Will Be Involved and
        What You Know about Them 212

Idea 36: Resolve Existing Contract Issues 214
    Specific Delivery Issues 215
    General Approach Issues 215

Idea 37: Price To Win 217
    Understand Your Customer's Budget and Expectations 218
    Review Your Competitor's Pricing Approaches 218
    Understand How Your Customer Will Evaluate
        Price Versus Other Factors 219
    Review Pricing Options 220
    Assess the Customer's Approach to Risk and Reward 222
    Summarizing Your Price To Win 225

Idea 38: Create a Green Field Solution 226
    Create a Solution from the Ground Up 228
    Building Your Green Field Solution 229

Idea 39: Understand Your Competitors 234

Idea 40: Create Your New Solution 238
    Your Customer's Future Strategic Goals and Needs 240
    Changes in the Breadth and Type of Work
        Involved in the New Contract 241
    Incorporating Your Green Field Solution 243
    Take the Competitions' Approaches into Account 244
    End Users Perspective 244
    Innovations and Changes in Process/Best Practice 245
    Learning from the Existing Contract 246
    Ideas for Improvement from Staff 247
    Partners and Supply Chain 247
    Financial and Commercial Options 247
    Transformation and Implementation 248

Idea 41: Influence Your Customer 249
    What Outcomes Might You Aim for? 250
    Align Your Own and Your Customer's Benefits 260
    Talk to the Right Customer Stakeholders 261

Idea 42: Prepare the Contract 261

SECTION VIII   Run the Recompete **265**
                What is the Run the Recompete Stage? 265

Idea 43:   Approach the Recompete as if It Is a New Bid **267**

Idea 44:   Review the Detail of the Published Requirements **270**
                Answer the Specification and Questions Set by the Customer,
                  Not the Specification You Think Is Best from Your Experience 270
                Understand the Changes the Customer
                  Has Made for the Next Contract 271

Idea 45:   Don't Assume the Customer Knows You **273**
                Get an Independent Review 275
                Be Professional in Presentations 275

Idea 46:   Use the Information You Have Gathered **276**
                Using Information about Your Performance on the Existing Contract.... 278
                Formatting Your Information from the Existing Contract 278
                Using Your Information from the Existing Contract to Best Effect 280
                Using Information about Your Customer's Future Needs 281

Idea 47:   Write from the Customer's Perspective **282**
                Win Themes and Discriminators. 282
                Storyboards 283
                Executive Summary. 283
                Reviews 284

Idea 48:   Be Future Oriented **285**

Idea 49:   Admit Mistakes **288**
                Ensure You Have Collected Information about Mistakes 289
                Make Sure Your New Solution Takes Account of Previous Issues 290
                Decide How Best to Use the Lessons You Have
                  Learned in Your Recompete 290
                Use the Lessons You Have Leaned to "Ghost" Your Competition 291

Idea 50:   Discriminators, Differentiators, Benefits, and Win Themes **292**
                Dangers for You as the Incumbent 294
                Use the Blind Proposal Test 300

Idea 51:   Become the Benchmark Bid **302**
                Ghosting or Knockdown of Your Competitors 303
                Planning for Being the Benchmark Bid 304

Idea 52:   Price to Fit the Specification, Not What You Know **306**

Idea 53: Alternative Bids **309**
    An Alternative Bid Is Additional to Your Compliant Bid. 310
    Find Out Whether You Are Able to Put in an Alternative Bid 310
    What Makes a Good Alternative Bid? 310
    Submitting Your Alternative Bid. 312

Idea 54: Use Risk Effectively **314**
    Understand the Variables. 315
    Know Which Risks Are Important to the Customer 317
    Demonstrating You Are the Lowest Risk Option. 318

Idea 55: Staff **320**

Idea 56: Asking Questions. **324**
    Informing the Competition of Costs and Risks
      Not in the Procurement Documentation. 325

Idea 57: Transition Plans. **326**

SECTION IX — Win the Recompete 329

Idea 58: Celebrate **330**

SECTION X — Mobilize and Last Day 331

Idea 59: Take the Transition to Your New Solution Seriously. **331**

Idea 60: Start Planning for the Next Recompete **333**

Index 335

Foreword

About This Book

This volume of the **Roadmap To BD Success** series, *The Recompete Guide*, focuses on the ideas and approaches needed to retain existing contracts. From the start of the contract through to final presentation, this book is full of tools, processes, and techniques that will help incumbents prepare for and deliver a successful recompete.

About The Author

Nigel Thacker has 18 years experience reviewing, running, and winning recompetes, as well as developing business-wide retention improvement processes and training contract and recompete teams in 13 countries. He has worked as a senior business development leader and Managing Director in some of the largest international outsourcing businesses, as well as smaller specialist contractors. Nigel is now Managing Director of Rebidding Solutions Ltd.

About Rebidding Solutions Ltd

Rebidding Solutions Ltd., based in the UK but operating through partners and associates in a range of other countries, focuses on helping incumbents win their recompetes and improve contract retention rates. The company delivers consultancy, advice, and training to help organizations deliver better customer experiences, better recompetes, and develop best practice retention processes (www.rebidding.co.uk). They also run the Rebid Centre, an online subscription-based repository of all the advice, guidance, tools, processes, and techniques needed to help businesses improve their recompete win rates (www.rebidsolutions.co).

Acknowledgements

Thanks to Kathy Carl of Avenue Design, Inc. Her work in turning my words and diagrams into this volume was excellent, as was her ability to adapt British English into American English. Thanks also to Susan Shealer for her valuable editing of the final draft.

About the Roadmap To BD Success Series

Effective government marketplace business development requires mastery and continuous improvement of a complex, multi-disciplinary set of activities. Most firms have developed and documented major pieces of their overall business development approach. It is, however, a rare contractor that makes the investment to unify all of the major pieces into an information-centric suite of modern guides to business development that all but guarantee improved performance in terms of successful capture activities.

Collectively, the **Roadmap To BD Success** series of easy-to-use-and-understand instructional texts was devised and created by CAI/SISCo to provide a modular, **how to** guide to government business development. Each volume provides a comprehensive foundation for one of the major activities that contractors can either use **as is** or adapt to their particular needs and circumstances. The overarching mantra of the series is "Spend Less, Do More, and Win More." The series supports this ideal by simplifying and standardizing capture processes across multiple pursuits to help reduce recurring and non-recurring expenses.

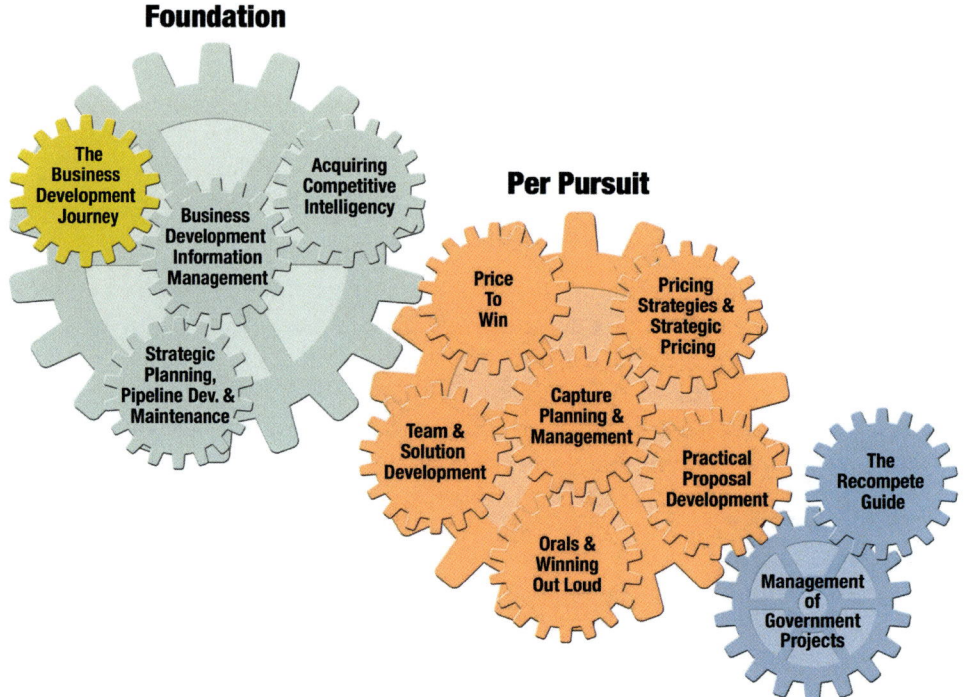

Foreword

The graphic on the previous page presents the scope of the series. Following is a high-level, volume-by-volume overview of the series that describes the relationships between and among the interlocking members of the constituent elements of the **Roadmap To BD Success**. Books in the series have each been developed by professionals for professionals. They are designed to convey time-tested processes, common sense strategies, and practical, yet effective implementation approaches to educate and reinforce best practices in a specific and an overall sense.

The books in this series will have special interest to at least these groups of readers:

1. Individuals and companies already doing a significant amount of government business and wishing to improve performance through knowledge of industry best practices;

2. Government employees, such as program managers, contracting officers, and subject matter experts wishing to know what is happening on the contractors' side—the *other* side of the fence.

3. Students of public administration wishing to know more about best practices related to government business development.

The additional volumes presently being produced are described below.

- *The Business Development Journey*, the keystone book of the series, provides a top-down view of the soup-to-nuts essentials of business development. It is an overview of the entire business development process and describes the relationships inherent in the texts that make up the volumes in the series.

- *Business Development Information Management* is devoted to the benefits of implementing a unified information management repository as the underpinning of all business development activity. This provides essential pre-positioned business development information of all sorts, from proposal boilerplate to competitor intelligence to pursuit post-mortems, building with every capture and avoiding having to pay more than once (in time and money) to learn the same information.

- *Acquiring Competitive Intelligence* examines the tools and techniques that can feed a successful capture activity with information to help capture teams develop winning solutions that can be bid at winning prices.

- *Strategic Planning, Pipeline Development and Maintenance* deals with the development and maintenance of an overarching Strategic Plan and the dynamics of the pipeline of business opportunities (task orders, contracts, etc.) that need to be pursued. This will cameo the Prologue approach to Strategic Planning and Pipeline Development.

- *Capture Planning and Management* deals with organizing and managing around the essential elements of capture by concentrating on the Four Cs: customer, competition, capabilities, and cost.

- *Price To Win* provides a practical guide to developing situational awareness and bid price targets based upon a detailed study of your competition, the opportunity at hand, and the price that the Home Team needs to come up with to prevail overall.

- *Winning Out Loud* shows you how to win your next oral proposal competition, and how to win 90 of your next 100. When a procurement calls for orals, that is where you will win or lose, and the guidance in this book will make you a winner.

- *Team and Solution Development* explains how the target prices developed by PTW should be used to develop teams and solutions that can meet and beat competitors.

- *Pricing Strategies and Strategic Pricing* explains how the target price-driven teams and solutions can be—through an effective and thoughtful pricing strategy—developed into a winning yet profitable bid price.

- *Practical Proposal Development* is a practical guide to the development of a proposal that demonstrates acceptability in terms of understanding, solution, team, and management approach within an affordable price.

About CAI/SISCo

CAI/SISCo is a very experienced business development support services and training firm operating primarily in national, international, and local government marketplaces. Our firm does not do or compete for government work ourselves—everything is done on an opportunity-exclusive basis to help clients capture major complex competitive opportunities. Since 1975, we have provided capture support to a veritable who's who of major corporations, covering well over 1,500 complex government programs with an aggregate value of more than $1 trillion. The majority of our work is derived from Price To Win (PTW) and strategic pricing engagements. As we see it, our job is to provide *outside insights* for client business developers charged with retaining or capturing major government contracts and other business opportunities.

Introduction and Idea 1: The Contract Lifecycle

Section 1

The markets that require companies to bid to government or private sector clients to provide services or products have grown hugely over the past two to three decades. With this growth has come a set of best practices, processes, and approaches based on the successes (and failures) of companies and contracts in the sector. This body of learning continues to grow, but at present it is significantly more advanced and established in some areas than others. Bidding for new business is establishing itself as a recognized discipline and there are a range of books, training courses, and qualifications devoted to the sales, capture, and bidding disciplines for winning new contracts. However there is relatively little information available on how to retain these contracts once they have been won.

You may find a few articles if you search. A small number of companies have developed their own in-house processes; and a number of business development, capture, and bid professionals have gained experience (and some scars) from running a number of recompetes amongst the new contracts they have also won. But the advice you will find on recompetes tends towards a few well-founded though general principles. Advice such as:

"Start the recompete from Day One of the contract."

"Begin your recompete preparations early."

"Take the recompete seriously—don't assume you will win."

All of this is extremely good advice and we repeat it in this guide. But how do you put this advice into action?

What processes, actions, and management systems should you be putting in place from Day One of your contract to help you win your recompete?

How early should you start preparing for your recompete—and what exactly are the preparations you should take?

What does taking the recompete seriously entail?

What else should you do to improve your chances of winning your recompete, whether you are responsible for a portfolio of contracts, managing a contract, a customer account manager, part of a recompete team, or a bid writer working on a recompete?

Where are the specific details, tools, and processes for recompeting compared to the plethora you will find when looking for ways to improve your ability to win a new bid?

This guide gives you those specifics—real relevant and proven actions you can take from Day One of the contract (in fact, from before Day One) which have been shown to make a positive difference in improving your chances of winning your recompete.

Actions Based on Experience of What Works

The Recompete Guide is based on our experience over the last 20 years of being involved in recompeting for some of the largest international outsourcing companies, small businesses, and businesses in between. We have written recompetes, managed recompetes, run companies with portfolios of contracts requiring recompeting, reviewed recompetes (won and lost), set up recompete processes, and trained teams in 13 countries on how to run recompetes. We have recompeted contracts for products, and for services, across a wide range of sectors for customers ranging from national governments and international businesses to individual schools. We have discussed recompetes with dozens of business developers, project leaders, and contract managers to gather their experiences and understand the processes and best practices they use. We have talked to customers about recompetes, read most of the articles written on recompeting, and have run our own surveys of what procurement professionals' experiences are with incumbents in their recompetes.

This guide and the ideas within it are the result. Each of the ideas we have either used ourselves or adapted from the actions others have found to work.

How Is the Guide Organized?

We have broken the guide down into 60 *Ideas*. They range from processes you can put in place for the life of your contract to approaches to a particular subject or event during the recompete. Some ideas we describe in a couple of pages, others take up several pages and include several steps to put them into action.

You can use each idea individually, or you can take any number of them together to create a set of approaches and actions that form a process for your business to help improve your recompete win rate, depending on which you feel best meet your needs or circumstances or which have a particular resonance with where you are now in your recompete. No doubt you will have a number of processes in your business already, whether they are processes for managing contracts, for implementing new contracts, or for bidding contracts. Our goal is for you to adapt the ideas in the guide to fit with these existing processes and actions; to add to them or perhaps modify them to better focus on the needs of the recompete. The choice is yours, depending on your own circumstances. What we can say with confidence is that even if you only use one of the ideas, it will help you with your recompete. And the more ideas you use, the more your chances of winning your recompete will increase.

For each idea, we have included a short summary of what the idea is and why it will help you win your recompete, as well as a list of steps to put it into action. Where appropriate, we have included examples to illustrate how the idea can and has been used. These are all real life examples, although we have anonymized them and in some cases changed some of the details to retain confidentiality. Many of the ideas also include tables or lists for you to use to fill in your own contract data or information. All of them can easily be copied into a spreadsheet or onto a whiteboard for you to test and complete as part of putting the idea into action.

To give some order to how we have organized the ideas, we have placed them into a *Contract Lifecycle*, which ranges from the day you win your bid through your contract and recompete to (having won your recompete) the start of your new contract. This lifecycle, which we introduce in the next few pages, includes a set of periods within your contract and a number of *events*—such as Day One of the contract. The ideas are placed within each stage of the lifecycle, both to give order and to give you a sense of the best time to use or introduce them. Again, this order is flexible depending on your own circumstances. You can use the lifecycle approach simply as a set of section headings, but it is an idea in itself to help you organize your own contract and what you focus on at different times during the life of the contract (not just with regard to your recompete).

Also spread throughout the guide are two sets of quotes. Some are quotes from contract and proposal experts on their experiences and ideas about the key actions to take to improve your recompete chances. Most are quotes from procurement professionals from around the world who responded to a survey we ran in 2012-2013 on their experiences and insights into incumbents at recompete. Some of these we have placed next to ideas that refer to the subject of the quote, but most are spread randomly throughout the guide. Many of these quotes only cover a single thought of one procurement professional as to what is important for incumbents to do, or the issues they have seen with incumbent recompetes (indeed, some of the quotes are only one word). Taken individually, some may seem at odds with the subject of the idea where they are placed. But as you read through the guide and read more of the quotes, we hope you will see a clear picture emerging of the issues, hopes, expectations, and sometimes frustrations regarding incumbents that this important group within our customer organizations feel and experience.

Using the Guide

We have designed the guide to be of use to anyone involved in running a contract that will be recompeted, or to anyone who is involved directly in a recompete.

You can use the guide in a number of ways, depending on your own role and focus and where you are with your recompete. You don't have to start at Idea 1 and work your way through in sequence to Idea 60 to be able to understand each idea.

You might want to start by reading through the contents list and picking any of the ideas that pique your interest. Each of the ideas is quite self-contained, and where any other ideas are relevant, we refer you to the idea number to help guide you to relevant information. Alternatively, you can quite quickly run through the ideas just by reading the summaries and quotes to get a flavor and then dig into any of the ideas that have particular relevance to where you are today.

However, to give you some guidance: if you are running a contract or are an account manager with one or more contracts presently in operation, you will gain most from starting at the beginning of the contract lifecycle. You can use the guide through the whole of your contract to get ideas for improving your contract's relevance to your customer and readiness for the recompete. The earlier you are in your own contract's lifecycle, the more this will be of use, as you will have longer to put the ideas into practice and gain from them. You can come back to the workbook at different times to pick out new ideas that fit where you are now or help with particular issues you are facing. But even if you are approaching your recompete, you will still gain a lot from working through the sections (even if you just read the idea summaries)—identifying things that you can do now and using the steps, tables, and lists within the ideas to identify actions you can still take on the contract, or information you can collect to help with the recompete.

If you are a bidder, capture manager, or business developer, or involved in a recompete team, you can use the earlier sections as a review tool for preparing for the recompete and collating information on the contract. You will gain more immediate help from the sections "Preparing for the Recompete" and "Running the Recompete" to give you ideas and approaches for your effort.

Whatever your role and wherever you start using the guide, we are sure you will find at least one idea to help you succeed in your recompete.

Idea 1: The Contract Lifecycle

Every contract has a lifecycle. At its most basic, it can be win, run, recompete (hopefully repeated). Looking at your contract in the context of its whole lifespan gives you the context to plan ahead, and knowing where you are in that lifecycle can give you a benchmark of what you should be focusing on now.

This Contract Lifecycle can form the basis of your contract's lifespan, whether it runs a few months through to a couple of decades.

Figure I.1   The Lifespan of the Contract Lifecycle

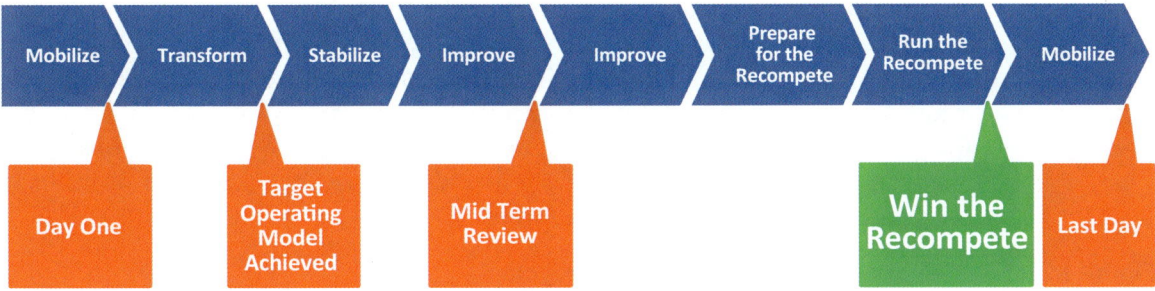

Why Look at Your Contract in Terms of a Lifecycle?

Running a contract is hard work. There are performance levels to meet, staff to manage, customer managers to keep on side, costs to manage and reduce, profit margins to maintain and most likely grow over the period. There will be pressures from your own company, from the customer, their staff and end users, Health and Safety inspections, environmental targets, other targets. There are reports to produce, write, and distribute; management and review meetings to attend, and a hundred other things that will keep you busy. There will be problems large or small that you will face every day and will need your attention.

With all these daily pressures and monthly targets, it is easy to become fully absorbed with the day-to-day and not spend time and effort thinking about and putting in place actions that address the longer term. Then after one, two, or five years, you look back and wonder what has changed and wish you had started projects that addressed underlying issues years ago, even though they involved an investment in effort or resources that you thought, at the time, you couldn't afford.

At the same time, the world and your customer are not standing still. Market conditions are changing, new technology is being introduced, new competitors with new offerings are entering the market, and new contracting techniques are being used. Your customer may also be changing; changing their strategy or ambitions, growing, having changes of management and direction, or facing new challenges. There are few things in a marketplace that don't change over a period of, say, five years.

If your contract hasn't changed just as significantly over that period and kept in line with the customer's needs and market best practice, then you could be very out of date come the recompete. Your customer could be looking for drastic change—and looking for a contractor that can deliver that change through new, innovative, and flexible approaches. If you are still delivering (even delivering well) a contract that was set in stone three, five, or perhaps 10 years ago and it has not kept up, why should they choose you again?

Seeing your contract in terms of a lifecycle helps you think ahead, put in place improvements, plan for longer-term goals—particularly the recompete—and focus on the key areas that are of importance at different points or periods in that lifecycle. Focusing on delivering improvement throughout the contract also means that you will be up to date when the recompete comes around; you will have a wealth of good information, data, and stories to show the improvements made in the recompete; and the customer should see you as the sort of business that they want to deal with in the future.

Figure I.2   The Stages of the Contract Lifecycle

Stage of Lifecycle	What Happens	Importance for the Recompete
Mobilize	This is the period from award to contract start. During this period, you will be preparing all the areas you require to be able to deliver the contract on Day One.	A good mobilization shows you can do the same next time. Being able to remind the customer in the recompete of how well you delivered this phase will add value and credence.
Day One	The first day of the contract. First impressions count. What key changes do you want to make that show different stakeholders you are better than the previous regime or things have changed? Some companies plan this day to include a range of impact measures that are low cost, high impact on stakeholders. This might mean repainting a grungy staff canteen the night before the first day, sending a new information pack to end users with information on new features of the service being provided, or a range of other initiatives that fit with your new contract and give stakeholders an immediate positive impression.	Getting stakeholders on your side from the start gives you the best possible start. Good impact measures are remembered and can also be used in the recompete—and give credence to the impact measures you put into your recompete document.
Transform	This is the period after the start of the contract when you are making all of the changes you couldn't before you had control of staff, were delivering the service, etc. You will have put in your bid a way of working, a cost model, and delivery structure. You need to have a clear plan to put this in place over a set period in the first weeks or months of the contract.	This period is more visible to the customer than mobilization. Delivering a competent transformation not only puts your contract into the position required to deliver ongoing, it shows the customer your ability to deliver. Being able to remind the customer of how effectively and efficiently you transformed the contract will help convince them of your ability to deliver the transformation you propose in your recompete.

Section I Introduction and Idea 1: The Contract Lifecycle

Stage of Lifecycle	What Happens	Importance for the Recompete
Target Operating Model	This is the point at which all your transformation efforts are complete. You should mark this point with a review to make sure everything is in place, that your solution has been enacted, that costs are what you forecast, and that you are delivering what you expected and promised the customer. There should be an internal sign-off that this is the case and, ideally, a similar sign-off from the customer.	A proper review and sign-off that you have delivered all the changes you promised sets you on the right path for the rest of the contract. The customer is content that you have delivered and are now moving forward. At the same time, setting this date and sign-off means your planned changes are all completed. Without this check, some might be missed and others drag on for long periods and may never be achieved. A proper review sets a benchmark for the contract profitability, costs, etc., and ensures future expectations internally are managed. Again, being able to show this to the customer in the recompete gives credence to your solution and contract processes next time around.
Stabilize	A relatively short period when you make sure all the new processes, management, etc., are settled in; that management and customer meetings and reports are running properly and normalized, staff are delivering effectively, and all the core policies and processes are in place and delivering.	To date, everything has been about change and setting up the contract. There may have been a transformation team working with the contract team. This period settles in the completed changes and makes sure the contract and contract team are working well together, small glitches are being ironed out, and everything is running smoothly.
Improve	You should move into this phase as quickly as you reasonably can and it should be running for the rest of the contract. Here, you are working internally and with the customer to deliver improved performance; find new ways of delivering the product or service, cut costs, improve end user satisfaction, etc.	This is the key stage. You move from stability to a proactive program designed to deliver improvement across the contract. Many contracts never enter this stage—remaining at Stabilize until the recompete. This is the stage where you make the difference between being out of date at the recompete—with your customer only seeing you as adequate—or being totally up to date with the latest needs of the customer and where they see you as the people they absolutely must have for the next contract period.
Mid Term Review	At least once during the contract, conduct a bottom up review using external reviewers (at least external to the contract—potentially using people from elsewhere in the business). This will review where you are in your improvement plan and delivery, what has changed in the market and customer, and how you need to change and improve for the rest of the contract to be in the best possible position for the recompete.	An in-depth review will help make sure the contract is on track and give valuable objective input from outside the contract team. The Mid Term Review will help reset direction, pace, and targets for the rest of the contract. This will help you be in the best possible position come recompete.
Improve	Continuation of the previous improvement period—but potentially with changes based on the Mid Term Review.	This period continues the previous improvement process—but with any changes or additions identified during the Mid Term Review to ensure the customer's changing needs are being fully met.

Stage of Lifecycle	What Happens	Importance for the Recompete
Prepare for the Recompete	This is the period when you start proper preparations for your recompete—looking at new solutions based on what your relationship with the customer tells you they are looking for in the next period, influencing what is in the recompete, bringing in recompete resources from outside the contract, creating and enacting a recompete strategy and capture plan.	Starting early on recompete preparations is vital. This period should start one year to eighteen months prior to the recompete date. Making sure there is sufficient time to put in place a proper process, influence the recompete, and implement a comprehensive recompete strategy that delivers real challenge to the existing way of delivering and brings innovative solutions—which is how competitors will be attacking the bid.
Run the Recompete	The process where the formal recompete is taking place—for your challengers, the bid; for your customer, the procurement.	While you will be using similar processes to a new bid, you need to add and adapt elements that are unique to your position as incumbent. Adding in the right processes and adapting your existing bid processes in the right way will help you make the most of your incumbent status—but avoid the mistakes some incumbents make at this stage.
Win the Recompete	The point at which the customer confirms you have won for another term.	Time to celebrate. However, you should not assume that the existing contract can continue as it is with no clear change plan and resources to put in place the new solution. Now is the time to start thinking about the next recompete!
Mobilize	The planned changes prior to the end of the contract when you put in place the changes you have promised for the next contract period.	As the incumbent, you are the low risk option in terms of change for the customer. Start the mobilization early to ensure the new solution you have put in is seamless and the contract moves to the new delivery model without a problem—just as you said in your recompete document.
Last Day	Mark this—whether the recompete is won or lost. Thank staff, thank the customer—leave the best possible impression and get ready for the next contract period. If you have lost, leave a final, positive impression with all stakeholders—you'll be back next time around!	If you have lost, ensuring that all stakeholders see you in a positive light on the last day of the contract means you should be well received again. Assuming you win, then this marks the change to the new contract, and thanking all involved for the work to date sets the new contract period off to a good start.

Review Your Own Contract Lifecycle

Every contract is different. Contract lengths vary; the size and complexity of the contract varies; the work you are required to do may be constant or change over time; the length and the extent of implementation at the start of the contract will vary; the flexibility you have to negotiate change with your customer (or for your customer to ask for changes) during the contract will vary; the length of time the customer takes to prepare for and run the recompete will vary: the margins you are making on your contract will vary; your customer's expectations will vary.

How you approach your contract will vary. Look at your own contract and compare the lifecycle we have described with your own situation:

- Do the stages we describe fit with your own contract or do you need to adjust them to meet the specifics of your own situation?

- What are the schedules for each stage and event of your contract?

- Where are you within this lifecycle?

- What is the next stage and when do you estimate it will start?

- Have you undertaken, even in part, the ideas and actions we will describe in the guide for the previous stages of your own contract's lifecycle?

While some of the stages of your contract lifecycle will have been set by the customer (for instance, when the contract starts and ends, when they start the recompete process), others are, to a greater or lesser extent, dependent on your own approach:

- Have you clearly set out when your contract transition ends and the contract reaches a Stabilize stage?

- Does your approach to the contract include an improvement stage and how seriously do you take this? Or is stability, with some minor ad hoc improvements or changes, the norm for most or the entire contract once it is in place?

- Is your approach to improvement based more on increasing your profit, or on improving provision to the customer? These goals are not mutually exclusive—indeed they often sit hand in hand—but the balance of your drive and motivation between the two will soon become clear to your customer.

- What promises did you make to your customer in your bid about the changes and improvements you will make during the contract? How strongly is the customer going to hold you to these? How committed are you to deliver them? Do you know how you can deliver them?

- How good was the bid that won you the contract? Has it set you up to deliver a great service to your customer, with room to maneuver as changes occur, and a healthy profit as reward for your efforts? Or were there errors that left you struggling to meet the promises made and the customer's expectations, and a pricing level or mechanism that prevented you from hitting your projected profit targets, or even caused you to lose money? Do you have a plan to "get well"? How long will this take and does it involve sacrifices to customer satisfaction or service delivery that will have an impact on the contract for a period of time? What actions can you take to resolve this once you have "gotten well" and before you get to the recompete?

Understanding the lifecycle of your particular contract and taking a proactive approach to planning for and dealing with each stage, rather than having a reactive (or even unreactive) default approach will make a huge difference—not just in how your customer reacts to and works with you during the contract to make it a success for all, but also to the chances you have for retaining your contract when the recompete comes around.

Write Down Your Own Contract Lifecycle and Plan for What You Will Do at Each Stage

By writing out your own contract's lifecycle, you will have to ask yourself many of the questions we have introduced. Don't just do this by yourself. Get your key management team members involved (you might even get your customer involved). By working through the exercise with your team, you will help generate a shared understanding of the context you are working in, help the team see beyond the day-to-day work of the contract, and give a sense of what your are aiming to achieve in the longer term. It will also give a context for planning ahead and putting in place a set of ambitions for your contract and the projects and programs you can put in place to achieve them. For more on this, see *Idea 8: Create a Contract Plan*.

The rest of this guide will use the lifecycle as a background to the Ideas covered. It will also look at some of the key steps in the lifecycle such as Day One, Target Operating Model Review, Mid Term Review and Recompete Preparation. If you have identified that your contract has a different lifecycle, you can still apply the subjects we cover to the way your contract is run—just place them into your own contract lifecycle.

What are the primary reasons incumbents lose recompetes?
   "Complacency."

Public Sector, UK

Section II

Mobilize, Day One, and Transform

The parts of the Contract Lifecycle that cover this period are the Mobilize, Day One, and Transform stages:

Figure II.1   The Contract Lifecycle Mobilize, Day One, and Transform Stages

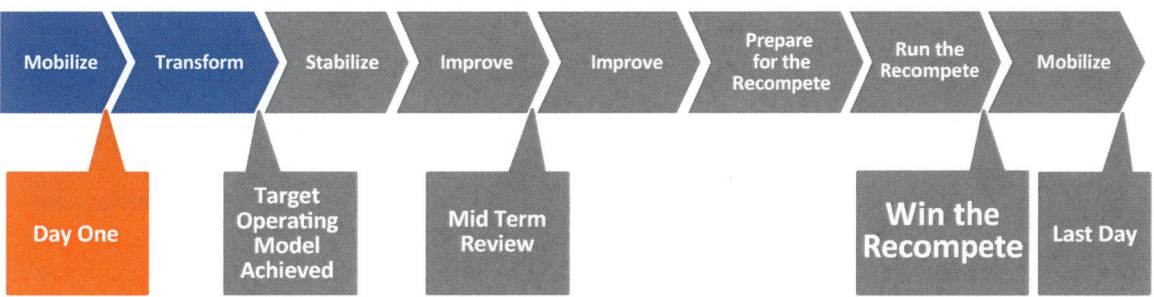

In this stage we will cover:

- Idea 2: Capture Information on Why You Won the Contract
- Idea 3: The Promises Register
- Idea 4: Capture and Record Previous Performance Information
- Idea 5: Set Up a Recompete File
- Idea 6: Day One Impact Measures

The ideas in this section should be put in place as early as possible in the Contract Lifecycle. Obviously Day One measures are fixed, however depending on the level of contact with the customer, the other ideas can be put in place during either the Mobilize or Transform stages.

Why Is This Part of the Contract Lifecycle Important?

Starting the contract well is important because:

- It gives the customer confidence you can deliver through the contract period.

- It builds early credibility with all stakeholders, which helps build relationships.

- Especially on a new contract, capturing information on how the contract or activities which now form the contract were previously run can give you further information on past performance levels that you can show improvement on in your recompete.

- A poor start can mean you are losing money early in the contract, which you may find difficult to make up later.

- Failing to get the new processes, people, or other parts of the contract in place during the Mobilize and Transform period can mean you never get them fully in place because the day-to-day of delivering the contract takes over.

- A good start gives you evidence of your capability in delivering change you can use with your customer in your recompete—but only if you capture it now.

We don't intend to cover all aspects of how to plan and run a mobilization or transformation. As with bidding for new contracts, there are many books, articles, and training courses that cover the project management and change management aspects needed to deliver this complex task.

What we will focus on are those aspects of this period that will be important for your recompete. Even though at this point in the contract the recompete may be the last thing on people's minds, there are a number of tasks that can help you win your recompete. These will be difficult to capture or come back to later in the contract if they are not done now.

Making sure you capture key information at the earliest stage of the contract means you will have it ready to present in a coherent and usable form for the recompete. Otherwise, it may be impossible to pull together when you are starting your recompete preparations in three, four, or five years as so much has changed, time will by then be short and you will have many other things to focus on.

What are the primary reasons incumbents lose recompetes?
   "*Complacency and/or arrogance.*"

Local Government, UK

Idea 2: Capture Information on Why You Won the Contract

> **Idea Summary:**
>
> **What:**
>
> Review why you won the contract. Ask the customer why they chose you—going beyond just the marks you achieved in the evaluation. Look at what the customer particularly liked about your proposal as well as what they may have seen as low value elements.
>
> **Why:**
>
> This will help you understand how the customer saw your bid; the elements of the solution they are particularly keen for you to deliver, and those they may be flexible on or would like delivered differently. Knowing this will help you fit the contract better to your customer's needs and so increase their satisfaction.

Most businesses review why they lost bids in order to learn what mistakes may have been made or lessons learned for future bids. Fewer take the same effort to review why a contract was won. Fewer still take this information and apply it to how they run the subsequent contract.

Understanding why the customer chose you above your competitors will help you understand what their underlying needs and preferences are and help you deliver the contract in a way that meets these. This will help you confirm the customer's decision to appoint you rather than disappoint them by not meeting their (often unspoken) expectations.

A good bid will have been based on:

- Gaining pre bid information on the customer's needs.
- Showing the customer you are the right company to meet these needs prior to the bid.
- Potentially influencing the form of the specification.
- Creating a solution that meets these needs.

- While being compliant to all the rules and specifications put into the procurement by the customer, clearly expressing why the customer should choose you through the use of win themes, differentiators, or discriminators (often interchangeably used terms for things in your solution that meet your customer's needs better than the competition. See *Idea 50* for more on this).

- Having the right price.

However, now that you have won and the formality of restricted communication with the customer during the bid process has ended, you should check again with the customer what it was they were really looking for and why they believe you will deliver this for them. This is best done with a range of contacts within the customer organization. Go beyond the procurement contacts to senior customer contacts (who will be looking at the organization's strategic needs) and others who were involved in the procurement decision, as well as your direct operational contact. Remember, they won't have the same perspective on the contract and might have different views. You may also be able to talk to any consultants who helped the customer with the solicitation process.

Most companies that do some review of won contracts look at any evaluation marks given by the customer to see where they scored better than the competition. This is a good starting point, but only the start.

Of course, price will also be important (extremely so for many customers) and understanding the differences in your price versus your competitors, not only at the bottom line but for different aspects of the contract delivery, will also be useful:

- If your price was significantly lower than the competition, was this because you have a unique advantage—or did you miss something in costing the delivery of the contract? Knowing this early may help you repair the damage to profit that mis-pricing of an activity, or different customer interpretation of the work expected (especially if it is in the signed contract), could cause.

- If your price was about the same level as the competition (and again, check the details if you can around different aspects of the pricing in the bid), what was the differentiator that gave you the edge? And was the decision clear and unanimous across the customer team? If not, are there people in the customer's organization who wanted a different winner and are waiting for you to fail in order to justify their own preference? These will be people whose opinions you may need to focus on and turn around to be positive towards you or they could damage your relationship-building and success through the contract period.

- If your price was higher than the competition, it is likely the customer saw something in your company and bid that really attracted and persuaded them. Or perhaps they saw something in the competition that really put them off. What was this? In any solicitation, especially in the government sector, justifying not choosing the lowest price is a tough process for the procurement team, even in best value solicitations, and a risk to their own credibility (even their jobs). They will most likely have had to go through some degree of challenge from seniors and potentially external auditors to get the decision approved. What was it that they were fighting for? You need to deliver on whatever it was or they will be quickly disillusioned with you—and those who challenged the decision could potentially step in and make life unpleasant. If there was a significant negative against the competition, what was it? Not only will it be good general intelligence for other bids, it will be something to focus on to show where you are different and better. Especially if the competition was the previous incumbent, there may be a range of embedded negative feelings across a range of stakeholders on the contract. What behaviors have these driven and how can you overcome them? For example, is a highly restrictive and penalty-driven performance regime in place because of consistent poor performance by the previous incumbent? Knowing why the regime is in place can help you work with the customer to get it relaxed and the burden of it lifted from you by showing it is no longer needed, though this may take time and consistently good performance on your part.

Questions to Ask

Of course, details will be specific to your contract. But the following is a list you can add further questions to, relevant to your particular contract:

- What are the main issues and challenges the organization is facing and how do you see the contract helping these?

- What are you looking for from the outcomes or outputs of this contract?

- What were the key reasons you chose our organization to deliver the contract?

- What were the relative weaknesses of the competitors' bids/solutions/organizations that meant they were not chosen?

- What were the key aspects of our solution you particularly liked?

- Were there any aspects of the bid/solution you are not sure of?

- Are there any areas we did not cover in the bid/solution that you think are important to delivering your needs successfully?

- Were there any aspects of the competitors' solutions you were particularly attracted to?

- Has anything changed during the bid period that will impact your needs going forward?

- What do you anticipate changing over the contract period that may impact your needs and the contract?

Collate Information from Your Review

Collate the information you have gleaned from the official feedback you have received, the scoring of your bid, and questioning of customer contacts. What have you learned? You should be in a better position to understand what the customer is really looking for in your contract and be able to compare this to your solution. Think about the following:

- What does the customer really want to achieve from this contract?

- What aspects of the solution are going to be most important to the customer?

- What aspects are least important—and can I save my company and the customer money by doing less/not spending as much resource on these aspects (or diverting resources to other more important areas)?

- Is there anything not in our solution that is important to the customer, and would ensure the contract is better run, delivers better, or better meets the customer's real needs?

- What, if anything, needs to change in my solution and how the contract is proposed to be run to better meet the customer's needs?

- What would be the impact on contract profitability if changes are made?

- What mechanism is in place to get these changes made and signed off by the customer?

List the potential changes that would make the biggest positive difference to the customer in how you deliver your contract from the start and look at how you might make them. Making these changes could have a significant impact on how the customer views you and the contract as it develops. Going through the process of asking the customer their needs and responding to what they say shows from the start you are a flexible organization concerned with meeting and delivering the customer's needs. Not only will this help build a positive relationship with the customer from the start, it will mean your contract is better suited to what the customer needs throughout its life—especially if you maintain this flexibility as the customer's needs change over the period of the contract and ensure you keep up with changes in their needs over this time (see the Contract Lifecycle stage: *Improve*).

Use at the Recompete

Keep a record of the questions you asked and the changes you made (in consultation with the customer) to ensure the contract met the customer's needs from the start. At the recompete, you will be able to refer back to how you have kept up with customer needs, been flexible and reacted to changes, and can show the changes you made to ensure the contract was relevant from the start and has continued to be so.

Customer Flexibility

Your ability to make changes this early in the contract will, of course, depend on the flexibility of your customer. Some customers will be highly flexible and wish to make changes early in the contract to reflect their needs. Others may not be so flexible. This could be due to their governance processes, or perhaps they don't yet fully trust you and want to retain the comfort of the signed contract and your bid commitments as a core of deliverables. At this early stage, they might not even want to be entirely open about the bid process—why you won and what they really want. They may even be suspicious that you are attempting to gain benefits for your own business by moving away from your bid commitments if they have had bad experiences in the past.

Even if this is the case, you should still attempt to find out all you can (without becoming a pain to the customer or alienating them at this early stage). The understanding you gain of their needs can influence how you approach the contract in the early stages, even if you are not in a position to change much about the actual committed deliverables.

As time passes and your relationship and trust grow, you can return to their initial needs and work with them on any changes you could be making to the contract to better meet what the customer really wants.

As the contract progresses, the customer should become more comfortable with talking to you about change. Over time, their own situation and needs will most likely be changing and they may want to look at renegotiating the contract or working through any existing change mechanism process to update the contract to their emerging needs. In addition, they may want to gain an understanding of what the contract is actually delivering versus what they now need. This will be a good opportunity to wrap in any of the areas identified at this stage to fully bring the contract in line with customer needs and expectations—and show you are the type of business the customer should want to work with over the long term.

Manage and Maintain Your Profitability

This is a caveat that applies for all the ideas and processes in this guide: while it is vital you are meeting the customer's needs as best you possibly can and are making the changes to your contract as it progresses that will keep it relevant for the customer, you should not just give away your contract profitability. You are in business to make a profit. The changes you make to the contract should be those you can make without destroying your profit. These might be changes that cost you little or nothing to make, or in negotiation with the customer divert resources from one area to another, or perhaps through an agreed process make changes the customer is willing to pay for.

This is an essential balance for contracts and managers of contracts and one it is easy to get wrong. The short-term pressures of your business will usually push towards a focus on profit maximization and increase. But many businesses fall into the trap of not thinking about the value of profit from a longer-term relationship with the customer during most of the contract and instead focus on maximizing profit in the short term.

To have an improved chance of winning your recompete and, as a business, improve your recompete success rate across contracts, you also need to look at the longer term. This means treating your contract as a long-term project and not just a series of single month (or even quarterly) projects measured by the profit or other measures at the end of that short period. In fact looking at customer needs over the longer term can bring you greater long-term profit and business as the customer sees you as a real partner and wants to put more business your way, reflecting your flexibility with their own.

At the same time, you don't want to lose sight of your own company goals and priorities. You are in business to make a profit, not a loss. The philosophy behind this guide reflects this, but takes a longer-term view that you will make more profit (during this contract period and by being the supplier for the next contract period) by thinking about the underlying progress that you can make over the contract period rather than just about this month or quarter.

What are the primary reasons incumbents lose recompetes?
"*Laziness, just expecting to be re-awarded.*"

Private Sector, Australia

Section II   Mobilize, Day One, and Transform

Idea 3: The Promises Register

> ### Idea Summary:
>
> **What:**
>
> Create a register of the promises you made in your bid. Use this to work through with the customer what they really want. Use it also to check off, with the customer, promises as you deliver them.
>
> **Why:**
>
> This will help you ensure you deliver the promises you made in your bid and enables you to negotiate with the customer to see if there are promises they are particularly keen on, some they may not want or others they may want delivered differently. The Promises Register also acts as a checklist for your customer to agree you have delivered your promises. When you get to your recompete, having a record of the promises you made last time around, and a record of how you achieved them, will give your next solution credibility that you will deliver.
>
> **Key Steps:**
>
> 1. Gather the bid documentation.
>
> 2. Collate all promises made.
>
> 3. Capture schedules for delivery of promises.
>
> 4. Organize to fit your contract (by contract stage, discipline, customer department, etc.).
>
> 5. Combine similar or repeated promises.

What Is a Promises Register?

A Promises Register is a table, spreadsheet, or list of all the promises you made in your bid of what you would deliver on the contract.

A Promises Register is sometimes created by the bid team during the latter stages of the bid process to keep track of all the promises being made so they can be cross-checked against costs, or sometimes as a summary in the bid documentation to help the customer see everything in one place. It is not just a compliance matrix showing that you have answered all the customer's questions.

Figure II.2   The Promises Register

Promises Register			
Section in the Bid	Summary of Promise	Delivered by When	Cross Reference with Other Promises

Key Steps to Creating a Promises Register

To complete your Promises Register, you may need to work with one or more of the bidders who put the bid together. This is the sequence you should follow:

Step 1: Gather the bid documentation.

Gather together the documentation you will need:

- Bid documentation created for your contract—the final signed off versions, not earlier drafts as things may have been changed.

- Any presentations made to the customer as part of the bid process.

- Any clarification questions and answers from the customer.

- Final copies of any negotiations and agreements made between preferred bidder stage and final signature of the contract.

- The contract that was signed.

Step 2: Collate all promises made.

Work through the documentation, noting all the promises made. For instance, wherever the bid said "we will…" count that as a promise. Add these into your register, making sure you carefully reference which document, section, and page it is from. Don't worry at this stage about repeated promises made in slightly different ways. Capture them all.

Step 3: Capture schedules for delivery of promises.

Capture schedules of when the promises made are supposed to be in place and delivered. This may not be easy, if deadlines have not been given in the documentation. If no schedule was given, keep this cell blank for now, but later you will need to put deadlines in based on discussion with your customer. A number of the promises will be around the start of the contract and transition period—separate these out into sections for these stages, as they will form part of the mobilization and transition processes and should be checked against the deliverables for these.

Step 4: Organize to fit your contract.

If needed, reorganize the register into relevant sections that suit your contract. You may decide to break down by subject (e.g. performance measures, staffing, IT) or by department or function (e.g. customer service department, procurement). If you have multiple customers or customer groups on your contract, you may find it useful to collate the promises by type of customer.

Step 5: Combine similar or repeated promises.

Collate and sensibly combine together those promises made in slightly different ways—but keep all the different references (document, section, etc.) even if you are combining several similar promises from different places into a single version.

You should now have a complete Promises Register.

Using the Promises Register

Your Promises Register will, of course, be a useful tool for managing the transition and the contract, and as such, you can use it as an aide memoir for internal purposes to ensure you are delivering what you said you would. But the Promises Register becomes much more useful if you use it with the customer.

Early Fine Tuning

First, it can be used at the start-up meeting, or even at negotiation stage. While your bid may be the one chosen by the customer as the winner, that doesn't mean they want everything you have said you will do, or perhaps not in the way you said you would do it.

Because the Promises Register pulls together in one place all the things you have said you will deliver, it becomes a powerful tool for working with the customer. While you should be intimately familiar with all the details of the bid and the contract, having a summary in the form of the Promises Register means you have a much clearer picture of the core of your solution that can be shared and worked on with the customer. You are able to go through it with the customer and get a much clearer understanding of what their real priorities are, what they are not so interested in, or what they would like changed.

The bid process may not have allowed this sort of open and focused discussion with the customer. It will also have been more dominated by the solicitation team than the operational team you will be working with, so now is an opportunity to fine tune the contract to really meet the needs of the customer, and start a proactive and closer relationship with them.

Health Warning!

While this may be a more informal forum than the bid period, be careful not to make informal changes to what has been agreed on in your signed contract without a clear and appropriately signed off change process. While some areas may be open to interpretation, you do not want to find yourself committing to costs not accounted for in your pricing. Also, you may find later in the contract that personnel on the customer side change and there is a return to the signed contract to check whether it is being delivered. You could find yourself in trouble if you have informally agreed with someone on the customer team not to deliver something in the way you contracted and then cannot justify this with clearly and officially signed off change notices or agreements you can turn to later in the contract to show these omissions were properly agreed on.

Ongoing Proof of Delivery

The other main use of the Promises Register is in your ongoing regular review meetings with the customer. As you progress in the contract, referring back to the Promises Register as you deliver each item and signing off with the customer the satisfactory completion of each promise gives you a positive ongoing record and shared sense of achievement. This helps you build strong and positive early relations with the customer, who will be able to see you delivering and developing your contract. Later reviews and reports can also refer back to the successfully signed off promises.

Later in the Contract

Things change over the period of the contract. People and managers will change in your contract and in the customer organization. If you are a new contract manager put in place part way through the contract, having a Promises Register to refer to can be useful as a learning tool. If there isn't one in existence, creating one can be even more useful, especially as it will require you to spend time going through the details of the signed contract and bid to ensure you are familiar with what you are contracted to deliver—and can highlight areas not yet delivered. Similarly, if new managers on the customer side arrive, the Promises Register can be a useful tool to help orient them.

At the Recompete

As you are preparing for the recompete, having the Promises Register in hand can be a useful aide memoir to help remind the team what was achieved in the early stages of the contract. It can also be used in the recompete (together with the customer sign offs of each promise being delivered) as evidence you delivered what was promised last time—and give credibility to your assertions of delivery in the next contract period. Again, putting a Promises Register for the next contract period into your recompete documentation will help the customer get a clear overview of all the positive changes you are proposing to make next time around.

> ***What is the most important thing an incumbent can do to improve their chances of winning?***
>
> *"Don't make assumptions. A decision has been made to change something within the service; just because you provided the old service does not mean you will automatically win the next one."*
>
> *Central Government, UK*

Idea 4: Capture and Record Previous Performance

Idea Summary:

What:

Capture what performance was on the contract prior to taking it over.

Why:

Capturing previous performance on the contract prior to your contract start helps give a benchmark of how well the contract was delivered before. You can use this to put your own performance into context as you go through the contract and at your recompete.

One of the more powerful pieces of information you can present to the customer at the recompete is the level of improvement in performance you have delivered over the period of the whole contract. Putting a table or chart into your recompete document showing the whole period of the contract and the improvement in performance from the start to the end of the contract is great proof of your ability to deliver for the customer—and evidence you will be able to further improve in the next contract period. Later in the guide, we will discuss performance measures in more detail (see *Ideas 11, 12,* and *13*).

But one of the things you can easily show is what performance was on the contract before you took over. Hopefully, you will have been chosen as the new contractor because you are offering a better (and for our purposes, better can also mean cheaper) service than was previously being delivered. Being able to show the improvement during the contract from the start to the end is powerful. Being able to add to that by showing how you improved performance over what it was before you started can be even more impressive.

The start of the contract is your best chance to get this information. Later it may have been lost, forgotten, or not seen as relevant. So even though you are busy setting up the contract, it is worth spending some effort to understand what performance was over the previous period.

Finding Information on Previous Performance

If you were the previous incumbent, this should be easy—you will have the information in hand. Otherwise, the customer may have included performance metrics either as public documents on the web or in the solicitation documents, or the bid team managed to gather it as part of its capture process. Check with them as a first action. However, it is more likely the information will be held either by the customer, or perhaps by staff transferring to you from the customer or previous contractor as part of the new contract.

Without breaking any data regulations or rules, you should spend time searching through the information transferred as part of the new contract for previous reports on performance. Ask staff, other stakeholders, and the customer for any information they can give you. You may be lucky and a full report of previous measures and performance against them is made available to you, or you may have to piece this together from different partial sources. Particularly if this is a first time outsourcing, the customer may not have had a formal measurement regime when the service was being delivered internally. Whichever is the case, collate what you can and analyze it to get the best view possible.

The customer may have set a different performance regime for the new contract, with different Key Performance Indicators (KPIs) to those previously used. If this is the case, it is worthwhile asking why they have done this. Perhaps the previous measures were not seen as useful or the priorities for the new contract are different from those previously set—of course, the work to be performed may also be different. Understanding the underlying reasons for changes in measurement can reveal useful information on the real level of customer satisfaction with the previous regime and their priorities for the present contract.

Relating Previous Performance to Present (and Future) Performance

If the measures previously used are different from those on the present contract, you should attempt to find the underlying data the measures are based on. The idea is to relate previous performance to your own performance now and going forward, so if translation of the data to fit existing measures is needed, you should aim to do this. As you will be presenting this information to the customer later, you should get their agreement to what you are doing, as well as the resulting numbers.

Section II Mobilize, Day One, and Transform

> **Example**
>
> *A previous contract performance measure on a Justice contract was set as "percent of detainees booked in within 30 minutes." The new measure was "number of minutes taken to book detainees in," with a maximum of 20 minutes. While the performance against the previous measure was 95%, to understand actual performance previously, the core data from the previous contract had to be extracted. Average time taken previously was in fact 12 minutes—giving a clearer understanding of previous performance versus expected performance, and an understanding of the level of changes required to hit the new target.*

You may find some of the previous measures useful for the present contract, even if they are not formally in the KPI regime, and you might wish to continue their use into the new contract, both to give continuity and as a useful measure of ongoing performance.

Compare the old information with the new performance regime and, wherever possible, tie the two together. Use the template in Figure II.3 to collate the different measures and relate them to your existing contract. Again, if there are significant differences in performance levels expected, check with the customer on the reasoning behind this—although, of course, poor performance in the previous contract will not excuse you from meeting the targets agreed for the future!

Figure II.3   Comparison of Previous and New Performance Measures

Previous Performance Measure	Performance Levels	Equivalent New Performance Measure	Target

> *What is the most important thing an incumbent can do to improve their chances of winning?*
>
> *"Approach the bid as if it were a new client for whom you really wanted to work, because you have true value to add to the client's operation."*
>
> *Private Sector, Australia*

Idea 5: Set Up a Recompete File

Idea Summary:

What:

A Recompete File is a place for you to record all information that could be relevant to your recompete.

Why:

Creating and starting to fill a Recompete File at the beginning of the contract helps ensure information from throughout the contract is not lost when you need it in your recompete.

When the recompete approaches, you will want to find a wide range of information about the contract. Some of it will be from the very start of the contract. Other information will be from regular reports made during the contract, or one-off items at different points in the contract. Over the period of the whole contract, many things change: people, managers, computer systems—perhaps entire offices can change once or several times over the years. Unless you have a clear place (electronic as well as physical) where you know you can find all the relevant information for the recompete, you will potentially waste huge amounts of time searching for and collating the information and evidence of how you delivered for your customer over the contract. And it is more than likely you will never find (or will have forgotten) some of the information that will be of real use for the recompete.

Starting a file for recompete information at the start of the contract, regularly ensuring you add relevant information to it, and keeping it in order may seem like a low priority now but will reap big dividends later.

Section II Mobilize, Day One, and Transform

What to Keep in the Recompete File

You will have your own views of what is important to your particular contract, and of course, you will have many files containing a huge range of information. Much of what you keep in the Recompete File may be a copy of information that is also kept elsewhere. The point of having a separate and distinct file for material likely to be useful for the recompete is to ensure everything relevant is in one place. The list on the following page is not comprehensive, but is a core set of folders for you to set up and continue to put material into as you go through the contract. You will no doubt be able to add sections relevant for your particular contract.

Keeping the Recompete File Up to Date

Creating a Recompete File and ensuring copies of relevant material are regularly added may seem bureaucratic and perhaps simplistic early on in the contract. But just a few seconds each week spent putting the relevant information away will save a lot of time, effort, and lost opportunity as the recompete approaches.

Tell your team the file exists and you want to put relevant information into it as the contract progresses. Make sure they are also looking for information that should be added and sent to you.

You might even turn the Recompete File into a motivational tool—telling staff their report/work is "one for the Recompete File" shows it is important and will be recorded and remembered as something contributing to the long-term benefit of the contract.

Figure II.4   Recompete File Contents Checklist

	Recompete File Contents Checklist	
	Subject	**Do we have?**
1	Copy of the original bid	
2	Copy of any negotiations	
3	Copy of the signed contract	
3a	Record of any changes agreed to the contract during the contract period	
4	Copy of the implementation plan	
5	Copy of any sign-offs by the customer of implementation completion	
6	Copy of the promises register	
7	A section for performance measurement:	
7a	Keep monthly reports, quarterly reports, etc.	
7b	Keep copies of any particularly good performance	
7c	Keep copies of whether performance fell, what the solution put in place was	
8	A section for innovation and added value	

	Subject	Do we have?
8a	Copies of ideas for innovation or added value that were not enacted or were turned down by the customer	
8b	Copies of any improvements or innovation delivered on the contract	
8c	Copies of any reports on weekly or monthly, or ad hoc added value that was added	
9	A section for compliments: Keep any compliments, or any positive publicity or mentions of the contract, letters of thanks, etc., whether these came from the customer, end users, or others.	
10	A section for accreditations, awards, achievements	
10a	Those gained by the contract	
10b	Those gained by staff for their work on the contract	
11	A section on risks and issues	
11a	Risk registers	
11b	The mitigations put in place and their results	
11c	Any issues that arise—and how they were resolved	
12	Section on the customer	
12a	Key customer initiatives and reports	
12b	Relevant publicity on the customer—press cuttings, etc.	
12c	Information on senior customer managers, organization structure, etc.	
13	Copies of key reports to the customer (monthly or ad hoc reports)	
14	Minutes of key meetings with the customer or other key stakeholders	
15	Records of regular management meetings on key subjects such as Quality, etc.	
16	Health & Safety section	
16a	Policy and any changes made	
16b	Audits and results	
16c	Incidents and reviews	

Other Useful Libraries of Recompete Information

You might find other useful libraries of information you can use to feed into your recompete and Recompete File. For instance, if you use a quality system such as ISO 9001, keeping the accreditation means the system needs to record a range of information that will be useful at your recompete such as customer feedback, quality improvements, etc. Setting up your quality system in the right way can mean you collect a range of information useful throughout the contract and especially at the recompete.

What is the most important thing an incumbent can do to improve their chances of winning?

"Give the best value for money before hearing about potential recompetes."

Private Sector, UK

Idea 6: Day One Impact Measures

> ### Idea Summary:
>
> **What:**
>
> Day One Impact Measures are a set of high visibility changes you make on the first day of the new contract.
>
> **Why:**
>
> They indicate to your key stakeholders what changes and improvements you will be making on the contract and create a visible start. Impact measures help with making culture changes and initiate an awareness that you have started the contract and things will now be different (i.e. better).
>
> **Key Steps:**
>
> 1. List key contract stakeholders.
>
> 2. Identify existing issues or problems.
>
> 3. Identify changes promised or required.
>
> 4. Brainstorm Day One impact ideas.
>
> 5. Review for cost, impact, and practicality and decide on the best few to put into practice.

The first day of a new contract is an important time for all concerned. The customer wants to see that the new contractor can deliver and the services or products are delivered with no reduction in quality. If you have retained staff, they will be nervous about the new contractor. Users will want to know they can still receive the service they have been receiving to date.

As the contractor you will have been preparing for this day for some time. Hopefully everything will work properly! You will, however, be starting a new way of doing things—you will want to ensure the customer and staff recognize you will be making a positive difference. You may want to change the culture of the contract from how it has been run in the past. If you don't immediately show you are different at the very start of the contract, then old ways of doing things may continue, people may conclude nothing has changed, and you will find it more difficult to make changes over time.

How can you show on the first day things will be different (and better) from now on? Day One Impact Measures are one way of achieving this.

Day One Impact Measures are highly visible changes made on the first day of the contract that give a sense of the key changes you want to make in the contract. They may not be massive changes—you perhaps haven't had time or resources to make huge differences yet. But they make a statement of intent and ensure that all relevant stakeholders see from the start you are different from what has gone before. And they go beyond the standard letters or brochures you will be sending out to stakeholders as a normal part of a new contract.

Examples of Day One Impact Measures

Below are some simple examples:

- Repainting and refurbishment of staff rest areas.

- New website for end users.

- Getting rid of reserved parking spaces for managers.

What's Different from Normal Communication Done on Any New Contract?

There is always a lot of communication being delivered at the start of a new contract. There may be a range of publicity materials sent to end users, staff, and customer contacts. There may be new uniforms, new logos, giveaways such as mouse mats printed with the company logo, etc. The difference with impact measures is they are additional to this standard and expected level of communication: they go beyond words and are a demonstration of the new regime you intend to bring to the contract. Rather than just telling people things are going to be different, they show things *are* different—and are focused on demonstrating the specific differences you want to make. That means they need to be linked specifically to the way your company does business, and the particular changes you want to make to the way the contract is run and delivers.

Day One Impact Measures therefore need thinking through well before you get to the first day of the contract—ideally as part of your initial thinking, project planning, and resourcing of the mobilization and implementation phases. To do this effectively, you need a simple framework to identify what impacts you want to make. Figure II.5 outlines how you could start this process:

Section II Mobilize, Day One, and Transform

Figure II.5 **Day One Impact Measures**

Stakeholder	Present Issue	Change Required or Promised	Potential Impact Measure

Key Steps for Day One Impact Measures

Step 1: List key contract stakeholders.

Start by listing the key stakeholder groups on the contract. These will include staff, end users, customer, suppliers, etc.

Step 2: Identify existing issues or problems.

Then identify any areas you have identified as problems or issues for each stakeholder on the present contract. There should be several sources of information you can call on:

- Look at what are often called "hot buttons" in the capture phase (the pre bid phase where your business development team will have been selling to the customer, identifying if this is an opportunity you could and should bid for, and talking to the customer to identify their needs).

- You should also look at the "win themes" in your bid (those parts of your offer seen as the most important and compelling reasons why the customer should choose you).

- Also take into account the promises in your Promises Register and any information gained from asking the customer why you won the contract (see *Ideas 2* and *3*).

Step 3: Identify changes promised or required.

Next—and this may also come from the above sources—identify the changes you need, want, or have promised to make as part of your solution for the customer.

Step 4: Brainstorm Day One impact ideas.

Once you have this information, you can start brainstorming ideas for potential impact measures.

Step 5: Review for cost, impact, and practicality and decide on the best few to put into practice.

Finally, review the ideas you have generated and look at the cost, practicality, time to achieve, and crucially, the message each potential impact measure will involve—and the total impact those "best few" ideas will have (at this stage, it is worth reviewing the message each measure might have on other stakeholders).

Once you are happy you have measures that will give the right messages and are achievable within budget and time constraints, they should be added to your mobilization plan—and cleared with the customer.

Example

The removal of managers' parking spaces listed above is a real example used as an impact measure on a contract. But this was not just a random action. As part of the capture effort prior to the bid, the winning contractor had realized the culture on the contract was seen as hierarchical with management not seen by staff as close to the contract. At the same time, there was limited parking space at the main work area and management's reserved spaces were often left empty as the management team was not in the office. The new contractor wanted to show they were bringing a less hierarchical culture with a more involved and open management team. Taking away reserved parking spaces was a small part of a program to illustrate this change.

What aspects of incumbents' proposals have been particularly poor?

"The incumbent thought they would get the contract without having to work too hard. They were complacent in their presentation of their offer. They didn't understand the strategic priorities."

Private Sector, Europe

Section III

Target Operating Model

The Target Operating Model fits in the place below on the lifecycle model:

Figure III.1   The Contract Lifecycle Target Operating Model Stage

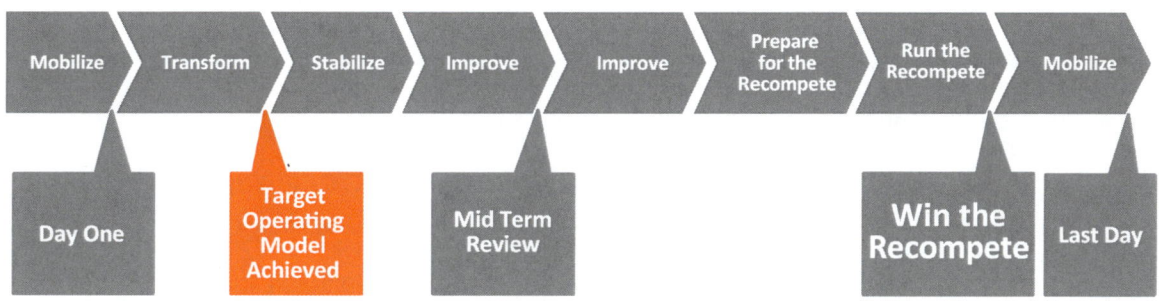

What is the most important thing an incumbent can do to improve their chances of winning?

"Perform the job well in the first place and provide accurate and honest bids."

Private Sector, USA

Idea 7: Conduct a Target Operating Model Review

> **Idea Summary:**
>
> **What:**
>
> A review at the end of the Transform stage to ensure you have everything in place on the contract, as per your bid, to progress to the Stabilize stage.
>
> **Why:**
>
> The Target Operating Model Review helps ensure you have completed your transition and all the elements of your solution are now in place. It ensures you have fulfilled all your promises for this stage and you are making the margins, etc., you anticipated. Marking this completion means you do not leave elements of your solution incomplete, which could lead to customer dissatisfaction as the contract progresses.
>
> **Key Steps:**
>
> 1. Are our structure and solution in place?
> 2. Are we performing to the levels we promised and the customer requires?
> 3. Are we delivering the financial performance that was signed off?
> 4. Summarize the issues and report.
> 5. Plan for delivery.

What Is the Target Operating Model (TOM) Review?

The TOM is the solution you bid to deliver. Reaching the TOM is the point at which the work of the mobilization and transition is complete: everything you put in your solution is in place and delivering. From this point forward, you will be delivering as you said you would—your staff, equipment, processes, offices, etc., are all in place. You should be delivering the level of services you predicted and achieving your contract margin.

The TOM review ensures you have indeed reached the point where everything is in place and nothing is outstanding. More importantly, the review shows whether your transition is actually completed and your solution is performing as expected—both in terms of delivery for the customer and in terms of profit for you. Without reviewing whether this point has been reached and exploring any issues that have emerged, you could carry on the contract with these issues unresolved, or elements of your promised solution may not be properly and fully put in place. Finally, you will not have a point at which you can feed back to the bid team and mobilization and transition teams what lessons should be learned for next time.

Why Is This Important for the Recompete?

Just as starting the contract well is important for the recompete in getting the customer on your side and setting a positive position from the beginning, ensuring you have properly reached the solution you promised the customer and have a clear plan to fix any issues quickly will make sure the contract doesn't underperform for a significant part of the contract without a proper resolution.

When Should the TOM Review Be Run?

When the transition is completed (note that the TOM review may conclude that the transition is not actually complete and more work may need to be done).

Who Should Be Involved?

- The contract management team.
- The mobilization and transition team.
- The bid team.
- Finance team members.

You may wish to involve the customer in parts of the review.

What Is Involved?

The basis of the review is to compare the solution promised in the bid, together with the forecast margin, turnover, and performance, against the reality of what the mobilization and transition periods and programs have achieved. You should therefore start with a review of the key points of the bid and solution and compare your position at the moment with those points, noting and analyzing any differences, their reasons, consequences and, if negative, rectifications. You will need:

- Your original bid.
- Your signed off pricing, costs and margin expectations.
- Your Promises Register.
- Your signed contract with terms and conditions.
- Any changes agreed upon during negotiations.
- Any issues faced during mobilization.
- Any issues or differences found at the start of the contract and during mobilization versus the assumptions or expectations made in the bid.

- Costs of mobilization and transition—and differences from those forecast.
- Levels of KPIs achieved from Day One to date.
- Turnover at present and the forecasts set.
- Margins being made at present and the forecasts set.

Key Steps in the TOM Review

Step 1: Are our structure and solution in place?

From your bid, Promises Register, and contract you should have the structure, processes, etc., you said you would deliver. Review the present situation against these. Identify where any areas are not yet in place or where changes have been required. Look at these differences and determine what the impacts of these differences are, whether there is still work to be done to get to the TOM you had in your bid.

Step 2: Are we performing to the levels we promised and the customer requires?

The customer will have set KPIs and a level of performance against these, which they contractually expect you to achieve. While they may have given a period of grace for the first few months of the contract, you should now be in a position to see if you are achieving the levels expected. You may also have promised other services and performance levels that go with these. Review your performance against the levels set and how quickly your performance has improved from Day One of the contract. Are you meeting the KPIs set, exceeding them, or are you not yet performing?

Analyze the reasons for any underperformance:

- Is this due to a delay in getting up to speed and you are confident that they will soon be achieved—if so, when?
- Is underperformance due to circumstances you have found on the contract that were not anticipated in the bid?
- Does it relate to any issues you identified in Step 1 regarding your structure?
- Are you going to face any penalties as a result of your underperformance?
- What is the customer's reaction to your underperformance, what are the consequences of this and what are you doing about it?

If you are underperforming, you need to have a clear plan to get to the levels agreed and required.

As part of this step, you should also review your Promises Register. Have you delivered all the things you promised to this stage in the contract? If not, why and what plans do you have to deliver your promises?

Step 3: Are we delivering the financial performance that was signed off?

The bid team will have created a cost model of the contract, together with expected turnover, margin and cash flow. This should have been signed off as part of the bid process by senior management. When the contract was won, and the transition into contract go-live complete, this cost model and the forecasts for profit, etc., will have become the contract forecast and budget. There should also have been a budget for the mobilization and transition costs.

In this step, you should review whether the bid costs, margins, etc., are being achieved and what the final mobilization and transition costs were:

- Are you on budget?

- Are you achieving the margins, etc., that were planned?

- If not, what are the reasons for this—is it a schedule issue or are things not as planned? If things aren't as planned, what are the issues and reasons for these?

- If you do have issues, can they be rectified—and if so, how and when?

- What will your revised forecast for the contract look like?

At this stage, you should also review your Risk Register (see *Idea 9* for more on this). There will most likely have been a risk register of some sort created during the bid. Ideally, it will have included other areas as well as risks such as assumptions, issues and dependencies (a RAID register). It is likely that the register will have covered risks for the bid, the mobilization and transition and for the contract. You should review this and revise it—any risks no longer relevant (such as for the bid, mobilization, etc.) should be taken out. Any that crystallized should be reviewed in terms of their impact. You should update the Risk Register based on the outcome of the TOM review, including the issues and situation you have uncovered.

Step 4: Summarize the issues and report.

In this step, you should summarize the position you have reviewed in the previous steps. If there are issues, it is possible they will be related—for instance, issues with your structure will most likely impact customer delivery and, in turn, impact your margin.

Set out the position. Summarize the areas where you are on plan and list any issues which mean you are not at your TOM as predicted in the bid.

For each issue you should write out:

- The issue.
- Its cause.
- The impact.
- The proposed solution, with actions, resources, and schedules.

This should form the report of your position that will be added to your Recompete File and be distributed as required to the relevant people in your company. You might want to get a sign off from management that you have reached your TOM. If there are issues, you may need to get support and agreement for how you are going to address them, as this is likely to impact the costs, margin, and potentially the relationship you are building with the customer.

Step 5: Plan for delivery.

Your report will include a summary of your action plan. However you will need to have a detailed, timed, resourced and costed action plan to overcome any issues identified that are preventing you from achieving your TOM. Unless, of course, you have achieved your TOM and can move on to the next stage of the contract—*Stabilize*.

It is more likely there will be some minor issues requiring work. These should not be lost in the day-to-day delivery of the contract. Your plan to deliver should be followed through and, once completed, your TOM formally signed off.

If there are serious issues, you may need to recommend a "get well" plan—or possibly an extended and revised transition phase.

How Long Should the TOM Review Take?

This will depend on the size and complexity of your contract. For a small contract, the TOM review might be a single meeting, in which case Steps 1-4 are the items to cover in the agenda. You will need to organize the preparation from each group so you can effectively review each area, ensure full notes are taken of the meeting capturing all the areas discussed, and then write out the report and action plan.

For larger contracts or if issues are already obvious, then the TOM review may be a more extended set of meetings—particularly the plan to revise.

Involving the Customer

The customer will be aware the transition phase is at an end. If there are issues impacting on delivery, they will also, of course, be aware of these and are likely to be pushing you to resolve them. Their views on how you have dealt with the contract to date will be useful input into the TOM review. The level of your relationship with the customer, and with whom specifically within the customer organization, should also be a part of the review. You will particularly want to ensure relationships built up by the capture, bid, mobilization, and transition teams have been effectively picked up and continued by the contract team (see *Idea 22: Constantly Build Customer Relationships and Trust*).

How much you involve your customer directly in the review itself will depend on your own circumstances and the level of relationship you have built up with them.

However, it will be wise to keep the customer informed of the result of your review: If you have reached your TOM, this is a positive message to give the customer assuring them that all is working on the contract. If you still have some issues to resolve, showing you have identified these (with the probable exception of your own internal margin issues) and have a plan to fix them will give the customer assurance you are in control. If there are serious issues and a "get well" plan is required, you are likely to need to involve the customer in this, as they will be only too aware of the issues themselves and will want delivery issues resolved.

If the contract is performing particularly poorly, you need the customer on your side, otherwise your relationship with them could be irreparably damaged. A get well plan may require further negotiations with the customer, and involving them positively will both be needed and may well pay dividends as opposed to keeping them at arm's length, wondering what you are doing and when you will fix all the problems they see.

Final Sign-Off of the Target Operating Model

If, after your review, you require further work to achieve your TOM, you should plan to revisit your review once this plan has been implemented. Only once you have fully achieved your TOM should you clearly sign it off. You may not need to review the whole contract again, but you should certainly hold a distinct meeting to sign off that all the issues identified in your original TOM review have been rectified and the contract is now at the position expected.

If circumstances mean you will not achieve your original TOM, and you have accepted there is nothing that can be done about it (you may actually be in a better position than planned) then this position, if accepted by your company—and **if** the customer is happy with the different position, should be signed off and you can move to the next stage in the contract.

What is the most important thing an incumbent can do to improve their chances of winning?

"Not take the procurement process lightly."

State Government, USA

Section IV

Stabilize

The Stabilize stage sits as shown below in the lifecycle model:

Figure IV.1   The Contract Lifecycle Stabilize Stage

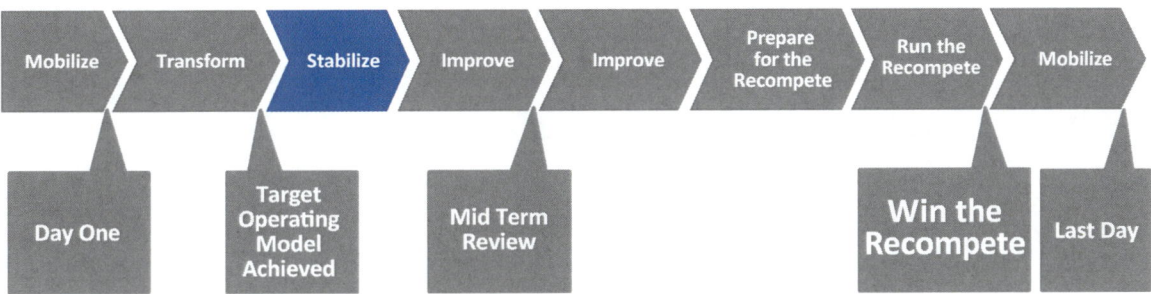

What Is the Stabilize Stage?

Once you have achieved your Target Operating Model and your transition is completed, you reach the position where the contract is operating as it was bid. There are usually several years to run on the contract and a period of relative stability has been reached. Many contracts continue this stage, perhaps with minor improvements, reacting to any issues that occur but with little proactively driven change until the recompete is imminent. This is not the approach you should take if you want to be in the best position to win your recompete.

Instead, the Stabilize stage should be a short period of two to four months when you settle in the contract staff, structure, and processes and ensure delivery is consistently and robustly working. While you are doing this, you should also be planning the main phase of your contract—planned and managed improvement.

The ideas included in this stage are:

- Idea 8: Create a Contract Plan
- Idea 9: Help the Customer Manage Risk
- Idea 10: Align to the Customer

What is the most important thing an incumbent can do to improve their chances of winning?

"Improve the quality and service outcomes while developing 'raving fans' for their responsiveness and steps towards service improvements."

Public Sector, USA

Idea 8: Create a Contract Plan

Idea Summary:

What:

A Contract Plan sets out your goals, targets, and strategy for the contract over its lifetime. It sets out the changes you want to put in place and what you want the contract to look like by the recompete.

Why:

Creating and implementing a Contract Plan means you are proactively managing change to a target over the contract period rather than simply reacting to day-to-day issues. By the end of the contract, your plan will have helped you make significant changes and improvements which will help you build strong and positive relationships with the customer and show in your recompete how you have been a proactive supplier.

Key Steps:

1. Create an initial aiming point.
2. Review where you are now.
3. Look at what will change over the coming years.
4. Set priorities and plans.
5. Review.

6. Communicate the plan.

7. Manage and govern the plan.

When you get toward the end of your contract and are preparing for the recompete, you will need to look back and review what you have changed and improved over the years that you have been delivering for the customer. One of the most difficult (and frustrating) positions to be in for the recompete is when the result of your review shows that very little has changed. You may have delivered a positive initial change at the start of the contract to reduce costs for the customer and/or improve performance as a result of your winning solution. But if you haven't used the years you have been running the contract to make further improvements, you have wasted a golden opportunity to improve your chances of winning the recompete. There are three main reasons for this:

1. By focusing on improving your contract performance throughout the contract, you will be building a positive reputation with the customer. They are likely to want to deal more openly and proactively with you. Those higher up in the customer organization will see the value you are delivering and feel positively towards you. This will mean you are building stronger, closer, and more positive relationships with a wider group of customer contacts, all of whom are more likely to be positively disposed towards you and will want to keep you as their chosen contractor (or even partner) in the longer term. This could lead the customer, if they are able, to not recompete your contract at all. It could make the difference between you being awarded the maximum number of extensions available on the contract and therefore postponing the recompete. And when it comes to the recompete, it will mean the customer starts the process favoring you over any potential competitors.

2. The world and your customer (and therefore their needs) will have changed during the contract. If you haven't changed, then the customer will recognize this. Your delivery will most likely no longer fit the customer's circumstances or goals for the next contract period, and any changes you propose in the recompete solution will need to be a step change, adding risk for the customer. The customer may wonder if you will be able to make those, considering the "outdated" level or type of performance you are presently delivering (especially compared to the more up to date offerings of your competitors).

3. Any assertions you make in your recompete about how proactive or innovative you are, or how you focus on continuous improvement, will ring hollow in the ears of the customer—after all, they have experience of your delivery over the previous few years and you haven't demonstrated these characteristics to date, even though you have had several years to do so (and remember, you may have made these same assertions last time around).

Even if you look back at your contract (or previous contracts) and see there have been some changes and improvement, look hard and ask:

- Did we proactively introduce these changes rather than react to them due to necessity or the customer pushing for them?

- Who benefitted most from the changes—us or the customer?

- Were these changes aligned to the most important needs of the customer as they emerged or developed over the contract period (if not, how much value to the customer did they really deliver)?

- How significant were these changes compared with what could have been delivered?

The difference at recompete between an incumbent that has delivered to the original contract specifications, but has only made marginal improvements or changes on an ad hoc basis (or as pushed by the customer), versus one that has planned and implemented a clear program of development can be dramatic—and can have a dramatic influence on their chances of success in retaining the business through the recompete.

The Contract Plan is the core driving tool you should have in place from as early as possible in the contract to ensure you are not standing still, or only reacting piecemeal to customer requests for change. A good Contract Plan, implemented effectively and updated proactively, will mean by the end of the contract your delivery will have:

- Changed significantly to meet your customer's changing needs.

- Delivered major improvement for the customer in areas of most importance to them.

- Positioned you to meet the future needs of the customer for the next contract period.

- Convinced the customer that you are indeed innovative, proactive, and a deliverer of continuous improvement they will want to continue their relationship with over the coming contract period.

If your contract is several years (or even, as in some cases, decades) in length, then the changes will potentially be so significant that the original contract delivery is almost unrecognizable compared to what is being delivered towards the end of the contract. But even if your contract is only a year or two long, you should still have been able to demonstrate you are a proactive and effective partner the customer would want to retain.

What Does a Contract Plan Look Like?

While the specifics will vary depending on your contract, industry, and product or service, the Contract Plan will look much like a good strategic plan any organization (like your company or your customer) would have. It will contain:

- An idea of where you want to end up and the type of contractor you want to be (often called the vision/mission or values in books on strategic planning).

- An analysis of the environment (i.e. the state of and changes likely in your and the customer's industry), a view of your customer and their own situation and plans and of your contract (what it is like at the moment, what capabilities and opportunities it has, and what challenges it faces).

- A set of ideas and priorities for future improvements addressing the first two points above.

- A plan of how to implement these ideas.

- A budget and forecast for now and the future, and how the changes in the plan will impact the future.

- A process for implementation, review, and updating of the plan, how it is going and how it may need to change over time, together with a view of who is responsible for managing and delivering the plan and the initiatives it contains.

As with any plan, this will all be iterative: as you initially develop the plan, you will revisit each part of it and potentially revise your thinking, and you will continue to review and update it over the period of the contract.

Depending on the size, length, and scope of your contract, the plan may be a very simple document of a couple of pages, or it may be a significant document with in depth analysis and a range of budgeted initiatives, much like a full company strategic plan. Bear in mind that a large contract can be bigger than many small, or even medium-sized, companies.

Whether your plan is simple or comprehensive, it is important that you have a proactive plan in place that you review regularly and implement over the period of the contract; it results in change and improvement in your contract; it delivers to the customer in areas that are important to them over the length of the contract; and, of course, it results in you being in the strongest possible position come recompete.

This guide doesn't purport to be a manual on strategic planning (there is a whole industry that focuses on this area alone), and you should at least read some of the literature and books on the subject. You may even decide to employ a consultant to guide you through the process. More likely, you may wish to work with your company's senior team who are producing plans for the business as a whole. What follows is a simple set of templates and advice to help you get started and aid in your delivery of a plan for your contract that will help you be in the best possible position for your recompete.

Objections and Limits to Your Contract Plan

Before we start to look at the details of how to start, manage, and implement a Contract Plan, we should review the limitations and potential objections to spending time and effort on a plan in the first place within the context of a contract:

"There is no spare money/resource/time."

It is unlikely that the contract was bid with any significant amount of "headroom" in the costs to give management the resources to do much more than deliver the specification. Especially when price is the dominant factor in the customer's decision of who wins the bid team, you will quite rightly have reviewed all cost areas and cut out anything not necessary to deliver the solution as set by the customer. So where will you get all the resources, time, and money to deliver this plan?

The extent to which you can make significant changes within the contract will indeed be limited by resources. Just as any business has limitations on the funding available to change (albeit less so in many circumstances than a typical contract). However, there is a range of activities that are still necessary for running the contract: regular management meetings, regular meetings with the customer, staff communications, and Health and Safety requirements. How you use these meetings and the inevitable work and projects that go with them can make the difference between being reactive and proactive.

Even if your plan is at first simply an outline of what is important to the customer and includes ideas that may make an impact on helping with these areas, together with a culture where you react positively to customer needs (rather than negatively or not at all), then you have the start of a set of priorities and a route to coordinating and driving events and the work you are likely to need to do anyway in the direction that will make the most positive impact. This prioritization will mean the work you do will be the most impactful and may help reduce spending time and effort on areas that will make little difference.

Section IV   Stabilize

"Contract margins are tight and the contract targets are for margins to increase, not be reduced by investment in schemes to help the customer."

On a tight contract, it can indeed seem that looking at ways to add value for the customer is just another way of giving away margins by offering further free services. However, there are a number of arguments against this:

- Not all changes cost money. Much of what may be in your plan will be how you do the things you might be doing on the contract anyway. Looking at how this work is delivered, while keeping the maximum value to the customer in mind, may well mean you make changes to how work is delivered without any impact on costs.

- Your plan is not just designed to deliver additional services. It should also look at how you can increase efficiency and reduce costs. While you might decide to share some of these savings with the customer (and we recommend it), there is no requirement for you to give all the savings away. A "gainshare" approach means you can increase your margins and still give the customer some benefits through a share of the reduced costs. In addition, you may find that the customer actually puts little or no value on elements of the work specified in the contract, or perhaps actually wants them delivered in a different way. You may be able to change, reduce, or even stop the work on some of these areas, being careful to ensure that an official change note is signed by the customer before you do. Again, you might not reduce your prices by the full amount of the reduced cost of doing this non-essential or under-valued work. While your turnover on the contract may decrease, your margin might increase. All this should also feature as part of your plan.

- The changes you identify in your plan, as those with the most positive impact for the customer, don't have to be given away free. If the customer can see their value, they may well be willing to pay for their delivery. As long as the cost of you delivering the change is less than the value the customer puts on the outcome, they will still see they are getting a good deal. There may be limits to the additional work the customer can give without going out to competition, however within these limitations the Contract Plan can also be a route to deliver growth to the contract and an increase in margin, rather than a cost to it. If both you and the customer recognize this is not your only motivation to seeking changes, and you are genuinely aiming to be a positive and proactive part of the customer team, they may be surprisingly willing to look at increasing payments to you for additional or better services than originally contracted. If the customer isn't willing to pay, this may be an indication that you have over estimated the value of the change or improvement to them, and you may wish to review it.

- Finally, you shouldn't underestimate the value in terms of motivation to staff that having a proactive plan focused on improving services can have, as opposed to just working on the same thing for years. Motivated staff are more likely to find the time to work on new and interesting projects on top of their day-to-day work if they feel part of a contract that is dynamic and has a positive purpose. You may find you can get more work or projects delivered by these more motivated staff than you expect, especially if you can combine this with a development process for individuals and teams. Developing your staff's capabilities should be part of your plan anyway, so they get additional experience, skills, and recognition for this work and are made a core part of the overall effort.

"The bid was too tight. We are losing money and not yet delivering what was promised. There is no appetite to look at improvements—we need to focus on "getting well""

This situation is becoming increasingly common as price becomes the dominant factor in procurement decisions and bidders are forced into taking greater risks to win, with lower margins and less room for error. The form of the problem—an inability to deliver the specification and/or an underestimation of costs leading to losses—will to some degree impact how you "get well," as will your company culture. Different companies have different approaches to this type of issue, and the approach can also vary by market. Some companies will focus first on ensuring that delivery for the customer is right and will then work internally on mending their own margins. Others will rely on contractual means to reduce their costs or required level of delivery.

Whatever the route taken, there needs to be a plan to achieve the "get well" position. And once this position is achieved (assuming it can be), what then? If, at the recompete, the customer's impression of the incumbent is simply one of poor performance at the start, then adequate performance once their own "get well" had been achieved it is unlikely to lead to the customer being positive towards retaining them. If however, the incumbent has pressed on to deliver positive change, then the impression may be very different.

If you are in a position where you need to "get well," you should incorporate the planning you need to achieve this into your overall Contract Plan (rather than have a separate plan)—but your plan should also ideally include some elements of low cost improvements that will have a positive impact for the customer. Having the customer on your side while you attempt to improve your position is key to helping achieve your get well position. Your plan should then move toward improvements for the customer, so by the time the recompete comes around, this improvement is the more dominant part of the customer's impression of you.

Section IV Stabilize

"The operational customer doesn't want change; they are managing the contract tightly focusing on delivery of what was specified."

Some customer contract managers and monitors are focused more on compliance than improvement. It is worth understanding the background to this for your contract. Is this standard procedure, or has the customer perhaps had a bad experience with a previous contractor and is reacting to this? If the customer is focused on compliance, there are options you can try to overcome this focus, depending on the specific situation:

- Is the compliance approach limited to the direct contract management team? If not, you may need to work with more senior parts of the customer to persuade them of the benefits of an improvement based approach. This, of course, needs to be done subtly so as not to annoy your direct customer contacts.

- You can focus your early priorities on cost savings and looking at how you can share these with the customer. Even a very compliance-focused customer team will find it more difficult to refuse an offer of a reduced cost than a proposed improvement/increase or change. Once trust has been more established over time, through a number of delivered reductions in cost (even if these are small), it is more likely the contract officers will be more open to other changes.

In addition, you should recognize that your Contract Plan does not only involve changes to your delivery. There is a range of internal changes which will improve your contract position. This may be in further efficiencies, improved staff training, succession planning, etc. All of these should form part of your plan and are independent of the customer. You can be enacting these changes even if your customer is still resisting changes to how you deliver the contract to them.

"There is no mechanism for coordinating this sort of plan with the customer or getting any changes put through the customer processes."

Some contracts will include specific processes and forums for driving change and improvement, such as partnering type contracts, while others have no specifically designated forums. However, all contracts have some form of regular contact or reporting meetings with the customer. Over time, these can be used to introduce ideas and delivery of changes. As the customer comes to recognize the opportunity for value being delivered to them, they can become more focused on improvement projects and programs. As with many areas of the plan itself, it is not just about adding new initiatives or meetings, it is about how the meetings already in place can be used.

As we have said, while there may be restrictions and limitations on the breadth and amount of change that can be introduced on a contract, it is the fact that you have a proactive plan in place that can make a difference, even if the changes delivered are initially small. Over time, once the initial improvements deliver, it is more likely that more will be enabled and progress can build on these early successes. Even modest changes can add up to, over the period of a contract, a very significant change.

Whatever limitations you may face that genuinely reduce your ability to deliver significant change on your contract can be incorporated into your plan. But they should not be used as an excuse for having no plan at all.

Key Steps to Creating Your Contract Plan

Let's move on to how to set up your plan. The following steps will put your plan in place, at least in outline. As your contract progresses, you will need to update this information. We deal with this in the Improve stage of the contract lifecycle. It is worth looking now at the processes, tables, and lists recommended in this stage, particularly the introductions to Performance Improvement (which precedes Idea 11) and to Added Value, Continuous Improvement, and Innovation (which precedes Ideas 15, 16, and 17).

Step 1: Create an initial aiming point.

Before you start analyzing, think about your contract and take your own view of what you would like the contract to be at the end of the period. This might be a qualitative aspiration relating to how your customer will see you; the impact your contract will have had on the customer's business or on end users; the performance of the contract; its value as a reference for other contracts your business will bid for; or some other position or achievement. Of course, this should be something that will put you in the strongest possible position with the customer regarding the recompete—ideally making you indispensible in the customer's eyes.

This becomes the draft end point. You might revise this as you do more analysis, but it gives you a start to your thinking.

Step 2: Review where you are now.

As with any plan, before setting off toward a destination, you need to understand your starting point. Review the present contract situation:

Start with your own contract abilities:

- What are the capabilities you have on the contract?

- Are there any weak spots you have discovered through the implementation of your solution that need addressing?

- What is your margin, cash flow, turnover, etc.—is it as bid, better, or worse?
- What skills, staffing, and resources do you have?
- How are you performing now on the contract—are you meeting all the specifications and KPIs? If not, what needs to be done to resolve this?

Next, look at your customer (the whole organization—not just the immediate department you may be contracted to):

- What is the purpose of the customer—especially if they are a government organization—what do they exist to deliver or achieve?
- What market or sector is the customer in?
- Are they a monopoly or do they face competition of any kind?
- Who are the customer's end users, and how does the work the customer delivers impact on these end users?
- How well is the customer performing its role—is it performing well or poorly?
- What pressures are on the customer, and how are they dealing with these?
- What strategic goals and plans does the customer have, and what programs or projects are in place to deliver these?
- Who has power within your customer—who are the decision makers, influencers, etc.—and how do these people relate to your contract? Are they close to it and interested in its performance and outcomes, or are they distant?

Looking more closely at the immediate department or area of the customer where you are contracted:

- Why has the customer outsourced the functions you are now delivering—what do they aim to gain—and why aren't they delivering in house?
- What is the role of the department or area you are contracted to—how does this relate to the customer organization as a whole and delivery of its wider goals?
- Who are the end users of the department—are they the customer's ultimate end users, a subset of these, or another department or set of employees within the customer organization?
- What are these end users' key needs and how (or how well) are these being met at the moment?
- What targets or measures of performance does the department have—and how well are these being met now?

- What plans, budgets, and projects does the department have in place at the moment—and how do the activity and outputs of your contract relate to these?

- Who are the decision makers and influencers within the department, and how do they relate to your contract and the customer's management of your contract?

Next look at the wider marketplace—both your customer's and your company's.

For the customer:

- What are the drivers in their marketplace? Are there budget restrictions, is competition growing, is new technology, regulation, etc., impacting the shape or structure of the market, and if so, how?

For your own company's marketplace:

- Is competition increasing? If so, what are the impacts of this (are prices decreasing, for instance?) and what are the strategies and offerings of your main competitors?

- What impact are new technology, regulation, economic factors, or other drivers having on the shape and structure of the market and what is being offered to customers?

Your contract:

- What are the key terms of your contract and what are you expected to deliver?

- What are the KPIs, performance levels expected, penalty regime, payment mechanisms?

- What, if any, changes or improvements over the contract period have been included as part of the contract?

- What governance procedures and processes do you have with the customer—i.e. is the contract set up with a clear process for managing and delivering changes, such as in a partnering arrangement, or is it a more static arrangement?

Pulling all this information together will give you a strong overview of the existing position for your contract. Some of this information could already be available from the Capture Team or Bid Team that won the contract. You may be able to gain other information from within your company and from reviewing your customer's own published plans, website, etc. In addition, you should be able to gain some information from the customer contacts you should already be building.

The answers to the previous questions will not all be clear. But together, the information will be a good start. It is likely at this stage you will have too much data and will need to narrow it down to what you see as the most important things relevant to your contract. List these as your key summary—but don't discard the wider information. It will be useful as you review your plan once you have moved through the next stages.

The next step is to look at the future and how the present environment is likely to change.

Step 3: Look at what will change over the coming years.

Looking at the future is always speculative, but without a starting idea of the most likely changes that are going to impact your customer, your industry, and your contract, you have no context in which to place your plan. The timeframe over which you are looking at change will depend on the length of your contract. You may wish to frame your approach to different time periods: what will change in one year, in three years, and, if appropriate, five years. Of course, the longer the timeframe, the more general your information is likely to be. As time progresses, the more it will need reviewing to update it with real events (see *Idea 19*).

Go through each of the questions set in Step 2 and review them from the point of view of the changes likely to happen over the timeframe(s). The key is to always look at the potential impact the change will have on:

- Your customer.
- Their needs generally.
- Their needs specifically in your contract.
- The contract itself.
- You are not yet looking at the changes your proactive work may deliver. At this stage, you are looking at what may require reaction.

Organize your information in the sequence below, listing the most important changes at the top of each area:

- How the market may change and the impacts this will have.
- How the customer may change and the impacts this will have.
- How the direct customer department may change and the impacts this will have.
- How the contract may change and the impacts this will have.

Of course, some of these areas will have an impact on others, so you may have a chain of changes. For instance, a change in the market may impact the customer, which in turn will impact your direct customer and therefore their needs of the contract. Following these links will be important to understand where customer changes in requirements have come from so you are looking at the overall cause—and therefore the impact of any changes you make on that cause rather than just the direct request that may come to you.

You might end up with more than one scenario. In this case, try to arrange each scenario as a separate option, with the changes that each of the areas would have in that scenario.

Step 4: Set priorities and plans.

From your review of the present situation and the changes likely to impact your customer and the contract, you should now be in a position to set out an initial list of priorities. These will be a set of what you believe will be the most important areas of change or improvement that will have a positive impact on your customer and your contract. The test of these should be:

"If we deliver improvement in these areas, they will make the most positive difference for the customer and their view of us come the recompete."

Now start to look at how you might be able to deliver these changes:

- What would it take to deliver the change?
- How long would the change take?
- What would the change cost to deliver?
- What would the positive impact of the change be?
- How would we measure the impact of the change?

In deciding your priorities, you should place all the options onto the matrix in Figure IV.2. At this initial stage, you might only have estimates of the cost and impact of the options, however this filter will at least enable you to take a view of the most likely priorities. Add in for each option the estimated time it will take to put in place.

Your priority areas will be those in the box marked 1—those with the most impact and least cost.

The next level of priorities will depend to some degree on the amount of funding and investment you and the customer (see figure on who pays) have available in budgets to deliver improvements. If there is little funding, then those with low cost and relatively low impact will keep the momentum of change and improve-

Section IV Stabilize

ment going. If budgets are available and the costs are seen to be worth it by the customer who has budgets available, then those with high cost and high impact might become a second set of priorities.

Those in box 3, with high cost and low impact, are unlikely to ever reach the stage where they become priorities for action. However, they shouldn't be discarded entirely from your analysis. Over time, you may find ways to deliver the change that reduce the cost, and/or circumstances may mean that the importance of the change may increase for the customer and so the impact may increase.

Figure IV.2   Priorities Matrix

	Priorities for Changes and Improvement	
High Cost	2	3
Low Cost	1	2
	High Impact	**Low Impact**

By adding an estimated time to deliver with each initiative, and taking those from box 1 and those you feel are achievable from either of the boxes numbered 2, you should now be able to set out a timed plan of your priorities over the next period of time.

Step 5: Review.

Now that you have an initial set of timed ideas and priorities, it is time to review what these could mean in total. Go back to Step 1 and your initial aiming point. With the analysis you have undertaken and the initiatives you have identified, does your aiming point still make sense and look achievable? Remembering that the priorities you have set for your initial plan will be followed by further opportunities, but that events may also slow or reduce your ability to deliver, should you look to change your initial aim, either in form (what you are aiming for) or ambition (the extent of what you are aiming for)?

Your aiming point is a qualitative one, so there should be some flexibility to how you achieve it. It should set a challenge and be ambitious—but it will also set expectations, so it needs to be realistic. Only you will be able to tell this based on the circumstances of your own contract.

Step 6: Communicate the plan.

Even if your plan is extremely short and relatively low level, it is unlikely to be achieved if you are the only one who knows about it and is knowingly participating in its implementation. Your next step should be to look at to whom you communicate the plan, and how you will bring them on board with the delivery of the plan. The following stakeholders should be part of your thinking:

- Your management team.
- The staff working on the contract.
- The customer.
- Your suppliers/partners.
- Customer staff and end users.
- Your own company.

The extent to which you give each of these stakeholders details of the plan and involve them in the day-to-day idea generation, planning, and implementation of the plan will vary. Generally, the more stakeholders involved in delivering the plan, the more likely it is to succeed in delivering the right outcomes.

You might decide to bring some stakeholders into your initial thinking, or you may introduce them to different aspects once you are clearer on their details or relevance to that group. Once you have communicated with a group about the plan, it is vital that you regularly keep them informed of progress. Otherwise, it may simply seem to be another short-term initiative that is not being followed through and will lose momentum and (along with you) credibility.

Step 7: Manage and govern the plan.

Your Contract Plan is not a one-off exercise. You will need to be able to drive, monitor, and revise the plan as the contract progresses. You need to put in place a mechanism to achieve this.

This will involve regular meetings with the relevant stakeholders to make sure you are keeping tabs on, and setting actions for, the projects and programs that the plan involves. You will also need to regularly review the plan and, if needed, revise it as you see the progress made and as circumstances change. You will need some form of measures to show how things are progressing, and the impact of what has been achieved (again, it is worth taking a look at *Idea 19: Keep Your Contract Up To Date* and the introductions to Performance Management and Continuous Improvement in Section V: *Improve* stage of this guide).

Section IV Stabilize

You can either create a separate mechanism for this management of the plan, or you can integrate it into the meetings, reviews, and governance that you have on your contract anyway. We recommend the second option.

You will have regular meetings with your management team, and with your customer. We recommend you add the Contract Plan to these meetings. Initially, it may be an item on the agenda (not the last item, as this is the one that can often be rushed or missed in many meetings). Over time it should, as the value being delivered by it becomes more apparent to all, become the focus of the meeting, with the usual items covered being encompassed within the overall Contract Plan.

It is worth reviewing the plan at least annually—although you may choose to do so quarterly if your contract is short or the environment dynamic. These reviews should go back through Steps 2–5. They should recheck the environment, the likely changes in the future, progress to date and the impact of this. The initiatives taken so far should be reviewed, new ideas added and the plan reprioritized as required. Your overall progress towards your aim should also be assessed.

You may wish at this time to write out, in some form, an "annual report" (see *Idea 18: Publish an Annual Review*). This will summarize your progress and successes to date, the positive impact made for the customer, and your priorities for the next period.

This report (or variations of it in staff newsletters, etc.) can be used to inform and motivate staff and also inform your customer of the progress made to date. The accumulated reports will also be an important part of the evidence you have for the recompete of the improvements you have delivered over the period of the contract.

Your Contract Plan will now form the backbone of other initiatives covered in this workbook. While each of them can be delivered without a plan, the processes involved in initiating them and their coordination and coherence will be significantly enhanced by being part of an overall plan.

What do you expect of an incumbent that is different from new bidders?

"Show that they are still hungry to have the contract. Show they have kept innovating and they know they are competitive."

Private Sector, Europe

Idea 9: Help the Customer Manage Risk

Idea Summary:

What:

Put in place a process for managing risks throughout your contract. Do this with your customer to create a joint process for risk management.

Why:

This will help you avoid risks and reduce the impact of them over the contract period. It will also draw you closer to the customer and help build a partnering approach to your relationship.

Key Steps:

1. Identify the most important risks.

2. Identify how you can reduce the likelihood and impact of risks.

3. Create a joint approach to risk with your customer.

4. Plan for your reactions to risks crystallizing.

We mentioned Risk Registers or RAID (Risks Assumptions, Issues, and Dependencies) registers in *Idea 8: Create a Contract Plan*. We will look again later in the guide at how to use risk to help persuade the customer that you, as the incumbent, present the lowest risk option for them (See *Idea 54: Use Risk Effectively* in Section VIII: Run the Recompete stage). However, you also need to manage risk during the period of the contract—and not just your own risks. The Stabilize stage of your contract is the ideal time to review your contract's risks and the wider customer's risks so you can plan and put in place a process for how you will manage, minimize, and react to risks during the contract.

Just as your bid team will most likely have investigated, reviewed, and aimed to mitigate risks during the bid (risks to the bid being successful, risks of mobilization, risks of the contract delivering and being profitable), so will the customer. Understanding and reducing risks will have been a significant part of the customer's preparations, evaluation, and outcome of their procurement process. They will have reviewed such things as:

- The risks of the project or activity overall.

- The risks of the procurement failing, or being extended or going over their procurement budget.

- The risks presented by each of the bidding companies (are they financially sound?).
- The risks of the solutions put forward.
- The risks of the prices and payment mechanisms put forward by bidders (for instance, are the prices sufficient to deliver the work effectively?).
- The risks to delivery of the transition stage.
- The risks of changing contractors.

When you won the contract, you were not only the contractor that offered the best solution at the best price, you were also the contractor deemed to present the lowest, or at least an acceptable, level of risk to the customer.

And just as the customer had their own risk management approach to the procurement, they will of course be managing their own risks throughout the contract period. And not just the risks related directly to the contract. Just as your company Board and senior management teams have a hierarchy of business risks they regularly review and seek to manage and minimize, the customer's organization will have their own set of wider business and strategic risks that you, your activities, and the area in which your contract operates within the customer are just a part.

If you can proactively work with your customer throughout the contract to help them identify, understand, mitigate, and effectively react to their risks, especially those they see as their most significant risks, you will be seen as the sort of contractor they want to continue to do business with. And you will have a horde of evidence to talk about in your recompete to show the recompete evaluators just why they should choose you as the winner.

Understanding the Customer's Risks

Some of the customer's risks will be publicly available through their website or annual reports. You may be able to identify others yourself. Ideally, you will be building a good enough relationship with your customer for them to share their risk management processes and key risks with you. If you explain your intention to work with them to align your risk management process with their own, there is a better chance this will happen.

As you build up an understanding of the customer's risks, you may find a number of them relate to your contract and the work you are delivering.

Key Steps for Risk Management

The following steps should enable you to integrate your risk management with the customer's:

Step 1: Identify the most important risks.

Identify those risks that are most important and those that already relate directly to your contract and the work you do. Understand the approach the customer is presently taking to these risks—whether they see them as high, medium, or low probability of happening; what level of impact they see the risks as having if they crystallize and what these impacts are; and what mitigations they have in place to reduce the probability and impact of the risk. At this point, you should also look at how the customer manages their risks and what sort of risk matrix or other way of summarizing their risks they use. You will want to align your way of summarizing and reporting risks to the customer's approach (even if you also use your own methods for your own purposes).

List those risks you see as most important and most relevant to your contract.

Step 2: Identify how you can reduce the likelihood and impact of risks.

Identify ways that you, through the contract, can reduce the likelihood or impact of these risks. You might not have an immediate impact—it may take time to be in a position where you can have a positive result. Or perhaps actions you have taken on the contract to date and the solution you have in place are already making a positive impact. Talk to your customer and see where there are, or could be, areas of their risk on which you have, or can have, a positive impact.

Step 3: Create a joint approach to risk with your customer.

If you can, work with your customer to create a joint risk approach. This should ideally involve:

- Having a joint risk register.
- Meeting on a regular basis to jointly review the risk register.
- Identifying whether there are any new risks.
- Agreeing whether existing risks have changed, or if risks have gone away (just as the risks to these areas will have passed once you have successfully completed your mobilization and transition phases).
- Working on ways to mitigate risks.

Step 4: Plan for your reactions to risks crystallizing.

Plan how you can help if risks do crystallize. If a risk should become an issue—for example, if there is a risk of a flood and a flood does happen—what can you and your staff do to help? Make sure you have clear and well-communicated plans in place for such events. You might even work with the customer on practices or drills showing what would happen if an event does take place and you need to work jointly to reduce the impact and recover as quickly as possible.

Caveats

There are two main caveats to note in working closely with the customer on risks (just as with all other joint endeavors you will be involved in through the contract):

1. Be careful that responsibility stays with the right organization. Yes, you should be helping your customer and working jointly with them wherever possible. But you do not want to take on responsibility for risks that are not in your power to impact. If something does go wrong, you need to be clear where responsibility and consequences sit. You do not want to end up with the customer (even unconsciously) stepping away from responsibilities that rightly sit with them and the issues become yours to manage or resolve—especially if you do not have the influence or power to effectively do so.

2. If there are additional costs over and above your contract pricing that are involved in reducing risks through mitigating actions, or in resolving the results of risks that occur, be clear what these are. Are you willing to take these costs on, or will you need to negotiate with your customer to ensure your costs are covered through contract changes? As with all the positive actions in the ideas in this guide, if you are offering something that has a real value to the customer, they should be willing to pay you for it. If they are not, either your actions are not adding real value to the customer or you should be careful to analyze how much you are willing and able to spend on them. You want to win the recompete. But you don't want to be running a loss-making contract in order to do so.

Managing Your Own Risks

While you are working with the customer to manage the risks of the contract and their wider risks, if appropriate, you must still proactively manage your own risks and the risks specific to your performance on the contract. Some see this as a purely bureaucratic exercise, with risk matrices that are out of date or cursory at best and often not related to the day-to-day of the contract. But come the recompete, you want to be able to show your customer you have proactively managed risks, actually prevented risks from becoming issues, and, if risks have crystallized, can show you have minimized their impact and learned from the experience to prevent them from happening again. At the same time, you should, of course, be minimizing those risks that will impact your own margins and ability to thrive.

The RAID Register

You will probably have your own standard internal risk approaches and matrices. The RAID register extends this to cover not only Risks, but also Assumptions, Issues, and Dependencies. RAID registers are often used for bids or transformations where information is incomplete, time is of the essence, and progress is required quickly. They are also useful for your contract.

Overview of Risks, Assumptions, Issues, and Dependencies

Risks will, of course, cover those potential issues that could impact your business. A typical Risk Register would include, for each risk, columns for:

- The area of the business the risk is in.
- What the risk is.
- What the potential likelihood is of the risk occurring (low, medium, high, or a numerical value).
- What the potential impact of the risk occurring might be (low, medium, or high, or again a numerical value).
- The overall risk level posed (a numerical value based on combination of likelihood and impact).
- A description of the potential impact.
- A potential cost of the risk if it occurred.
- What is being done to mitigate the likelihood of the risk occurring.
- What plans are in place to reduce the impact of the risk if it occurs.
- What the residual risk likelihood is, with the mitigating action in place.
- What the residual risk is, with the mitigating plan in place.
- The overall mitigated risk level.
- The owner of the risk (who is responsible for managing the risk, watching for its likelihood, planning for minimizing its impact).
- If the risk has a time period in which it may take place, or after which it may disappear, what this is.
- Whether the risk is increasing or decreasing in level, likelihood, or imminence, or is stable.

Section IV Stabilize

Assumptions are usually included in the bid for the contract when full information is not always available. They may be assumptions about volumes of work or inflation that form the core of cost calculations or about customer needs or a range of other factors. They will have been tested, revised, and moved from assumption to known information as the bid progresses and then as the mobilization and transition teams test them in the reality of the contract. Assumptions are often necessary so some form of solution or plan can be created. But they are also dangerous. If they are poor assumptions and are acted on, the solution or the action taken based on them could be flawed and lead to serious problems. Even more dangerous are those assumptions which, over time, start to be seen not as an "educated guess" but as a known or obvious truth that stops being tested or questioned. When this happens, the contract can go off track without the team understanding why, or thinking to check whether the assumptions being made do, in fact, reflect reality.

For each assumption, your Register should include a column for:

- Description of the assumption.

- Basis for the assumption (reasons that justify the assumption).

- What is based on the assumption (e.g. cost growth may be based on inflation assumption).

- Owner (who is best in place to test it).

- When the assumption should be rechecked and perhaps revised.

Your RAID Register should include those assumptions made during the bid, together with the facts that emerge when information becomes available. As other assumptions are made on which plans, forecasts, or actions are based (for instance, in your initial Contract Plan), these should also be added to the register. The point of the Assumptions Register is:

- To make sure the assumptions you are making are clearly written down as assumptions, not facts.

- To check that you are not making conflicting assumptions in different areas or at different times.

- To enable you and the team to question, challenge, and test your assumptions regularly.

- To show how close or far out your assumptions have been when the facts emerge, and help you make better assumptions as the contract progresses.

Issues are problems that are happening now. The Issues Register ensures that you are keeping focus on all the issues you are facing on the contract, large or small, and are progressing toward the resolution of all of them. You should also be checking your issues against your risk register: were the issues you are facing anticipated on your Risk Register and are they having the impact you expected? You should be looking at the issues and adding their potential to reoccur as risks to your Risk Registers. Seeing issues occur and dealing with them helps you understand their impact and their causes. This should help you figure out how to reduce their likelihood and impact in the future.

While keeping your Issues Register live, you should also keep an Historical Register of all the issues you have faced and resolved. This will be a great learning tool for the team (who, over the contract period, may change) and will help if issues reoccur. When you get to the recompete, this will also be a good source of information: knowing what issues have been faced will help build a better solution; and being able to show the customer you have positively resolved issues on the contract shows you as proactive and experienced.

Your Issues Register should include columns for:

- What the issue is.
- When it occurred.
- Why it has arisen.
- What the impact is now.
- Severity (high, medium, low).
- What the impact will be if not resolved and severity (high, medium, low).
- Owner.
- Actions to resolve.
- Dates for actions.
- Date for resolution.
- Status (red, yellow/amber, green).

Dependencies are things you rely on to happen in order to achieve your plans or deliver your services. Usually, they will be things that others outside the contract are delivering to you. Examples might be timely information from the customer on requirements, or payment of invoices on time, or suppliers delivering in a certain timescale. They may, however, be areas of your own contract work that impact other areas in order for these, in turn, to deliver.

Section IV Stabilize

Again, your bid will most likely have a list of dependencies, and they may have been made explicit in your contracts with customers and suppliers to ensure you have some comfort that they will be delivered. Make sure the dependencies in the bid have been checked and processes and agreements are in place to ensure their delivery. As the contract progresses and more dependencies are identified, these should be added. When you get to the recompete, this will form a helpful list of areas for the new solution.

The Dependency Register should include columns for:

- Who is included in the dependency.
- What the dependency is.
- Issues that would be caused if the dependency fails.
- What your backup plan is.
- How the dependency is covered in contracts or agreements.
- Owner.

Summary

Rather than a paper exercise, your risk management should encompass reality. Things will happen on your contract. They might be problems or issues or they might be crises. Your RAID Register should be a learning document: whenever an issue occurs (large or small, whether it was on your Risk Register or not), the issue should become "live" on your RAID Register. When it is resolved, its impact and what you did to resolve it should be added to an historical Issues Register—and the potential for it to reoccur added to your Risk Register. The mitigating actions you have learned will actually prevent or reduce the frequency of it happening again (see *Idea 20: Resolve Any Problems Quickly and Effectively*).

By the time you get to the recompete, this should be a rich source of information for you to use to:

- Show how you have managed the risks of the contract.
- See how you have proactively resolved issues.
- Determine how and what you have learned from the risks and issues you have managed: so you are the contractor who will have fewest issues in the future (and be the lowest risk for the customer)—and how your new solution for the next contract period has been designed with this learning in mind.
- Point out your detailed understanding of the contract to the customer—and use this to show them that perhaps challengers have not thought of the issues in depth.

We will return to the subject of risk and how to use it in your recompete in *Idea 54: Use Risk Effectively*.

> ***What is the most important thing an incumbent can do to improve their chances of winning?***
>
> *"During the term of their existing contract, they need to communicate constantly what it is they are doing and also show the value they are providing. It is too late at the recompete to then tell everyone what you have been doing for the last 12 or 24 months."*
>
> *Private Sector, Australia*

Idea 10: Align to the Customer

Idea Summary:

What:

Align as many of your processes as possible with those of the customer.

Why:

By taking a joint approach, you will be able to help the customer achieve their goals and address their issues. You will also build a closer relationship with the customer and bring yourself closer to their strategic goals and issues.

Aligning as closely as possible to the customer's wider goals goes beyond sharing risk management agendas (see *Idea 9*). Wherever you can align with the customer, get close to them, be seen as a partner, or add value—through your normal activity on the contract or the wider governance and business activities you undertake—this will help in your relationship through the contract, and at the recompete. For instance, it is likely that both you and the customer will:

- Have business continuity and disaster recovery plans.
- Be working on Corporate Responsibility (CR) initiatives.
- Work on reducing your impact on the environment.
- Sponsor events, organizations, or other activities as part of CR and marketing initiatives.

As part of your integration with the customer, you should look at how you can align your own initiatives with the customer's and how the activities on your contract may help the customer achieve their own goals.

For instance, any issues requiring a business continuity response are likely to impact both you and the customer:

- Is your business continuity plan fully aligned with (indeed part of) the customer's?

- Do you have facilities, capacities, or capabilities on your contract or perhaps within your company as a wider business that could be used in helping the customer if a business continuity or disaster recovery situation arises?

- Can you participate in, or even help organize, any exercises that test readiness for potential crises?

What are your customer's goals, targets, and programs for reducing their environmental impact? Could you:

- Participate in any of these programs?

- Look at the work you are doing on your contract to see if it also helps the customer's environmental targets?

- Also work towards a particular environmental accreditation that the customer is working toward?

- Align your environmental policies with the customer's?

What CR activities does the customer undertake? Could you:

- Participate in these?

- Encourage any of your staff to join customer CR committees—or enable them to participate in activities the customer's staff are also undertaking?

- Align your CR policies, procedures, and targets with those of the customer?

Do you have access through the work on your contract to end users of the customer? Could you:

- Use this contact to help the customer understand these end users in a way that will help them?

- Conduct end user surveys, perhaps of satisfaction (see more of this in *Idea 14: Measure End User Satisfaction*)?

- Through your activities, collect information on the end user that will be of use elsewhere to the customer—either in understanding the end user or in providing other services to the end user?

There may be a range of other areas where you could align yourself with the customer. Use the Stabilize stage to:

- Understand all these types of activities and goals that the customer has—look at their website, annual reports, etc.

- Think about how you might be able to align with the customer.

- Think about how you may be able to actively help the customer meet their goals.

- Create a set of possible areas of alignment.

- Approach your customer (both your direct customer contact and, if you have agreement from your direct customer, those directly responsible for these other areas) with your ideas.

- Set out a plan for alignment with the customer.

Not only will these activities help build a general sense of partnership with the customer, they will open up a range of other contacts and relationships across the customer organization that you and, if they are able to participate, your staff, will be able to build over the contract period. It will also give you a broader insight into the customer and what is happening more widely across their organization, and give a richer perspective on their business and priorities, which could be vital as the contract progresses and approaches the recompete.

What are the primary reasons incumbents lose recompetes?

"Not becoming a partner in the enterprise. Work with me and I'll work with you."

— Private Sector, USA

Section V

Improve

The Improve stage sits as shown below in the contract lifecycle:

Figure V.1   The Contract Lifecycle Improve Stage

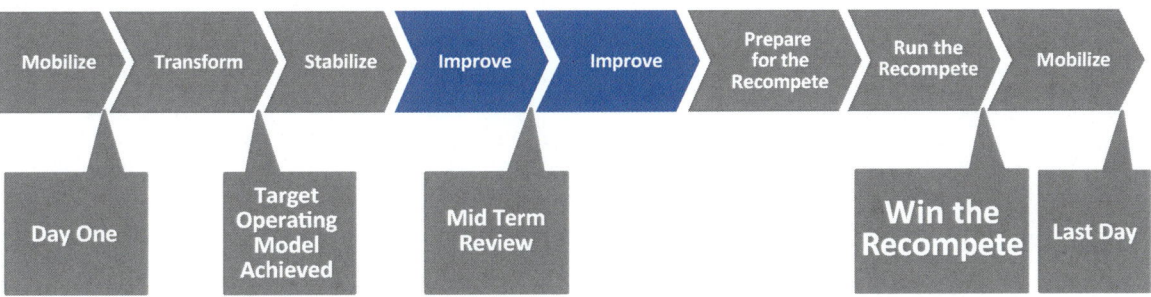

What Is the Improve Stage?

The improve stage should cover the majority of the period of your contract. It is the phase where you will **proactively** be improving your performance, the added value you deliver, your customer relationships, putting into action and revising your Contract Plan (see *Idea 8*) and a range of other improvements. It is the phase where you will be making the differences that will, when you come to recompete, have put you in the strongest possible position with the customer in their appreciation and (well founded) belief that you are the type of contractor they want to choose for the next contract period.

Unfortunately it is also the phase that many incumbents skip. They move to the stability stage and never really step out of it until the end of the contract. While some improvement may take place, it is likely to be sporadic, not part of a wider plan or perhaps driven by the customer.

The difference between this and the proactive, planned, and coordinated approach we will take is a huge cumulative difference in performance by the end of your contract—and a huge positive difference in your position come recompete.

In the Contract Lifecycle, the Improve stage is actually two stages: it is split by the Mid Term Review. We will cover how to run a Mid Term Review at the end of this section on Improve. However, it is worth giving a short explanation of how it fits into the overall Improve phase.

The first half of the Improve stage will be based on your Contract Plan set up in *Idea 9* and modified as you progress through regular internal reviews, monthly meetings, and through the changes and successes you achieve and the changes you perceive in the customer's needs and situation. The Mid Term Review is an external and significant review of the place you have reached, as the name suggests, halfway through your contract period. It will involve people from within your business who will audit where you and the customer are, what you have achieved to date, what the customer's situation is, and what has changed. It will be conducted by people within your wider business who can take an objective view of where the contract stands. The outcome of the review will help determine both your progress and any changes in direction you may need to take in your Contract Plan, based on where the customer is now. This will provide information for the second half of the Improvement phase—you will still be looking at the same areas of activity (performance measurement, added value, etc.) but the pace, priorities, and direction may change.

The Improve phase actually continues to the end of the contract. Even when you are preparing for the recompete and are actively in the recompete process, you should still be improving.

Ideas included in this section:

- **Idea 11:** Measure the Things That Make a Real Difference to the Customer
- **Idea 12:** Balance Consistent Measures with New, Relevant Measures
- **Idea 13:** Benchmark Your Measures
- **Idea 14:** Measure End User Satisfaction
- **Idea 15:** Add Value for the Customer
- **Idea 16:** Deliver Continuous Improvement
- **Idea 17:** Innovate
- **Idea 18:** Publish an Annual Review of the Contract
- **Idea 19:** Keep Your Contract Up to Date

Section V Improve

- Idea 20: Resolve Any Problems Quickly and Completely
- Idea 21: Know and Use All Available Contract Change Routes
- Idea 22: Constantly Build Customer Relationships and Trust

What is the most important thing an incumbent can do to improve their chances of winning?

"Stay competitive in pricing and technology of product. Talk to me about what is going on in the industry, including competing products, and call on me more than just when it is time to place an order."

Public Sector, USA

Measuring Performance

Introduction to Measuring Performance

The USA Federal Acquisition Regulation (subpart 42.15) states that:

> "Past performance information is relevant information, for future source selection purposes, regarding a contractor's actions under previously awarded contracts. It includes, for example, the contractor's record of conforming to contract requirements and to standards of good workmanship; the contractor's record of forecasting and controlling costs; the contractor's adherence to contract schedules, including the administrative aspects of performance; the contractor's history of reasonable and cooperative behavior and commitment to customer satisfaction; the contractor's record of integrity and business ethics, and generally, the contractor's business-like concern for the interest of the customer..... Agency procedures for the past performance evaluation system shall generally provide for input to the evaluations from the technical office, contracting office and, where appropriate, end users of the product or service."

Why Is Performance Measurement Important?

Measuring your performance on the contract will most likely be required by the customer. They will have set performance measures and levels of expected performance against those measures and told you in the procurement procedure what these are, together with the penalties you might incur if you don't achieve them. On many contracts, there will also be a direct relationship between the key measures of performance and how, and how much, you are paid for the contract.

In addition to getting paid correctly for the work being done, one of the vital parts of building a positive reputation with the customer during the contract is being able to show throughout the contract that you are meeting or exceeding your performance measures. Consistently showing the customer you are performing to (or above) the levels set by them will build your reputation as the sort of contractor they want to do business with, giving you a positive position as you approach the recompete. Being able to show in the recompete your record of excellent performance throughout the contract will be proof to those evaluating the recompete that they should choose you as the winner.

But there are several aspects to measuring performance you could miss if you just stick to what the customer has imposed on your performance regime.

Before we look at these, let's quickly review some of the key types of performance measures.

Types of Performance Measurement

While there are many things that can be measured, in many different ways, for our purposes we will focus on three categories of measurement: input, output, and outcome. There are grey areas between them, but being able to categorize your performance measures will be important for managing your contract.

Input Measures

Input measures refer to the amount of resources applied to a particular task. On a service contract, this might equate to the number of people employed (and showing up) to do a particular task. Some contract formats will pay the contractor on this basis and potentially penalize the contractor if they don't deliver a certain level of input.

A simple input measure might be: 20 cleaners, to do 8 hours work per day, 7 days per week.

Output Measures

Output measures quantify the amount of a particular task achieved, though not directly the results of this work. In contracts which are predominantly output measurement based, the amount of input required to achieve the output will be up to the contractor. And on contracts that are paid based on outputs, the risk of the amount and cost of input required to deliver that output sits with the contractor.

So taking our example above, a (very simplistic) output measure for the same contract might be: All wards in a hospital to be cleaned every day of the week (in reality there will be significantly more detail around what is to be cleaned and to what standard, etc.).

Section V   Improve

> *Proposal expert advice*
>
> *"Make sure that the client experiences good service and value through the life of the contract. It is important that this is regularly articulated in terms of client service improvements and value throughout the contract. If these are left to be consolidated at the end of the term and presented as part of the bid solution, in my experience this is less effective. Build trusted relationships with clients at the right levels ('suits' arriving once a year won't cut it to build exec relationships). Collaboration is a very current concept, look at how better integration with client side staff will reduce waste and cost. Some people (including clients) will need to cast off their egos if real progress and savings are to be made. Next is an old one, but still very valid—make sure you KNOW what the client's drivers and needs are long before the recompete arrives."*
>
> *Director, Business Services Company, UK*

Outcome Measures

Outcome measures do not directly measure the work done. Instead, they focus on the result of that work. They will often be strategic or policy outcomes for the customer, or will be directly related to important results which themselves contribute to these overarching objectives.

In our example, a possible outcome measure might be the reduction of certain types of hospital-acquired infections related to a lack of hospital cleanliness.

Development of Contract Measurement

There has been a general shift over the past few decades from contracts being contracted and measured via input-based models to more output-based arrangements, and now a relatively small but increasing emphasis on outcome-based measurement and even payment. This is not to say that all contracts, customers, or markets have moved steadily through this process. Different customers and different circumstances still require different arrangements, and it is not unusual to see input-based contracts in many areas. In the past few years, a small number of contracts procured on a payment by outcome basis (sometimes called Payment by Results) are being tested in a number of areas to achieve social outcomes. Contracts already in existence in 2013 include those where at least part of the contract payment is based on increasing the number of unemployed getting and keeping jobs, and others where payment is based on reducing the reoffending of those released from prison.

Different Customer Stakeholders Have Different Priorities

When it comes to the recompete, you will have a real advantage if you can show the customer you have delivered benefits to a range of stakeholders in their organization (and if relevant, beyond). Recompete evaluation processes often involve a wider set of departments and people than the customer contract team, which manages and monitors the contract on a day-to-day basis. Ensuring this wider group has built a positive view of you and the contract will give you an advantage. And in any organization there are those who might not be directly involved in the evaluation, but who have some form of influence on the decision makers. These might be individuals, groups, or departments who are the end users of your services, for instance. Being able to show during the contract that you are delivering a great service to them will help build a good relationship and reputation for you during the contract. Being able to present evidence in the recompete showing how you have done this—and the results—will prove you are the sort of contractor who has gone beyond the basics of delivering the specification and has worked to give the wider customer real benefits.

What do you expect of an incumbent that is different from new bidders?

"That all issues and SLA requirements have been met. That we have already been offered any innovations (technical and commercial) should we NOT have come out to bid."

Private Sector, UK

Idea 11: Measure the Things that Make a Real Difference to the Customer

Idea Summary:

What:

Don't restrict yourself to measuring the KPIs set in the contract. Understand where you can show how you are making important contributions to the customer's business and measure (and report) on these.

Why:

By measuring those things most important to the customer's own success and showing your contribution to this success, you will show you have the customer's strategic goals in mind and are contributing to those. This will increase your value to the customer and open up a wider range of relationships within the customer organization, as well as give you powerful evidence of relevant performance at the recompete.

Key Steps:

1. Review your existing performance measures.

2. Understand the link between your existing performance measures.

3. Review the customer's priorities.

4. Build a map of the actions that lead to achieving the customer's outcomes.

5. Define the measures you can use to show your impact.

6. Talk to the customer.

You will most likely have two sets of performance measures on your contract:

- The measures the customer has set.

- Your own internal measures (such as cost related measures, margins, etc.).

But are those measures the customer has set the best ones to enable you to:

- Show during the contract that you are making the maximum positive impact on the customer's organization?

- Understand what drives performance so you can effectively manage the efforts of your contract to deliver improvements?

- Show at the recompete the contribution you have made to the customer's goals and objectives most important to them?

- Gather the type of information on the contract, its operations, and demands which will help you develop a winning solution for the recompete, even if the customer changes the way they want to pay for and measure the contract in the next contract period?

To be sure you are measuring the activities which will have the most impact on the above points, you need to review the measures the customer has put in place, decide whether you should (and can) add other measures, and work toward improving these.

The following steps will help you focus on what you measure and report to the customer, and the areas you focus on to improve your performance in ways which will have the most positive impact for the customer.

Step 1: Review your existing performance measures.

List out the performance measures the customer has set and break them out into different groupings:

Input	Output	Outcome
Measure 1	Measure 4	
Measure 2	Measure 7	
Measure 3		
Measure 5		
Measure 6		
Measure 8		

This will give you an initial view of where the majority of measures stand. Where there are several measures, you should also break them into the different parts of the services you deliver on the contract. For example:

Service a	Service b	Service c	Service d	Service e	Service f
Measure 1	Measure 2	Measure 3	Measure 5	Measure 6	Measure 7
Measure 4			Measure 8		

Step 2: Establish any links between your existing performance measures.

Next, look at the links between the performance measures. For instance, in the tables above, are any of the measures in the input column linked to the measures in the output column, or are different service measures linked in such a way that:

- If you are required to deliver a certain number of hours work in an activity, this is linked to an output of the number of tasks completed?

- In terms of the services you deliver, service *a* must be completed before service *b* can start?

- Missing target levels in service *d* will automatically mean you will fail to deliver the required level in service *e*?

Understanding these areas and links between the performance measures you have set will enable you to prioritize efforts, focus staff and management teams on achieving what is required of them, and help you predict where your performance will be ahead of the final results. For instance, if performance has fallen in service *d* and it is linked to service *e*, you can predict you will also suffer there and hopefully be able to reduce the impact.

Section V Improve

Step 3: Review the customer's priorities.

Your performance measures might reflect the priorities of the contract. But how do they link with your customer's wider strategic priorities? As discussed, if you can show at the recompete you have had a real and positive impact on the customer's strategic goals, you are in a much stronger position than if you just show you performed the contract well.

List out the customer's strategic priorities and the outcomes they are aiming to achieve. You might find these from a range of sources:

- The customer's own published annual reports.
- Their website.
- Internal documents that you may have access to.
- Conversations with senior customer contacts.

The types of priorities you may find will, of course, vary with the type of customer and their particular goals. But they might include:

- Growth in particular markets.
- Customer satisfaction.
- Meeting environmental targets.
- Being the lowest cost supplier to their customers.
- Being the highest quality supplier to their markets.
- Being innovative.

For government customers, there may be particular outcomes they are aiming to achieve related to improvements such as:

- Reducing unemployment.
- Improving health.
- Reducing crime.
- Improving educational outcomes.
- Supporting foreign policy.
- Defending the country.

Step 4: Build a map of the actions which lead to achieving the customer's outcomes.

There can be a big gap between the goals and outcomes the customer is aiming to achieve strategically and where they are now. There may also be a big gap between the services you are providing on your contract and these higher level goals. But the customer will usually have their own set of projects, actions, or strategies to help them achieve these goals. These might be included in projects or programs they are putting into action themselves, or there may be some obvious links you can build from your own research to show how these goals could be delivered. These drivers to achieving the customer's outcomes could be areas you can have more influence on, or be able to link your contract's services to, and measure your impact.

Build your best view of the main priorities and drivers the customer is, or could be, using to deliver their strategic outcomes. These links might not be obvious, so here are two examples which might give you some ideas:

Example 1:

A roofing contractor had a contract with a Local Authority to deliver the customer's program of replacing and upgrading school roofs over a five-year period as part of the customer's estate management program. The contractor's key performance measures set by the customer were based on:

- *Cost per roof;*

- *Completion of each roofing project to times set;*

- *Quality of work as inspected by the customer's surveyors.*

The contractor, on reviewing the Local Authorities priorities and targets on their website, discovered the customer had set itself a target of reducing CO_2 emissions by 20% over the next five years. They also saw on the environment section of the website one of the main areas of CO_2 emissions was related to the buildings under the Authorities' control, and a significant proportion of these were schools.

Part of the specification for the new roofing the contract required was a higher level of insulation than presently on the school roofs being replaced. The contractor, using standard building and environmental formulas, calculated the new roofs they were installing reduced the heating requirements and therefore carbon emissions of each school by over 10%. They fed this back to the Authority's environment team each quarter as an ongoing new measure of the contract's contribution to this key customer target to be added to the customer's published progress towards its goals.

Section V Improve

> **Example 2:**
>
> *A company delivering contracts to police forces to replace police officers in custody cell blocks with civilian staff for administering the detention process of those arrested and detained by the police was being measured on a mainly input basis. This involved how many staff were available for set shifts together with basic compliance and quality checks on their work to the standards set. When the contracts began, they replaced warranted police officers doing these administrative duties with civilian employees—freeing these police officers up to be used on more public facing duties. However, this was only a one-off benefit for the customer resulting from the initial outsourcing of the contract. While a useful piece of information, it said nothing about how the contract was performing or improving outputs for the customer through the life of the contract.*
>
> *However, the contracts also had another benefit not measured by the customer: they reduced the time taken to book in detainees brought in after arrest by police on duty. The company measured how much time was saved for each detainee brought in by the police—and the reduced time off the streets this meant for the arresting officers. Over a year, this figure added up to several thousand hours—the equivalent of having over 20 additional officers on the streets—which was one of the police's key targets. This measure helped relate the work on the contract to one of the key targets of senior officers who may have had little to do with the custody environment in which the contractor operated, and it was something the company could work on to improve during the life of the contract.*

Build a picture of where your contract activities could impact the strategic goals of the customer, or at least the programs the customer has for achieving these goals:

Contract activity helping deliver program	Customer programs leading to strategic goal	Strategic goal
	Program a	Goal 1
Activity u	Program b	
	Program c	
Activity v	Program d	

Activity w	Program e	Goal 2
	Program f	
	Program g	

	Program h	Goal 3
Activity x	Program i	

Step 5: Define the measures you can use to show your impact.

Once you have a clearer idea of where you can show the positive impact your contract can have on these customer goals, you need to decide how you will measure this impact. You need to understand the link you can demonstrate, and also how you will go about measuring it.

In the two examples we used on the previous pages, the answers to these questions were relatively simple.

The roofing contractor measured:

- The type of material used in the old roof being replaced and how many inches depth there was on the roof.

- The new material being used and the inches depth of this.

- The square foot size of the roof (which they had to do anyway).

- The old and new materials used in both had known insulation levels which were common industry knowledge.

- The amount of heat lost through the roof of the schools was also an accepted percentage of the total lost from the buildings taken from building industry standards.

- There was also a standard industry (and environmentally) accepted formula for calculating how much the increase in insulation would impact reduced fuel to heat the building—depending on the type of heating the school used—which was also captured for each school by the contractor.

- This gave the measure of CO_2 saved for each school. Which was added up each quarter from all the schools where roofs were replaced by the contractor.

Each roofing project could take from two weeks up to a month. By simply taking a few minutes to capture the type and amount of material used on the old roof and a few minutes calculating the other figures and setting the calculations up on a spreadsheet, the contractor could show their positive impact.

The police contractor measured:

- The time that it had taken before they took over the contract to book a detainee (see *Idea 4*).

- The time each detainee arrived at a police station (which had to be noted anyway).

Section V Improve

- The time each detainee was taken to a cell, or the time one of the other relevant outcomes for the detainee was completed (again, these had to be noted anyway).

- The number of arresting officers for each detainee.

- These times were collated each week and the total time for booking for each detainee calculated.

- This was added up for all the detainees that week to give the total time taken by the arresting officers in the police station (using an average of the number of officers per detainee).

- This was compared to the total equivalent number before the contractor started. The difference was the total hours saved.

- The hours worked per week by an officer was taken from the customer's own numbers.

This measurement involved significantly more calculations, as there were hundreds of detainees a week per contract, but a simple system was created to capture information already being recorded as part of the work on the contract and a simple spreadsheet was used each week to produce an internal report. This was shared with the customer each month to show the total and cumulative savings being made in police time.

Note: It won't always be easy to find a causal link between all the aspects of work you do on the contract and strategic customer outcomes. The work might be too far removed; there might be limited information of the interim measures linking the work and the outcomes; or there might be a number of causes for a particular outcome, making it difficult to link improvement on the contract with improvement in the outcome. If this is the case, it is still worthwhile making the link for your own purposes, even if there is limited evidence you can quantify. One qualitative benefit, even of a link where you can't find measures, is when staff connect the work they are doing with a real customer outcome or benefit, it will help them understand the importance of their tasks and, managed well, give them a clearer sense of purpose and a chance to deliver the work in a way that enhances these benefits. You may, across your entire contract activities, only find one or two measures you can quantitatively link with a customer outcome. But that may be enough to transform how the customer sees your impact and efforts, and provide a focus for improving your performance and the impact you are seen to be having for the customer.

Step 6: Talk to the customer.

Obviously, the end point of this process is to give the customer information showing how you are helping them achieve their goals. When you involve the customer in your deliberations will vary depending on a number of things:

- Your relationship with the customer.

- Who in the customer organization will benefit most from the information you are producing (and the benefit you are delivering).

- The attitude of the customer and their attitude towards you (are the customer contacts and contract manager proactive, how open and positive are your relationships at this point, what are their motivations towards introducing new information and measures?).

- How you are presently performing on the core contract activities.

- What forum you have to introduce your thinking on new performance measures—or the results of your thinking.

- Whether you need additional help from people within the customer to gather information or validate your own thinking or results.

You may be in a position to present the customer with your first set of completed measures and talk the customer through what these measures mean, how you have collated them, the benefits you think they show, and the measures themselves can deliver. Or you might need the customer's help in gathering information only they hold, or want them to participate in the whole set of steps to bring them into the process from the start and get their insight and buy in early. Exactly which stage and to what extent you involve your customer contacts is up to you. The one thing you must not let happen is if the customer tries to block your drive to find new measures. Even if your direct customer contact is unreceptive, you might (without alienating your main contact) find others in the customer organization able and willing to help.

Usually your direct customer will be only too pleased to find you are supplying them with information enabling them to show the positive impact the contract or service area they are responsible for is having on the organization and goals of their superiors and colleagues—they, too, will gain from this heightened involvement in delivering corporate or organization goals.

Section V   Improve

Finally

At the end of this process, you should have a clear idea of how your existing measures relate to the work you are delivering to the customer. You should also have a set of additional measures showing the positive impact you are having on the customer's key organizational targets. These will make you more relevant to the customer as a whole over the period of the contract. They may bring you to the attention of, and help you build relationships with, other perhaps senior figures in the customer organization. And they will help show in your recompete how you have proactively made a real impact throughout the contract when you collate the overall benefits you have delivered over the contract period. Of course, once you have found the right measures, the most important thing will be to focus your effort on how you can improve your performance in these areas. Being able to show over the period of the contract that you are improving performance in strategically important areas for the customer (as well, of course, as delivering the basics well) will be where your real advantage lies in the recompete.

What do you expect of an incumbent that is different from new bidders?

"Their familiarity of our customers and needs, an awareness of emerging trends and values, that they have a focus on the pulse of their existing relationship with us as a customer."

State Government, USA

Idea 12: Balance Consistent Measurement with New, Relevant Measures

Idea Summary:

What:

Ensure you manage your set of performance measures over the period of the contract. Retain key measures throughout the contract to show overall improvement, but add new measures as circumstances change or you introduce new initiatives

Why:

At the end of the contract, you should be able to show, through consistent measurements, how you have delivered over the whole contract period. In addition, as you introduce new initiatives, you will be able to show the positive impact they are having.

At the end of the contract, when you are compiling what you will present in your recompete, you will want to show a set of measures which illustrate how you have consistently delivered, and improved, over the whole period of the contract. Therefore, you need to have this set of core measures kept the same, or at least easily comparable, over the whole contract period. If you change how you measure core information halfway through a contract, you will have a disconnect; you won't be able to compare performance at the start of the contract with that at the end.

At the same time, you shouldn't set in stone what you measure at the start of the contract and not add new measures as things change, as new services or ideas are introduced, or you are able to focus on improving particular areas of your work.

As you introduce new improvements, changes, or innovations to your contract, always look at how you will be able to measure the impact the improvement will have. Maybe it will have an impact on an existing measure; or you might add a new measure to test, validate, manage, and illustrate the performance and impact of your new idea.

As your contract matures over its lifecycle and as your Contract Plan (see *Idea 8*) brings changes and improvements, you may find that some measures are less relevant to managing your contract and showing the customer how well you are doing. For instance, the set of measures you used during the Transformation stage will no longer necessarily be of use when you have achieved your Target Operating Model and are in the Stabilize phase. If that is the case, you should agree with your customer when these measures are no longer relevant and you can stop reporting on them. But don't just abandon them. Gather the information surrounding the process which led to that measure and summarize a short report, even if you don't share it with the customer (which, in most cases, you should). File this report in your Recompete file (see *Idea 5*). You might find it useful when you come to the recompete.

Your report should include:

- What was being measured.

- Why you were measuring this aspect of work.

- What the measure was.

- How you collected the information.

- What the performance was (and, if possible, keep the data that was behind the reported performance).

- How this compared to the targets you set for performance—and if there was a variance, why.

Section V   Improve   85

- The outcome of the activity being measured—what benefit was delivered.

- Each of the reported measures over time (e.g. the daily, weekly or monthly figures) and summarize on a chart, diagram or table the total set of measures for the period.

- When and why you stopped measuring this activity.

- What you learned from the activity or process.

- Add copies of the reports you may have created for the customer at the time, and any feedback from the customer.

This doesn't need to be a huge report—a couple of pages with the relevant appendices may suffice. But as you write the report, bear in mind you (or someone else) may want to use it in the recompete in several years' time when the original reason for, and delivery of, the activity may be long forgotten and those involved may have moved on. Make it clear and obvious. Don't assume those reading or using the report will have prior knowledge of the surrounding context and what was happening at the time.

As you instigate new measures to fit with new activities or changes in focus, think through not just how you will measure the activity, but how it might be used with the customer and how you may be able to use the measure in the recompete.

What do you expect of an incumbent that is different from new bidders?

"Would have expected continuous improvement during current contract delivery bringing delivery up to current standards."

Federal/Central Government

Idea 13: Benchmark Your Measures

Idea Summary:

What:

Find external sources against which to compare your own performance.

Why:

This will help you understand the potential for improvement. It will also illustrate to your customer how well you are performing against industry best practice.

Performance measures on your own contract will allow comparison against some criteria, such as:

- How good are they against performance in the previous contract (if you have captured that information)?
- How are they changing over time?
- How do they compare to the levels of performance set by the customer?

But these are only part of the picture. How does your performance compare with industry standards, with your competitors, or with your own company performance on other similar contracts?

Being able to compare your performance with other external measures can give you powerful information that can drive you to find ways to improve. If you are performing particularly well against others it can also be a powerful message for your recompete.

It can often be difficult to get reliable information of competitors' performance, and in most cases this is the least available or reliable benchmark. While in some industries, competitors do share this sort of information, it is rare. However, you should look to see if you can obtain this information if it is available.

Industry standards can be found in some areas. Search out any benchmarking forums, websites, or industry associations. If you can find this information, it will give you a useful and often well-researched and qualified benchmark to use. Of course, you need to be sure you are comparing like with like, as other members of the industry may perform tasks in different ways or measure things differently.

The most likely and most usable information will probably come from other contracts within your own company. You will probably have several contracts performing similar tasks for different customers. Not only can you benchmark against these, it is easier (and competitively more beneficial) to share best practice within your own company. You are already likely to be using common measures for the financial returns across contracts. Even so, it's surprising how few businesses actively compare operational performance across contracts and use this information to help drive up performance for the customer to the levels of the highest performing contracts.

The following table lists some common objections to benchmarking together with some challenges to these objections:

Section V   Improve

Figure V.2   **Barriers to Benchmarking Performance Measures**

Barrier	Challenge
Different contracts are required to perform tasks differently.	Which is most effective? If by benchmarking you find one method is more efficient or effective than another, it would make sense to adopt this across other contracts. We will look at innovation in later ideas. This sort of benchmarking can be a good source of innovation and improvement ideas.
Different customers want different things.	How different are these really? If the differences are minor, any benchmarking measurement can account for this. And even if performance is different, over time the improvements can still be compared.
Customers want similar tasks measured differently.	There are two challenges to this: First, the final measures may be different but the underlying data could still be compared and translated into a similar measure. Second, one method of measuring a task may be more relevant and revealing of real performance for the customer. Once you have compared measures, you may wish to talk to your customer and see if they have thought of using the alternative measure used elsewhere.
My contract is performing less well than others—I don't want to tell the customer this.	There is no requirement for you to tell the customer immediately—you have time to look at why performance on your contract is lower, how others are achieving higher levels, and adopt any good processes and ideas. The customer will initially see your performance improve and when it is at a comparable level, you can show benchmarking data going forward.

Benchmarking is not a one-off exercise. While the initial information will show any differences in performance, the real value comes over time when these differences are analyzed to understand their causes, the reasons for better levels of performance are understood, and improvements are put in place to bring all contracts up to higher performance levels. Once this process is in place, the improvements can be measured over time and adopted not just for existing contracts but also for solutions put into new bids—and potentially for your next recompete.

What aspects of incumbents' proposals have been particularly poor?

"*Incumbents that deliver poor, overpriced or sloppy bids generally have performed the same in the previous job. In most cases, they will be aware of the dissatisfaction and are not really interested in reclaiming the contract.*"

Private Sector, USA

Idea 14: Measure End User Satisfaction

> **Idea Summary:**
>
> **What:**
>
> Find ways to regularly measure end user satisfaction and ways to improve the levels of satisfaction over the period of the contract.
>
> **Why:**
>
> Measuring end user satisfaction is a powerful tool for improving services and showing your customer you are delivering to their own important stakeholders. At the recompete, you will be able to use this information to evidence how you have helped the customer business, how you have taken into account end user needs in focusing your own improvement efforts—and the results of these activities.
>
> **Key Steps:**
>
> 1. Identify whose views you want to measure.
> 2. Identify how you will measure satisfaction.
> 3. Decide what questions to ask.
> 4. Test your process.
> 5. Analyze and present results.
> 6. Create an action plan of how you will respond to any issues.
> 7. Repeat the survey.

There are few more powerful messages you can give in your recompete than proof that the users of your service are extremely happy with what you are doing. Especially if these users are the customer's customers, you will be showing that you have focused on delivering real benefits to your customer.

As with the rest of your performance measures, you should make sure you are measuring this information from as early as possible during the contract; measuring it regularly, using it to improve your own performance, and making sure your customer is familiar with your performance as the contract progresses. If they only see it in the recompete documents, it will be new to them; they may not believe it, and you have not built the positive view going into the recompete to make sure the customer is on your side from the start.

Section V   Improve

It may not simply be direct users of your service whose satisfaction with your services you should review. There may be other stakeholders you interact with whose views you will also want to understand.

Your goal should be to have relevant, regular, and reliable information showing the views of users in a way the customer can understand and appreciate, and you can use to improve your services (and motivate your own team).

There are many consultants, companies, and books that focus exclusively on satisfaction research. If you are going to spend time and effort on surveying stakeholders, especially in larger numbers, it is worth talking to one of these businesses or reading up on the subject. You may not need or want to use an external company for all aspects of the work (although you can for a reasonable cost). For a small fee, consultants will advise you on key aspects of the process or set up a process you can run yourself. The process can be as complex as you wish to make it. The process that follows is a simple overview of the key stages and some of the main areas of focus.

Step 1: Identify whose views you want to measure.

Your first step will be to identify the key users of your service and any other stakeholders whose views you want to know. If your service is being provided to the customer's customer, this would be a clear group of people whose views you need to obtain. But there may be others.

List the potential groups you could survey for their views of your work. Identify the most important for you, depending on their closeness to the impact of the work you do and the potential impact as influencers on the customer. Prioritize the most important one or two groups. You should start with these. Once results from surveys of these initial groups are having an impact, you may decide to come back later in the contract to review the potential to survey other groups.

Example 1:

The roofing contractor whose work on performance measures is given as an example in Idea 11 recognized that the Principals of the schools they were reroofing were a key group of influencers for their contractual customer. While the schools did not pay the contractor, they were key influencers of the local authority with whom the contract was held. The contractor visited a number of Principals who had had their school's roofs replaced in the past year. They asked a range of open questions about what was important to the Principal in running the school; what impact the reroofing had on the school; the main worries and issues the Principals had prior to the work being done; and what they had experienced during the work process. Only toward the end of the meetings did the contractor ask how the work had gone; what was good about the work and the process; and what could have been improved.

The results of these interviews revealed a number of aspects of the work not recognized in the contract with the Local Authority as being important:

- *The Principals often felt alienated from the decision on when their reroofing project would be done and were uninformed of what the process would entail.*

- *The Principals were worried about disruption to the school timetable while the reroofing was taking place—but some were full of praise for the teams of workmen who completed the work for stopping work when requested if the school had particular events on such as exams, assemblies, etc.*

- *The Principals were also particularly worried about interaction between pupils and the workmen, but were again very positive about how the work teams on site managed their interaction with pupils and ensured sites were set up with safety in mind and interaction with pupils was managed by the contractor's on-site staff.*

- *Some Principals were critical of the long time it sometimes took for the site to be cleared after the work took place and the final clean up of the surrounding areas at the end of the project.*

- *The Principals were generally unaware of the benefits in additional insulation the new roofs delivered, but some did mention they thought the school felt a bit warmer after the new roofs had been completed.*

As a result of these interviews, the contractor created a short survey to be sent to all Principals of schools where work was completed. This was sent retrospectively to those who had had work done over the previous year, and then at the end of each project going forward.

The contractor also identified a number of simple changes and additions to its processes to resolve many of the issues identified in the initial research:

- *They initiated a meeting with each Principal prior to the work taking place, to take them through the process, identify any particular issues the Principal had and any key periods during the project when the school would appreciate work stopping or schedules for the work being managed (for instance, stopping from 9:00 to 9:30 each day for assembly, or understanding when exams may be taking place—and incorporating these into the project plan for the work). They also produced a simple leaflet the Principal could distribute to staff about the work. On some occasions, they also agreed with the Principal to present to staff at a meeting prior to the work commencing, and even ran occasional presentations as part of lessons to pupils on aspects of the work.*

- *A manager was identified for each project and their details given to the Principal so they could call or email at any time during the project if an issue occurred. The foreman for the site was also introduced to the Principal as an on site contact prior to the work commencing.*

- *Payment of the work teams on site was reviewed and a small bonus added depending on the results of the survey completed to the Principal—the teams were made aware of the issues the initial research had identified and what the company wanted to achieve regarding Principal's satisfaction.*

The initial results of the retrospective survey and the interviews were shared with the contractual customer and a quarterly report produced covering all the results from projects completed in that period. This resulted in a move from purely technical, timing, and budget measures to a service quality element being added by the customer in the recompete—for which the incumbent contractor had a strong answer, with plenty of evidence to give.

Example 2:

A contractor working for a mental health organization to deliver refurbishments and small rebuilds to the customer's estate recognized the outcomes of their work impacted the ability of doctors and nurses to complete their jobs effectively. They initiated a survey of those who worked in the areas they refurbished. The results of this survey identified a range of details in how the new or refurbished areas could be improved to enable better working practices. Presenting this to the Estates Division—the contractual customer—led to a process of involving doctors and nurses in the planning stages of projects and an increase in satisfaction in the finished works by these influencers. When the recompete process came around, representatives of these groups were included on the customer's procurement evaluation committee.

Step 2: Identify how you will measure satisfaction.

Once you have identified the groups you want to survey, you need to decide how you will get their input.

Ideally, you will be able to put in place a process which will give you regular, relevant information and data that has credibility with the customer.

There are a number of ways you can ask stakeholders about their views, but the most appropriate will depend on considerations such as:

- How many stakeholders there are in a particular group.
- How closely they interact with you.
- How often they interact with you.
- How important the service you are providing is to them.
- The methods you have for holding a database of information of who they are and contacting them (bearing in mind data protection rules).

As we said in the introduction to this idea, there is a whole industry of research companies you may want to turn to for advice on the best ways to survey your stakeholders, and the more stakeholders you have, the more likely you will gain from using a third party to conduct a survey. Not only will this ensure the methods used are effective and accurate, using a third party may help with the credibility of your survey and the results in the eyes of both those completing the survey and your customer. Some of the options for surveys might be:

- A quarterly survey of a random percentage of your total stakeholder base. Getting quarterly or even monthly information gives you more regular input than a yearly survey and helps you see more quickly the impact of changes to the services you make so you can vary and experiment with new ways of working and quickly see the results. However, your stakeholders will tire of responding if you survey them too often—hence asking a percentage of them each time (as long as the number of responses you receive gives you statistically representative information) will save cost and the patience of your stakeholders.

- Asking a set of questions at the point when your stakeholder receives your services. Especially if you only deal once, or irregularly with each of your stakeholders, getting their input immediately after they have interacted with you will both increase your response rates and the likely accuracy of the answers you receive.

- Adding relevant questions to surveys your customer might be taking of your stakeholders. Any survey you do of your stakeholders should be done with your customer's permission anyway (they are, after all, your customer's staff, customers or users). If they are conducting their own surveys, sharing the expense with them can reduce your own costs and help with the credibility of the results you receive.

Section V   Improve

> **Example 1:**
>
> *A company contracted to provide safety devices for 30,000 members of staff nationally for the National Health Service was contracted to run surveys of the entire user base once a year to collect information on usage, satisfaction, and areas for improvement. The company recognized that yearly information would simply give an occasional snapshot of information. The company would not be able to effectively react or show the customer improvements with a year's gap between feedback from users. So they agreed with the customer to survey a quarter of the users every three months. This fulfilled the customer's needs but also meant the company could get a faster return of information as they made changes and improvements to their services based on the surveys run.*

> **Example 2:**
>
> *A company providing software to schools piloted a new online support tool for customers as an alternative to telephone support. The final stage of each support event gave the customer a chance to comment on the support they had received. The comments combined a short set of questions with fixed answers (yes/no or unhappy, ok, happy, very happy) together with a space for comments by users. The results and comments were collated weekly and reviewed by the support team. In the first two months, these comments and results were used to tweak the online support tool to fit the customer responses about what they liked (and disliked) about the tool. After three months, the responses from users were so positive the company started publicizing the tool to all users and migrating more users to the tool and away from telephone support. The move increased customer satisfaction and enabled the company to reduce the costs of their telephone support—but was based on known results from customer feedback, rather than being a guess that it would work, which could have backfired.*

Step 3: Decide what questions to ask.

Asking the right questions may seem an obvious point, but it is still something many organizations seeking customer feedback get wrong the first time they try. You don't simply want to understand how you are delivering your existing service. You will gain far more by understanding what is really important to the customer about the type of service you are delivering. This is how you will learn new ways you could deliver the service, or new additions (or even reductions) you could make to significantly improve the stakeholders' satisfaction.

Rather than starting to list questions you should ask, the first step is to talk to a sample of the stakeholder group you are going to be surveying (this is often called Qualitative Research). Like the school contractor in Step 1, Example 1 (page 89), find out the context for the stakeholder of the service you are delivering:

- What work are they doing, what is important to them in this work, what worries them, what are their own goals and targets?

Next ask about the service you are supplying—but initially in general terms. Don't start asking closed questions about specifics yet:

- What does the stakeholder see the service contributing to their life or work, what worries them about it, what would a good service help them with, what is important to them about the service and how it is, or could be, delivered?

Now you can turn to the process of how the service is delivered. Unless it is brand new, it is likely the service is delivered in some way at the moment, so ask about that. If the service is new or a new way of delivering a particular element for the stakeholder, ask about the existing service as well as how you are proposing to deliver:

- What is good or bad about the service overall, what about each stage of the process, what impact does the good or bad delivery of the service at each stage have on the stakeholder, how could it be improved?

- What about the people delivering the service—are they helpful or not, how could they be more helpful?

You should now have a broad range of information from your stakeholders about the service you provide, its context, what it means to them and what they see as important about it and how it is delivered. You might already have learned a lot: both about the stakeholder and what they see as important about the service. This might already have given you some ideas about improving the service. Before you act, start surveying your stakeholders now so you can compare (and show your customer) the results of the improvements you will be making.

Now you can move to putting together your questions so you can get a sense of how many stakeholders think particular things about your service, and you can do statistical analysis of this information (usually called Qualitative Research). Perhaps the customer, or your bid, has defined some aspects of how you should be delivering the service and require you to ensure you are complying with these requirements. If so, you might need to add questions showing you are doing this work. But the main thrust of your survey should be to focus on the aspects of the work which are most important to the stakeholder. For instance, if you are required to answer the phone within three rings, fine. But this might be the least important aspect of the service to your stakeholder—or they might be quite happy with four or five rings. The key is for the stakeholder to be satisfied with the service, not just confirm you are delivering it to a particular specification. If you only focus on predetermined specific mechanics, you will learn nothing that will actually help you improve satisfaction.

Set out those few questions that focus on the most important aspects of your service to the user. Try to keep them to less than ten if you can, which will prevent you from going into too much detail and will increase the likelihood of stakeholders responding. Give the customer choices in their answers: ask what level of satisfaction they have with the service rather than a simple yes/no answer to whether a specific aspect of the service was delivered. Finally give the customer a chance to comment in their own words—typically about what was good about the service, but also what could be improved. You won't be able to turn these final answers into statistics, but sometimes they are the most interesting and powerful responses you will get and give more depth to the information you receive. Positive comments can also become quotes you can use when presenting to your customer—and in your recompete.

Finally, it will be useful to know more about the individuals who are responding. Different segments within your stakeholder group may have differing needs or views. However, only ask the type of information that is genuinely useful. You are not looking for every detail about the respondent's life—and you should not be asking for their name or details of their address, etc., that are likely to cause data protection issues. Ask these questions at the end of the survey and keep them to a necessary minimum. Many experts will tell you the more personal details you ask for, the fewer respondents you will get.

Step 4: Test your process.

It is always a good idea to test the whole process of a survey. There are a number of aspects you won't realize could be improved until you actually go through the whole process. For instance:

- Are you getting the survey to stakeholders in the best way?

- How many are responding?

- Do the questions you have asked actually make sense to the stakeholder and give you a relevant answer?

- How will you collate the answers and analyze them?

- What do the answers tell you—can you take any actions as a result?

Testing these practical aspects of your process will help you fine tune your survey. You may need to change a number of aspects to get the process working for you. Don't be afraid to do this in the testing stage—once you have your process in place, you can reuse it throughout the life of the contract, so it is worth getting right. It is particularly useful to analyze the results you get from your test. Even if the results are not complete, this will show you what analysis you can do with the answers to your questions. If you can't find a useful way to analyze the information you have received, you may need to look again at your questions—or how you are asking stakeholders to answer them.

Step 5: Analyze and present results.

Once you have completed your test, made any adjustments, and run your first full survey, you can begin to analyze the results. You will hopefully have found a number of different ways to look at the results when you ran your tests. You are aiming for analysis that gives you clear information—and you can take action on. Breaking the data down in different ways will often show different and useful patterns—for instance over time, or type of respondent. The more ways you look at the data, the more likely you are to find something useful and perhaps unexpected.

Once you have completed your analysis and have some initial views on what you can do with the information, you should present it to your customer. How you do this will depend on your relationship with the customer, the type of results you are getting, and what you believe you can do to improve the results (see below).

One of the keys is not to keep the results to yourself until the recompete. As with much of the information you will gain through the ideas in this book, you should make sure your customer is fully aware of it throughout the contract. Assuming that the information is positive, it will help build your relationship with them and their wish to keep you on the contract. And surprising the customer with information at the recompete could mean they don't believe it, or discount it and you don't gain the benefit in the evaluation.

Step 6: Create an action plan of how you will respond to any issues.

Once you have analyzed your results, you should have identified a number of areas where you could make changes to improve the satisfaction of your stakeholder group. You may have found areas in your initial interviews that are confirmed by the results of your survey. There may be a pattern to the comments you get as part of the survey, or you might find a particular level of dissatisfaction with a specific part of the service you are providing. These may not immediately lead you to the answer to the issue raised. You might need to focus on a particular area and understand the issues better before you can take action. However, you should take action. While you can use your survey to simply emphasize the good results you are getting in some areas, this is not what will lead you to improve your service over the period of the contract.

Set out a list of possible actions you might take as a result of the information you are receiving. Prioritize it and start to make changes. Subsequent surveys will show you the results.

Step 7: Repeat the survey.

A one-off survey is better than none at all. But you will only be able to track changes in your stakeholders' needs, their satisfaction, and the results of actions you take on the contract if you repeat your survey regularly and compare the results. How regularly you conduct your survey will vary with the contract, but once a year should be an absolute minimum frequency to get a genuine view of patterns of change.

Once you get to your recompete, being able to show high and increased satisfaction of stakeholders will be powerful information to help you win. Being able to show the actions you took during the contract and relate these to the increased satisfaction delivered will be even more helpful.

> *What do you expect of an incumbent that is different from new bidders?*
>
> *"A solution that clearly matches the purchaser's environment and a bid that is very realistic rather than over promising and under delivering. Changes in their offer that show they are aware of the worst elements of their performance and have addressed them."*
>
> *State Government, Australia*

Added Value, Continuous Improvement, and Innovation

Performance measurement is an important part of the activity on your contract and evidence for your recompete. But improvement in this performance is the vital element. The following three ideas look at how you can deliver this improvement. But before looking at them, lets define the differences and similarities between continuous improvement, added value, and innovation. Each is important, but the terms are often not clear and are sometimes used interchangeably by suppliers and customers. For the purposes of the recompete, we will be looking at each of them and how you can deliver them separately.

We will use the following definitions (our own) of each area:

- *Added Value*: ad hoc or one-off benefits delivered to the customer, and any benefits delivered to the customer outside the direct performance of the contract. The value to the customer must be greater than the cost to them of delivery.

- *Continuous improvement*: an ongoing effort to improve products, services, or processes. Typically delivered incrementally over time, although can lead to breakthroughs in improvement. Usually cumulative and leading to a permanent increase in performance or reduction in cost of the contract.

- *Innovation:* a new method, product, idea, or way of doing things. Differs from continuous improvement in that it typically involves doing something different (or differently) rather than the same thing better.

All of these areas require a proactive management effort to achieve. Your Contract Plan (see *Idea 8*) should include processes and goals for delivering in each area. But as well as being run through top down approaches, you can also encourage staff to look at opportunities to deliver in each area. In an ideal world, you will be able to deliver significant amounts of all three over the period of your contract, however the proportions will, in reality, vary with the type of contract, customer, and services or products you are delivering and the sector and market in which you work.

Common Themes

There are a number of common themes and priorities to delivering added value, continuous improvement, and innovation on your contract. Rather than repeat them for each area, we will deal with them first in general and then look at the specifics within each of the following ideas:

- As mentioned above, all require a planned and proactive management effort.

- All can also be generated "ad hoc" by staff at any level in the contract. Putting in place a culture that encourages and recognizes ideas and can put them into place will be worthwhile.

- All can require some level of investment, although this may be small.

- All can be used to save you costs as well as deliver improved performance to the customer. Indeed, it is likely that reducing costs to the customer will be one of the main positive impacts in the eyes of the customer. For each, you will need to decide how much you take as additional profit and how much you share with the customer as reduced cost to them.

- All, because you don't want to waste money, time and resources, should be targeted to focus on specific areas:

  - Quick and easy wins.

  - Areas that will have the greatest positive impact on the customer and their opinion of you.

  - Areas where the impact can preferably be measured; and the cause of this traced back to your work to deliver a particular piece of added value, continuous improvement or innovation.

Section V   Improve

- Different stakeholders may have different priorities and views as to what is important. For all three areas, you should think about the needs of key stakeholders and stakeholder groups in setting your priorities.

- For all, the effort should cover the whole contract period; in each area, some may need to be planned for later in the contract rather than all delivered at once.

- Documenting and evidencing the process for generating and delivering each of them is as important at the recompete as the improvements they deliver—as it is this process which you can show as evidence that you proactively delivered the improvements, and it is the (by the end of the contract proven) process that you will take into the next contract as a way to deliver further improvements.

- It will be beneficial if you can create a regular forum with the customer where you can:
  - Discuss all the areas.
  - Generate and discuss ideas.
  - Gain customer input, commitment and perhaps involvement and investment.
  - Potentially test ideas out in practice.
  - Report back results.

Let's go through a couple of these areas in more detail.

Targeting

As we have mentioned above, you should focus your improvement efforts on areas where you will get the most return for the least investment. These will tend to be areas where your key stakeholders are focusing themselves and see as particularly important. Spending money and effort on improving an area where the customer has little interest will get limited appreciation. Conversely, delivering even a small increase in performance in an area of vital importance to the customer will reap dividends. The process for understanding these areas is similar to that described in *Idea 8: Create a Contract Plan* and *Idea 11: Measure the Things that Make a Real Difference to the Customer.*

Step 1: Review what is driving the customer.

The drivers on the customer which will impact what they see as most important will come from a range of sources:

- The customer's market or sector, and the Political, Economic, Social, Technological, Legal, and Environmental (PESTLE) factors impacting the customer organization—as well as the impact of competitors.

- The customer's response to these drivers, and its own goals and objectives will also have an impact on what they see as important. Understanding the customer's own mission, strategies, and the programs in place to achieve these will help you understand what their "hot buttons" are likely to be.

Figure V.3   Drivers and Pressures on the Customer and Contract

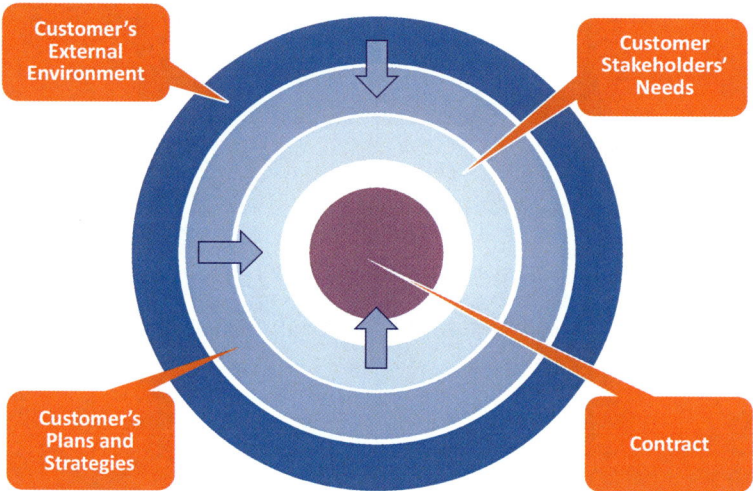

- Within the customer, different departments and stakeholders (including end users and customers) will have their own areas of responsibility and needs. Understanding these will give you a more clearly segmented view of the areas that will be seen as important by different people.

Section V Improve

First, list out the external drivers on your customer, the impact these might have, and the level of importance the driver and impact may have for the customer:

External Drivers			
Area	Driver	Impact	Importance 1=low to 5=high
Political			
Economic			
Social			
Technology			
Legal			
Environmental			
Competitive			
Other			

Then list out the strategic goals and programs the customer has in place and the impact these might have on the contract:

Customer Goals and Strategies		
Customer Goal or Strategy	**Impact on Areas Relevant to Contract**	**Importance 1=low to 5=high**

Next, look specifically at your key stakeholders on the contract and within the customer—different levels of seniority, different departments, users of the services or products you are delivering, and potentially the customer's customer. Each is likely to be affected by the external and organizational drivers in different ways, and each will have their own local issues, goals, and "hot buttons" where different improvements in different aspects of your contract performance could make a difference.

Stakeholder Needs Analysis			
Stakeholder	**Key Needs**	**Impact on Contract**	**Importance 1=low to 5=high**

Section V   Improve

From these lists, you should be able to gain at least an initial understanding of what the most likely areas of importance are to your customer and how they relate to your contract. They will, of course, link together, as the external influences you identify for the customer as a whole will impact their goals and objectives and then, to some degree, onto the different stakeholders for your contract—although of course, if you include your customer's customers, their needs will impact back to the customer itself.

Figure V.4   Sources of Impact on the Contract

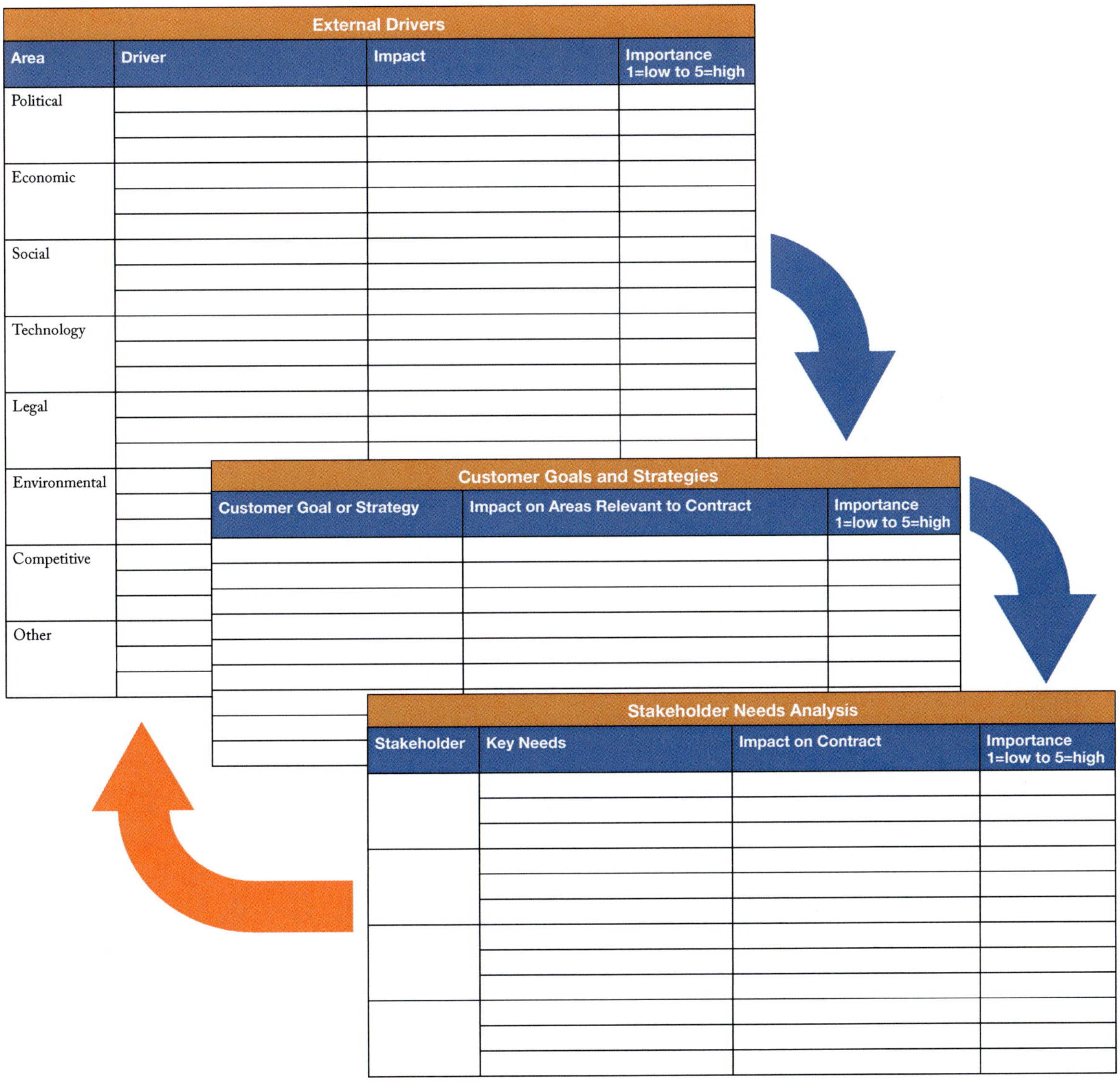

External Drivers			
Area	Driver	Impact	Importance 1=low to 5=high
Political			
Economic			
Social			
Technology			
Legal			
Environmental			
Competitive			
Other			

Customer Goals and Strategies		
Customer Goal or Strategy	Impact on Areas Relevant to Contract	Importance 1=low to 5=high

Stakeholder Needs Analysis			
Stakeholder	Key Needs	Impact on Contract	Importance 1=low to 5=high

From these lists you should now be able to pull together a core list of the main hot buttons—areas and aspects of your contract that, if you focus on improving, will have the greatest positive impact on your customer—and therefore gain the greatest appreciation and so the greatest return on your investment (be that in terms of money, time or management focus).

Now you can start looking at the specific improvements you might be able to make—through added value, continuous improvement, or innovation. But there is one final filter to put these ideas through before you enact them: how much investment are you able to make and where will you get the biggest return?

To start this process, test your list of ideas against a simple matrix:

Figure V.5   Importance vs. Cost Matrix for Improvement Ideas

	Low Importance to Customer	High Importance to Customer
Low Cost to Deliver	?	✓
High Cost to Deliver	✗	?

You will already have weeded out those areas with little, if any, relevance to the customer. Initially, you may only have an outline idea of costs for each idea. However, even an outline view will give you a set of ideas that should, by being in the "high importance/low cost" part of the matrix, be those to examine.

Those ideas in the low cost and (relatively) low importance sector should not be ignored. If they are particularly simple to put in place and can be done without distracting from your main target actions, they will add to the sense the customer has of your proactive approach to improvement.

Finally, those ideas in the "important to the customer but high cost to deliver" area of the matrix may be longer term opportunities to work on with the customer and gain their investment to help you implement.

Putting Targeting into Action

At first glance, the above process may seem like a lot of work. Taken seriously, it will involve some initial investment in time and effort. You might need to work through the process over a number of weeks through a set of meetings, as an agenda item on your internal management meetings, or through bringing staff, managers, or others together and running brainstorming sessions to generate ideas. But the outcome should give you a focus, rather than wasting significantly more time putting management effort into improvements (either through added value, continuous improvement, or innovation) which get little appreciation or support from the customer. As always, if you can involve your customer in the process, you will gain their buy in and more insight into their needs (remembering that who you involve may bias their input toward their own needs at the expense of other stakeholders).

Obviously, this should not be a one-off exercise. You should constantly look for new trends or events that will impact your customer and what they see as important. At the same time, you should be delivering new ideas throughout the contract, not just in a flurry at the beginning, followed by nothing later on. You should formally review your targeting once a quarter and always be generating, evaluating, and testing new ideas for improvement: for instance, by regularly running user groups from your end users, asking for their views on the service, where it could be improved, and what is driving them at the moment.

With this initial targeting process now explained, let's move on to the specific areas of added value, continuous improvement and innovation.

What are the primary reasons incumbents lose recompetes?

"In the public sector, they don't appreciate the balance of professional relationship building and the procurement process. Both play an important part for the incumbent supplier."

Local Government, UK

Idea 15: Add Value for the Customer

Idea Summary:

What:

Added value can come through initiatives from staff, reactions to one-off events, and by reviewing the contract to identify where you can add value, or from using your company's wider capabilities.

Why:

Adding value for the customer throughout the contract shows you are responsive to customer needs and issues and are willing to go beyond the basics of delivery to help your customer. By adding value throughout the contract, focusing on areas important to the customer but inexpensive to deliver, you will build a positive customer perception and will have significant evidence at the recompete of how you are the type of contractor the customer will want to retain.

We defined *added value* as: ad hoc or one-off benefits delivered to the customer, and any benefits delivered to the customer outside the direct performance of the contract. The value to the customer must be greater than the cost of delivery.

As with continuous improvement, and avoiding confusion with the definition above, while any one event of added value might be one off, you should have a stream of added value events being delivered on your contract. You should always be on the lookout for ways to add value for the customer, and creating an environment where your staff are doing the same.

We will look at four routes by which you can deliver added value to your customer:

- Bottom up added value.
- Ad hoc added value.
- Reviewing the contract for value to the customer.
- Using your company and contract capabilities to add value outside the contract specification.

Bottom Up Added Value

This is the basic added value the customer should receive from your staff. On a simple level, it could be called good customer care. It is the everyday flexibility, willingness to help out, and general proactive approach to delivering great service that comes from senior management on the contract creating an environment where staff are motivated to help the customer, understand the benefits of doing this, and feel recognized when they do. At the same time, staff should be feeding ideas for added value to whatever level of management can assess it and put it into action. As they are delivering the work on the contract and have the most interaction day-to-day with your customers or end users, front line staff will be delivering most of the initiatives you put in place and will have a valuable perspective on the customer.

While you are targeting the areas important to your customer and looking at ideas for added value and other routes for improvement, you should make sure you are involving your staff, both directly and through two-way open communication. Your staff should understand what you are expecting and why in order to feed information back to the management team.

You also need to make sure staff and managers at all levels on the contract understand why you are making this effort. If they think the recompete will be won by the company that just puts in the cheapest price, regardless of how you have performed during the contract, they will be less likely to see any reasons for putting in the effort to improve performance throughout the contract.

While a lot of bottom up added value will be difficult to record and collate directly, you should always be looking for examples where staff have gone above and beyond the norm to deliver better service. Capturing examples or even better, any customer commendations for staff, will add up over time. When you do customer satisfaction surveys (see *Idea 14*), ask for these examples and give as many opportunities as you can for customers and end users to provide feedback on great service experiences. No single example of added value from a member of staff will make a huge difference, but dozens will, and by creating the right environment, setting the right example, and capturing the results, you should be able to generate hundreds over the period of the contract.

Ad Hoc Added Value

Ad hoc added value comes from one-off events where you can help the customer above and beyond the norm. It might be when the customer has a problem or even a crisis, and you and your staff can help out.

An example that has happened on more than one contract is where the customer's premises were flooded over the weekend and contract staff, who had no role in facilities management, came in to help clean up so the customer could continue work as usual on Monday.

Another example of ad hoc added value would be where the customer had a rush of work and you recommend staff from the contract to help deliver it, even though it is not directly related to your work on the contract.

These events may be small or large. They are typically short term, unexpected, and often when the customer has a problem (when customers have problems, helping even on an otherwise low level task can be particularly important to them).

By being unexpected, it is difficult to plan for ad hoc added value opportunities. Your focus should be on flexibility, reaction speed, and a willingness to help, even if you may not have arrangements with the customer to pay you for the help you give. If the issue is short term, the cost should also be short term. If the issue continues for a longer period of time and is costing you money, then you may need to review the situation with the customer: you shouldn't get caught by a positive addition of value becoming an expectation you can't continue to meet.

Again, you should make sure you collate the added value delivered and report it to the customer—and file the information for the recompete. Over time, these one-off events can add up and are likely to be remembered by the customer, but as with all things in the recompete, you can't rely on the customer remembering; you will need to remind them in your proposal.

The true monetary value of ad hoc added value events can be difficult to quantify; but if you can do so, you should. Even if the value is "non cashable" (i.e. the customer won't see a direct saving on their accounts), if you and the customer agree that the help you gave had value, then it is possible to quantify later (even if you are not going to charge the customer).

Reviewing the Contract for Value to the Customer

The specification the customer set for the contract will have been laid out in the bid process and will define a set of tasks you are contracted to deliver. At the same time, you will have made a number of promises and set out how you will deliver to the specification in your bid. But once you are delivering the contract and have a much clearer understanding of the customer's expectations and needs, you may find some of the tasks you are committed to, or the processes you have agreed to use, are not actually adding value to what the customer really wants.

Reviewing what you deliver and how you deliver it for the value it adds to the customer can reveal a number of opportunities to make changes that would add value for the customer. These might be doing things in a different way to better meet a need, doing things more efficiently to reduce costs, or even not doing certain things that cost money but add no real value. As with bottom up and ad hoc added value, it might be your staff who see this on a daily basis and they may be a good source of ideas for doing things better. You might have done an initial version of this work at the start of the contract by using the Promises Register (see *Idea 3*). That should be just the start of a constant review of what the customer needs and how the contract allows you to deliver this most effectively. This, in turn, should become more developed as you get to know the task and the customer better, and as things change for the customer over the period of the contract.

Customers will all start at different points in their willingness to look at changes to the contract. Some will be wary of a new contractor coming into the contract and immediately talking to them about changes. They may have been caught off guard before by a previous contractor who was just looking for ways to get out of certain tasks to reduce their costs, or was aggressively looking for growth in the contract from the start. With these customers, it is sensible to wait until you have proven you can deliver the existing requirements through the Transform and Stabilize stages of the Contract Lifecycle (see *Idea 1*) and built up a relationship before approaching them with changes. Others will have a greater drive to change and improve the contract from the start and may have put in place forums and processes to discuss and drive this; in which case you have a ready-made route to introducing ideas.

Section V　Improve

As with the other elements of added value, continuous improvement, and innovation, the process for finding and assessing which changes add the most value to the customer will be a variation of the process we introduced at the start of this section. The first step is understanding what is of value to the different stakeholders in the customer. You can then list your ideas on a table similar to the one that follows:

Figure V.6　Reviewing Your Contract for Added Value Ideas

Reviewing Contract for Added Value				
Area of Contract	**Idea**	**Stakeholder**	**Improvement Added Value**	**Cost Reduction Added Value**

Some simple examples to illustrate the table above:

> ### Example 1:
>
> *In a contract held with a customer where the contractor supplied services to 40,000 end users, there was a specification that a survey of all users was to be conducted annually to ascertain their satisfaction with the service and views on its benefits. The contractor recognized an annual survey would be difficult to use to test the impact of any changes they put in place. They therefore discussed the option of running a survey quarterly, to a quarter of the total end user population each time. This also meant the customer could report more frequently to their own customers on the progress of the service and positive reaction of end users, thus keeping the service more "front of mind" with their own customers. The cost of running the four smaller surveys was marginally greater than a single yearly one, and this was split between the customer and contractor. The contractor gained from more regular feedback on improvements and changes to the contract, allowing them to test changes rather then putting them in place and waiting a year before understanding whether they had made a positive difference.*

Example 2:

A business running a contract with a housing trust to refurbish the kitchens and bathrooms of their stock of houses had specific types of taps requested by the customer. A year into the contract, a new supplier came onto the market offering similar taps at a significantly lower cost. The contractor approached the customer contract manager, who was increasingly under pressure to reduce cost. They demonstrated that the new, cheaper taps were of equivalent specification to the make and model in the contract. The customer agreed to the change and the contractor agreed to split the cost reduction of the new taps between themselves and the customer—reducing the price to the customer and increasing profit for the contractor.

Example 3:

A contractor was required by their customer specification to report monthly on a wide range of measures of volume, performance, and other aspects of the contract. Some aspects of this report took significant time and cost to collate and prepare. Over time, it became obvious that many of the measures were not being used or even read by the customer. The contractor suggested a review of what was reported. After some discussion and testing with the direct customer contact and her superiors, a new format of report was developed with some data reported monthly, while some was reported quarterly or annually. This reduced the cost for the contractor and made their monthly reports briefer and more relevant for the customer.

Example 4:

A company contracted to deliver reactive maintenance for a local authority for its housing stock had, over the first years of the contract, built a detailed database of the properties to which they were regularly called, and as part of their work, undertook a simple inventory of the state of repair of parts of the houses to which they conducted maintenance. Their customer was looking for ways to target their planned refurbishment of the housing stock in a more effective way, rather than just replacing bathrooms or kitchens after a set period of time (work that was separately contracted). By slightly altering the fields on their database and getting their work teams delivering repairs to add a short additional line to their repair reports, the contractor was able to give the customer a clearer view of the state of repair of the bathrooms and kitchens in many of the houses in the estate. The customer was then able to target their refurbishment program on those houses that needed it most, leaving for later those still in good repair, without the cost of having to do their own audit of the housing estate. As an added benefit, the refurbishment of those bathrooms and kitchens in the poorest state of repair also meant there were fewer calls to fix out of date and constantly breaking items in these highest users of the maintenance contract, thus reducing the cost to the customer and the turnover of the maintenance contract. While this may seem to be a downside for the contractor, it reduced their costs, so didn't impact margins, and they won their recompete with a very happy customer.

While these examples show quite low level amounts of added value, and might be seen by some as standard tasks in ongoing contract management, they all either saved the customer money and/or improved the contract performance in the eyes of the customer, either directly or indirectly. By constantly looking for opportunities to make changes that benefit the customer, you will be, over time, adding value for the customer—and be seen as proactive and customer focused.

To enhance your recompete, capture these initiatives, large or small; report them to the customer regularly to remind them what you have done and the value delivered to them; get their agreement that this value has indeed been added; and then collate all of these actions over the period of the contract for the recompete.

Adding Value Through Your Company or Contract Capabilities

As a business, you may have a number of systems, processes, or advantages that the customer does not. These might not form part of your delivery of the contract. But see if you can use these capabilities or capacity to help your customer and add value for them.

As with all the above types of added value, the specific actions you take may not be big or expensive, but if they add value for the customer, they are definitely worth doing.

The specifics will as always vary depending on your customer, contract, and your own business. However, the following examples may help illustrate some of the possibilities:

- Letting the customer use your company offices for their meetings.

- Giving the customer access to low prices or special deals your procurement department may have negotiated.

- Using your company's marketing or research expertise to help the customer in its own marketing or surveys.

Any added value you can deliver using your wider company capabilities has a number of potential advantages beyond just a happy customer:

- The interaction with other departments in your wider business may build a broader and stronger set of relationships with customer stakeholders not normally involved in your contract.

- As these are not contracted areas, it is difficult for the customer to replace them contractually at the recompete—giving your business a significant advantage over those just putting forward benefits related directly to the contract.

More Points on Added Value

Added value can initially cause issues with some businesses. The concept of adding value for the customer is usually recognized as a strong benefit to deliver during the contract to help win the recompete. But some see practical difficulties in giving away potential profit: *"Why are we giving this free to the customer? We are under pressure to increase our margins, shouldn't we take savings to profit or take the opportunity to expand the contract by charging for these extras?"*

The answer to this will depend, to a degree, on your business culture. Delivering added value and managing contract profitability are not mutually exclusive. The answer lies in the balance of what you take in short-term profit and what you give to the customer, and whether you are willing to share with them the gains you make. If a culture of finding and assessing added value opportunities is created on the contract, there will be a range of opportunities throughout the contract. Some, you may choose to "give" to the customer. Others, you may choose to share the benefits with the customer. Some, you may decide to take as additional benefit internally. As long as this balance is in place, you should be able to deliver to all your stakeholders, internal and external. And remember: added value does not need to be given "free" to the customer for them to perceive it as added value. As long as the cost to them is considerably lower than the value they gain or would gain from contracting for it separately, then you are delivering what you need to help build a strong, positive, and trusting relationship with your customer, and a stream of evidence for your recompete showing that you are the best choice for the next contract period.

> *What aspects of incumbent's proposals have been particularly poor?*
>
> "Some good incumbents fail to elaborate on their experience and qualifications. Instead of detailed resumes, they provide summaries. They tend to brush over the submission requirements, making them, in some extreme cases, non responsive."
>
> *State Government, USA*

Section V Improve

Idea 16: Deliver Continuous Improvement

> **Idea Summary:**
>
> **What:**
>
> Continuous improvement is the constant drive to improve the performance of your contract for your customer.
>
> **Why:**
>
> Delivering continuous improvement over the period of the contract can lead to significant improvements over time. By focusing on areas important to the customer, you increase the positive impact these improvements have. Having a clear process in place for identifying, analyzing, implementing, and measuring the impact of improvements will show your customer you are the type of contractor they will get more value from over the next contract period. At the recompete, being able to evidence how you have delivered improvement gives a strong reason for the customer to pick you as the winning contractor for the next contract.

We defined *continuous improvement* as: an ongoing effort to improve products, services, or processes. Typically delivered incrementally over time, although can lead to breakthroughs in improvement. Usually cumulative and leading to a permanent increase in performance or reduction in cost of the contract.

Continuous Improvement is the engine and the outcome of the main ongoing effort to deliver improvements to your contract throughout its lifecycle. You probably promised in your bid that you would deliver improvement during the contract. The customer probably asked in their solicitation that you do so, and most likely wanted you to show how you have already delivered it elsewhere. It may even have been part of the questioning of references taken in the selection process. Some customers will even set targets for you to deliver a certain amount of improvement over the contract (even if this is in terms of reduced costs over time) or will ask you to offer reductions in your price over the period of the contract as a result of your "learning curve" of getting better at delivering the tasks of the contract over time.

As the incumbent at the recompete, being able to clearly show how much you have improved your performance on the contract and the benefits this improvement has given the customer will be a real advantage. You will have kept your promises to deliver improvement (and so probably have a happy customer), been able to give real examples and evidence of the improvements made, and also realistically and believably been able to promise you will do more during the next contract.

Conversely, if you haven't delivered any significant improvement or can't document or evidence it, you are going to be at a real disadvantage. The customer will already be aware of this lack of improvement and probably be unhappy with you because of it. And you will a have a difficult time talking credibly about how you will deliver improvement throughout the next contract: you have already proven by your actions (or lack of them) over the past few years that you don't deliver improvement, so why should the customer evaluating the recompete believe you have suddenly had a change of heart or capability for the next contract?

There is a library of books on continuous improvement and a significant number of established methods (including, for instance, TQM, Lean, Six Sigma, Kaizen, and the various quality management accreditations) which give a range of ways for delivering continuous improvement in various circumstances. So this idea is not going to try to compete with a whole industry. What we will do, however, is focus on some of the key aspects of continuous improvement, and how to address it on your contract, which will be of most use for your recompete.

Focus on Areas that Are Important to Your Customer

As we have been emphasizing in this wider section on added value, continuous improvement and innovation—improvement in areas which are important to your customer—will gain more positive reaction than improvement in areas that are not seen as important. Your first step should be to review the process we have described above to identify which areas you should be focusing on improving. While you shouldn't ignore any quick and easy wins elsewhere, these will only give you limited benefit and should only be worked on if they don't divert you from the main areas of effort.

Link Your Performance Measurement Regime to Your Continuous Improvement Effort

Idea 11 on performance measurement emphasizes that you should put in place a performance measurement regime measuring what is important to your customer. Make sure you align what you are measuring to your areas of focus on continuous improvement. Not only will your performance measures be one input to your efforts to tell you where you might need to focus, they will be the way you can judge whether and how much your improvement efforts are delivering—and, of course, be the evidence you can use to show your customer that you are indeed improving as you progress, and particularly at the recompete. Before you spend time and resources putting an improvement program in place, make sure you know how you will measure the improvement you hope to be making.

Clearly Set Out Your Continuous Improvement Process

At the recompete, you will want to show the results of the improvements you have delivered during the previous term. The implication and claim you will be making is that you will provide further improvement throughout the next contract period. As the incumbent, you are the only bidder with the evidence to back this up for this customer on this contract. This will be much more powerful, however, if you can show how you will go about delivering more improvement in the next contract, and again give the customer the confidence that this will work. Your evidence of improvement will gain more credibility if you can demonstrate to the customer that there was a coherent process you used to deliver the improvements you have made—and that you will use this same process to deliver the improvements you are claiming for the next contract. This is your continuous improvement process.

To some degree, the exact form and detail of the process is not too important, as long as you can clearly and credibly describe it—preferably adding a diagram to show the process. Most of the established methodologies for quality management and improvement we mentioned above have processes clearly set out for delivering their methods. You don't necessarily have to use one of these, but you do need to show you are using a clear, credible, and repeatable process.

Typically this would include:

1. A set of routes or inputs for understanding the issues or getting input or ideas where improvement can or should be delivered: for instance, customer satisfaction surveys; complaints processes; quality audits; staff suggestion schemes; focus groups; review meetings with the customer; benchmarking.

2. A process for evaluating ideas and deciding which are feasible (probably involving the customer).

3. A testing and implementation stage.

4. A measurement process to help you understand the progress and impact of the improvement (see performance measurement above).

5. Review and feedback stages, sometimes looping back to the start so the process can begin again.

Link Your Improvements to Your Process

To complete your credible, fully evidenced claims for continuous improvement, you should be able to clearly link your actual improvements to your continuous improvement process. Show how each improvement was generated by the process you have used—perhaps giving a number of examples or case studies of how an idea came about or where the input for it came from, how it was evaluated, tested, implemented, and measured and then the lessons learned fed back into the continuous improvement "loop" to generate more ideas and improvements. Again, the exact process you are using is not the most important point. What will make the difference is that you clearly link the improvements to the process. That means you need to have a real, practical process you are actually putting to use—not a theoretical process you pay lip service to, but actually generate your improvements in a different way. If the process you start with isn't practical or isn't producing results, then adapt or change it to fit what works; for instance, if your ideas are coming from a route that isn't in your described process, add this route into your process.

Of course, you don't need to (and shouldn't) wait for the recompete to be communicating your process and the links to improvements to the customer. Your regular reports to the customer should include this linkage as you progress with your improvements though the contract. This will encourage a more active and positive involvement from your customer and potentially help generate even more ideas, as well as bring a closer, partnering type of relationship, which can only enhance their view of you.

What is the most important thing an incumbent can do to improve their chances of winning?

"Stay involved with your business and act as a partner."

Private Sector, USA

Idea 17: Innovate

Idea Summary:

What:

Innovation involves new products, services, or new ways of delivering. While continuous improvement involves improving what you are doing, innovation involves doing new or existing things differently.

Why:

Finding and implementing new ways of delivering the contract should not just be left to the recompete. By implementing innovations during the contract, focused on areas of key importance to the customer, you can transform the worth of the contract to the customer and encourage them to extend your contract or choose you as the winner in the recompete.

We defined *innovation* as: a new method, product, idea, or way of doing things. Differs from continuous improvement in that it typically involves doing something different (or differently) rather than the same thing better.

Sometimes the difference between innovation and continuous improvement can be difficult to define, and the two terms are often confused—after all, both should result in the same things: a reduction in cost and/or an improvement in the delivery of your contract. But at the recompete, you will want to show how you have delivered both, and describe them separately (so you get credit for both).

Let's look at a couple of examples to illustrate the potential benefits innovation can bring:

Example 1:

A contractor with a wide-ranging facilities management and operations support contract for an airbase near the Arctic Circle introduced a new chemical for de-icing the airbase runways. The same machinery and method of spreading the chemical was used as before, but the new chemical worked at lower temperatures, enabling the customer to keep planes flying at temperatures of 10 degrees centigrade lower than before—a significant benefit for them.

Example 2:

A government contractor with a contract to repair and upgrade major highways introduced a new method of repairing and replacing central reservations that involved scraping off top layers of concrete rather than digging out and replacing it. Not only did this reduce the costs of the work, it also reduced the time taken to conduct the work (reducing traffic congestion while the work took place) and meant that less concrete and other materials had to be taken off site or new brought on site, again saving money and time but also reducing the environmental impact of the work. Reduced cost, reduced traffic congestion, and improved environmental impacts all fit well with the customer's key needs.

An innovation on a contract doesn't have to be something that is a first in the world to count as innovation (although if it is, then you should make the most of it!). Usually, it will be the application of a technique, product, or process that has been invented elsewhere but is applied on the contract to deliver a change in the way the contract is delivered, and leads to real benefits for the customer.

Some sectors are delivering regular innovation (such as IT), but you should always be looking for new approaches and ideas no matter what your service or market. The amount of innovation you are able to apply to a contract over its period will depend on a number of factors such as:

- The length of the contract: a short contract period might mean you are less likely to be able to make the investment and changes that will show the benefits of innovation during the contract. If your contract is, for instance, three years or less, you may be better off waiting for the recompete to introduce significant innovations. However, if your contract is over five years long, then introducing no innovation during this time is likely to put you behind the market and cause you issues at the recompete (see *Idea 19: Keep Your Contract Up to Date*).

- The attitude of the customer: introducing innovation can be a risk. The changes innovation can require to how the contract is run, or the investment required to deliver the innovation, can cause some customer contacts concern. An innovation might also require a change in the contract specification or require the customer to make changes in their own processes or organization to fully benefit. Some customers may not want to make these changes initially. Others, of course, will welcome the opportunities innovations can bring. Make sure your customer is fully on board and understands the impact of the changes an innovation will bring.

- The investment required to put the innovation in place: some innovations need upfront investment in development and in implementation. Staff may need retraining, new equipment might need to be bought, new ways of working devised and embedded. Perhaps you can share the cost with your customer if they see the benefits they will gain, or you may even be able to expand your contract as a result. But you may be in a position where you don't have the margin or funds to invest prior to the return you should make from having the innovation in place. You need to be able to clearly understand the upfront costs that go with the innovation and be able to justify these against the returns you will make.

Whatever the apparent barriers, you should always be on the lookout for potential ways to introduce innovations to your contract. As with added value and continuous improvement, you should follow the process we have outlined at the beginning of this section to focus on your customer's needs and look at how you can deliver improvements there. And again, as with all the improvements you make on the contract, you should be measuring and collating the improvements so you can report them to the customer during the contract and use them in your recompete.

Searching for Innovations

As we said, an innovation does not have to be invented by you. Innovations are being introduced constantly around the world, or ideas from one industry transplanted into another. At the same time, innovation does not have to be large scale. A series of small innovations can be just as effective (and potentially lower risk) than a single large innovation. Finding innovations and seeing their potential application on your contract is more a matter of being open to ideas than necessarily being "inventive." Always stay alert for new developments—reading industry magazines or websites, talking to suppliers or your colleagues on other contracts, understanding what your competitors are doing in the marketplace or the solutions your own business developers are putting forward on new bids could all open up ideas for new ways of delivering your contract or elements of your service. You may have identified a problem and be looking for the solution, or you may simply see an idea that you relate to what you could do on your contract. Whichever route the idea comes from, the more you look and listen, the more likely you are to see possibilities.

Testing and Implementing Innovations

As you identify potential innovations for your contract, review the benefit it could deliver for the customer and the likely cost of introduction. When you talk to your customer about the opportunity will vary, depending on your relationship and the particular innovation. You might find that your customer wants to hear about innovations but will rarely wish to implement them. This shouldn't put you off. As long as you are putting forward sensible ideas, it is, to a degree, the process and approach of being proactive and showing your customer options for improvement which will gain you credibility and a positive reputation with the customer, even if few ideas are put in place.

By their nature, innovations can be riskier to initiate than continuous improvement. They tend to replace existing methods of working or products presently in use. Wherever possible, find a way to test the innovation first, with a backup plan to return to existing delivery if there are issues. Ensure the customer is aware of and has backed the test so they are comfortable with any potential issues you may find during the implementation. Perhaps they are willing to accept a temporary reduction of performance levels while the innovation settles in. If there are costs to the implementation, perhaps they are willing to pay for or share these costs (and perhaps share the benefits with you)—depending on the level of benefit the innovation will provide them in the future.

Always put in appropriate measures for testing and monitoring the benefit the innovation may bring (see *Idea 12*). You will want to show as early as possible the improvements delivered by the innovation and, if you have the information, the improvement in performance will be something you can use at the recompete.

Again, work with the customer on this. It may be that the innovation brings a benefit to them outside your normal contract delivery measures—and it may be that the customer needs to act in order to turn the potential benefit into reality (or to turn it into cashable savings or benefits). For instance, in Example One above, the potential to have the airbase open longer would also impact other staff on the base beyond the contract, involve communication with the airbase customers regarding the change, etc.

Introducing significant innovation during the contract period may also be a route to gaining an extension on the contract (or perhaps, in the private sector where the option is often available, suspend the recompete). If there is an investment in bringing in an innovation, the payback period may extend beyond the core length of the existing contract and, as the benefit provided by the innovation may be great enough for the customer to prefer that benefit to the benefit of seeking a new competition, they may be willing to extend your contract to get the benefit offered.

Idea 18: Publish an Annual Review of the Contract

Idea Summary:

What:

Publish an annual review of progress, performance, and achievements on the contract. Make this available to the customer and potentially your staff.

Why:

Publishing an annual review is more likely to show the total improvement delivered than would be the case with the more incremental improvements or variations in monthly reviews. The document is more likely to be read by senior customer influencers. It also provides a useful summary of achievements for reviewing performance and activity as you prepare for the recompete.

As we have mentioned several times in other ideas, you need to have all the information of the good work you have done throughout the contract ready for your recompete. But you will get much greater value from consistently sharing this information with your customer throughout the contract. It will help build trust and positive relationships with the customer; when the recompete comes, they will already be positively disposed toward you, and the information you put in the recompete will not be a surprise that might not be understood or even not believed.

But at the same time, it is easy to lose the trends and cumulative value you are delivering when it is only being incrementally shown in monthly or even quarterly reports—which might also include a lot of other information required by the contract or the customer.

Creating and "publishing" an annual review of the contract helps you pull together the key information you want to convey, and gives you the chance to show the cumulative improvements you have delivered throughout the year. Monthly performance might not show a dramatic change in each period (in some cases, it might even go down in particular months if there is a problem, or there are seasonal fluctuations in activity on the contract), but over 12 months you should be able to show the full impact of improvements during the year.

A single, concise report covering a whole year is also more likely to be distributed to and read by a wider audience of senior people in the customer organization who might not read more regular reports. These are potentially the people who are more likely to be involved in the strategic activities around the recompete rather than the day-to-day operation or customer management of the contract. You might also find that your direct customer is required to write an annual summary of their own activities—including management of the contract on a yearly basis—perhaps for planning and budgeting. Collating the information you feel best reflects the delivery of your contract over the year could help them with their own report—gaining you more credibility with, and support from, them.

You can also use the annual review within your business and with your staff to give them an overview of what has been achieved, and what your plans are for the next year.

And pulling together the results of your work for the year gives you a clearer view of the progress you are making in your Contract Plan (see *Idea 8*) and a chance to review that plan and recalibrate what you need, or can do, for the rest of the contract.

Finally, having a set of annual reviews for each year of the contract is a useful way to collate information as you arrive at the recompete. It is much easier to pull together four annual reviews than 48 monthly reports (on a four-year contract) when totaling up the achievements and improvements over the contract period for your use in your recompete.

What to Put Into Your Annual Review

Your review should be a summary of the important changes, improvements, and events of the year. It needs to be concise. A long, detailed document is less likely to be read. The key sections should include:

1. A short introduction with a few of the key highlights from the year. This is your executive summary for the document.

2. A short section on key facts and figures for the year. For instance, how many end users have you delivered service to over the year, or what is the total number of projects completed? These need to be impactful, interesting, and relevant to the customer and representative of the key deliverables of the contract. As with all the other information in the summary, you should challenge yourself with the question "so what?," thinking not just from your own viewpoint, but also from that of key people in the customer organization, otherwise you may begin to go into too much detail not of real value in the document.

3. A section on performance. The goal is to show the improvement over the year. Key figures such as performance at the start of the year versus at the end of the year for some of the key measures (and/or those which have improved the most!). Where you can, include charts showing this pictorially, as these have impact and break up the text. As the contract progresses, you can also include cumulative improvements over the period of the contract. Wherever possible, show the outputs and what the improvements have meant for the customer (see the introduction to performance measurement above, and *Idea 11*)

4. Summarize the key added value you have delivered over the year. You may want to highlight one or two of the areas that have had particular impact, but you should also (perhaps in an appendix) create a list of all the added value activities you have completed in the year. And if you can include against these a monetary estimate of the value to the customer each has delivered—together with a total—you might be surprised when completing this list just how much you have done.

5. Include any innovation you have introduced during the year and the improvements this has delivered. Investments you have made, if any, to deliver this innovation should be included as well.

6. Issues. While the review should be positive, it will have little credibility if you don't include any issues you have faced during the year which have impacted, or are known by, the customer. Acknowledging these issues will give a balance to the review. The key is that for any issue you cover, you must show the solution you put in place to overcome it, the learning from it, and the changes you have made to prevent it from happening again.

7. Staff. A section on your staff should include personalizing any particularly outstanding performance by highlighting key staff members who have delivered particularly well. You should also include training given to staff, any accreditations gained by the staff, etc. Again, these need to be relevant to the customer and the contract.

8. Accreditations, achievements, recommendations, and quotes from end users and/or stakeholders.

9. Outline the plan for the coming year—what you see as the key targets, what projects or programs you are committed to, and any other key items. Of course these should be included in a way you are sure you can achieve. You don't want to set expectations you are not going to be able to meet.

Quality of the Document

This is potentially the only document senior customers will see from your contract. As the point is to promote the quality of the service you have given in the year, ensure the document is of good quality. If you have a central marketing team, enlist their help with layout, design, and production. However, the report should be appropriate to the size and context of your contract. A full color, multipage, hardcover report for a small contract or one where cost reduction is a major target would not perhaps be seen as appropriate. Equally, a two-page stapled black and white Word document would not fit with a large multimillion contract. Ideally, the annual review should be the highest quality document you produce in the year. The level of quality depends on the context of your contract.

Involving the Customer

As with most things you will be doing for the recompete, the report should not come as a surprise to your customer. Let them know you will be producing a document ahead of time, and if you are able to show them a draft before production that receives their positive involvement, they will also feel some ownership of it and will be more likely to endorse, support, and pass it to a wider stakeholder group within the customer. They may even agree to participate by writing a section themselves or include an endorsement of a particular improvement or achievement—particularly useful to have in the recompete.

Other Stakeholders

Depending on the type of service you provide and the end users you provide the service to, you may also want to provide a variation of your annual review to other stakeholders—particularly end users and potentially your supply chain, if it is extensive. Again, these could be used to build positive relationships with these stakeholders and can be used in the recompete as evidence of this. Think about the information that is relevant to each of the stakeholders and whether you should be giving them an annual update on the previous year's activity and performance.

What aspects of incumbents' proposals have been particularly good?

"Very clear strategy (organizationally and process) to fit in with client's organization and objectives."

Public Sector, UK

Idea 19: Keep Your Contract Up to Date

Idea Summary:

What:

Particularly on longer contracts, the market conditions, customer needs, and best practice can change considerably between winning the contract and the recompete. Keep in touch with these changes and adapt your contract and delivery to stay up to date.

Why:

Keeping your contract up to date with customer needs and market best practice builds a stronger relationship and reputation with the customer and may postpone the need for them recompeting the contract. You will also be in a much stronger position when the recompete does come, as you will not be delivering in an out of date way. This will reduce the need for significant change in your solution and the danger of the customer perceiving you as inflexible or out of date, compared to your competitors.

Key Steps:

1. Regularly review changes that might impact how the recompete could be formatted and run.

2. Relate changes to what impact they might have on your customer and your recompete.

3. Look at what actions you could take as a result of these possible impacts.

4. Involve your customer.

5. Incorporate changes in to your Contract Plan.

Section V   Improve

The format of a competed contract, with set specifications, tasks, terms and conditions, agreed costs, and payment mechanisms will usually mean there is only a certain amount of change that can be delivered through the contract period. Even with a customer who has put in place partnering and continuous improvement processes, and a flexible contractor delivering improvements and innovation during the contract, the restrictions of the original contract will create a barrier to making very significant changes. This is particularly the case in the public sector, where regulations restrict the customer from making significant changes to a contract between competitions.

The wider world, of course, isn't restricted in this way: change is a constant factor and while some changes can be slow, others can be fast or even immediate (for instance, a change in legislation).

If your contract gets out of step with these changes—either in the wider world, in your sector, with your customer, or end users—it's likely you will see some major changes to the contract at the recompete. If you aren't ready for them, you can be at a real disadvantage. This could take a number of forms:

- If your competitors have been moving forward by taking on more recent contracts which have required them to put some of these changes in place, they will be able to show evidence that they are working in more up to date ways than you have been able to because of the restrictions of your contract. By comparison, the customer might see you as out of date and unable to deliver in these new ways at the recompete (after all, they will only have seen you delivering what they have been asking you to until now).

- If the contract is expanding at the recompete in terms of the geography or the type of tasks it requires, you might need to look at partnering with other suppliers who can cover these areas. If you haven't anticipated this, you might not be able to build these relationships or agreements in time for the recompete.

- If new technologies mean the work you are doing can be delivered in a very different way, you might not have had the chance to test this technology or the changes it enables. Even if you can put a coherent solution together in your recompete, you won't have the evidence (for the customer or yourself) you can really make these changes and meet the new levels of speed, quality, or reduced costs these could enable.

To avoid these potential problems, you should make sure you are keeping in touch with all the potential changes that might impact the customer, their needs, and the form of the contract at the recompete. Ideally, you should also be anticipating or even introducing as many of these changes as possible on your contract while you are still the incumbent in order to be ready—and crucially seen by the customer as ready—to bring in these changes in your recompete.

So what might some of these changes be?

Supply Side Changes

Over the period of a reasonably long contract (let's say five years), there could be a lot of changes in your own competitive environment, meaning you would be facing a very different set of challenges, and challengers, at the recompete compared to the last competition:

- New competitors could have entered the market.
- Competitors could have merged or acquired to gain greater economies of scale, new capabilities, or greater geographical coverage.
- Competitors may have introduced new products, services, or processes (indeed, your own company might).
- Some competitors might have grown significantly: winning new contracts, giving them more references and the ability to leverage the capabilities or capacity of these contracts to offer a better or cheaper service to your customer.
- A competitor may have won a contract with your customer in a different area, giving them a degree of incumbent advantage in terms of relationships with, knowledge of, and references for your customer.

Customer Changes

Your customer will probably have changed over the past five years:

- They may have grown or indeed shrunk.
- They may have merged with another organization.
- The budget pressures on them may have changed.
- Their objectives and strategy may (most likely will) have changed.
- They will have delivered some programs of work and have started others.
- Their own customers' needs may have changed.
- Their structure and management may have changed, and with it their local priorities.
- Their own competitors or other external stakeholders may have changed.

Market or Social Changes

The impact of changes in the wider world are likely to drive changes for your customer and their needs of the contract, as well as your contract directly—changes which might not impact until the recompete when the customer, you, and your competitors will have to take them into account. Potentially significant changes to the form of the next recompete and contract compared to the present one might include:

- The economic climate will change—for instance, putting greater budget pressures on your customer and so potentially the emphasis on cost savings as key to the next contract—and potentially increasing the emphasis on price in how the next procurement is evaluated at recompete.

- Legislation might change. On many contracts, there will be provisions for this, but it is possible the full impact of the change will not be put into practice until the recompete.

- Trends might change—for instance, the requirements around environmental and social sustainability, which could become more important in the next contract period and so the recompete.

- There could be a change in government, which could impact policy toward contracts.

- Technology will change, which might impact costs or how the contract is structured.

- Trends in outsourcing could change—new forms of procurement might be introduced or become more popular, which could change the form of the next contract (for instance, a move from input-based contracts to output- or even outcome-based contracts, the expectations around upfront investment by contractors, contract lengths, Low Price Technically Acceptable type contracts, contracts focused on either performance delivery or cost reduction, etc.).

All of these changes could mean a major difference to the requirements that the customer sets out in the recompete compared to what you are delivering now, for instance:

- The geography the contract covers could expand or contract.

- The range of tasks included in the contract could expand—or be broken down into different lots that are recompeted separately.

- The performance measures used on the contract could change.

- The evaluation criteria could change—for instance, increasing the importance of price (and decreasing the importance of quality) in deciding who wins the recompete.

Let's pick out a few examples to illustrate the impact these changes could have:

> **Example 1:**
>
> *This first example is based on a decision taken by the U.S. Government Accountability Office (GAO). The GAO is responsible for deciding on the validity of contractor protests regarding Government procurements. The GAOs decisions, and the reasons for these, are published on the GAO website and can make interesting and informative reading for all bidders, incumbents included.*
>
> *GAO decision on a protest by CYIOS Inc., published July 13, 2012. CYIOS protested the decision of the Department of Defense (DOD) to bundle together three existing Information Technology support contracts into a single contract, and to not set these aside for smaller businesses. The customer wanted to bundle the three contracts together, as the existing ones were difficult to coordinate, and a single contract would save up to $5m. The GAO denied CYIOS's protest and the changed recompete went through, being offered to a larger contractor acting as a prime for the now consolidated contract.*

> **Example 2:**
>
> *A government healthcare provider had separate contracts for refurbishment building contractors, surveyors, and architects. At the recompete, the customer changed their requirements to create two contracts (one for smaller works and one for larger works), but required bidders to provide all building, surveying, and architecture services together. The incumbent building provider had to partner with an architect and surveyor in a consortium to be able to bid for the new contract.*

> **Example 3:**
>
> *The move for many contracts to be procured under Lowest Price Technically Acceptable (LPTA) terms means that many incumbents who may have been contracted based on high levels of quality delivery are having to change how they approach their recompetes to provide a set level of service at the lowest possible price to win.*

Actions to Keep Your Contract Up to Date

As an incumbent, you can wait until the recompete to see what changes the customer makes. But if you do, you lose some real advantages that keeping your contract up to date could give you:

- You might not have collected all the information you need to have an advantage at the recompete. For instance, if the contract moves at recompete from an input-based contract to an outcome-based contract, you might not have the information available to help you understand the connections between what you provide (inputs) and what the customer outcomes are (outcomes) and how varying the inputs (level of resource) or processes you use could lead to changes in output or outcome.

- You won't have been able to demonstrate to the customer through your existing contract provision that you are also able to deliver in the way the customer wants next time around. This could put you at a disadvantage twice. First, you have lost an opportunity to put evidence in your recompete of how you can deliver the new way of working (or understand the costs and processes of what that entails). Second, the customer may get the impression that you are not capable of delivering differently from how they have been asking you to date. This could put you at a disadvantage against competitors who could, because they are not known so well by the customer, claim to be able to deliver the new way of working and so gain more credibility.

- You won't have been able to influence your customer in how they specify the details of the new way of working in the recompete by demonstrating to them how it would work in practice.

- If you need to partner with others to deliver a broader service, you won't have the advantage of having more time to build relationships and solutions with these partners.

Following the steps below will give you an opportunity to anticipate and react early to the potential changes in the recompete:

Step 1: Regularly review changes that might impact how the recompete could be formatted and run.

This doesn't need to be a monthly task; once a year is likely to be enough. As some changes will be immediately obvious, others will be slower and perhaps only evident over a period of time.

Review the headings covered above to determine what has changed in:

- The supply side.
- The customer.
- The wider environment.

Initially, you may have a long list. This is good at this first stage, as you may find links between different areas.

Look also at what is changing in the way your customer is procuring, as you can sometimes see trends and indications of what is more important for the customer. If your customer publishes solicitation invitations or other solicitation documents, even if they are for services significantly different from your own, try to obtain these to see the format—for instance what, if any, are the trends in how they weight different aspects of bids, such as price?

Similarly, look at other solicitations in your market for trends. Your company is likely to be bidding for other opportunities similar to your own—is there a trend here that might reflect changing needs in your market and give an indication of what might be coming at your recompete?

Of course you should also be talking to your customer. What do they see as the trends and what impact do they think this will have on their needs, and therefore what they would ideally like the contract to look like in the future?

Step 2: Relate changes to what impact they might have on your customer and your recompete.

Even if your recompete is several years away, having an outline view of what might happen at the recompete (even if this changes over time) will give you a sense of what you should be looking to do on the contract to prepare.

List the changes you have spotted from Step One, then look at the potential impacts they could have on your customer and what the needs might be for your contract and the recompete. One way of viewing this would be to ask, if the recompete were being run now, what impact on the solicitation and the specification for the next contract term would this change have?

Change	Impact on Customer	Potential Impact on Recompete

Step 3: Look at the actions you could take as a result of these possible impacts.

Once you have a view of the potential impacts on your customer's needs for your contract and potentially on your recompete, the next step is to decide what you can do to prepare for these changes.

As with the ideas on added value, continuous improvement, and innovation (*Ideas 15, 16* and *17*), filter the potential changes you could make by testing them against those which directly relate to the most important of your customer's needs (you can also add to this analysis those that will have the greatest impact on the recompete) and those which will cost least to implement.

At a minimum, you should be gathering the best possible information to enable you to present a winning solution for the changed recompete. For instance, if you anticipate your next contract could be moving to an output-based model, collect data to help you put an output-based solution together.

You might anticipate that your customer will extend the scope of the contract—either geographically or in the breadth of services included. If so, look at how you might be able to deliver these skills or across this wider geography. Does your business already have these areas covered? Do you need to develop them? Do you need to build relationships with possible partners?

Finally, look at the changes you could make on the contract now to bring your services closer to what you anticipate the recompete might require. While this might not immediately seem to be a good investment, you should balance the cost and effort against the potential benefits:

- If you are showing the customer you are being flexible and attempting to meet their changing needs, this will help build a better relationship with them and improve their view of you as a future preferred contractor.

- Making these changes demonstrates to the customer your ability to deliver in the ways they are likely to be asking for in the next contract period. This will again improve their view of you and address any doubts they may have about your ability to deliver differently in the next contract.

- It gives you the opportunity to understand what these services or ways of working entail in practice—their costs, benefits, issues, training required for staff, etc. This will help you put a more coherent solution together at the recompete, and show evidence you are able to deliver for the customer.

- If your customers feel their changing needs are being met by you on the existing contract, they may not feel the need to run a recompete exercise at all, if they have no requirement to do so. They may at least use all the potential contract extensions available, so you gain a longer period of running the contract without a recompete.

Step 4: Involve your customer.

No matter how good your analysis of the changes happening (or likely) in your surroundings, or the benefits of the adjustments or improvements you feel you can make to the contract to meet these changes, you will not gain the full benefit unless your customer is fully involved, supportive, and working with you to achieve them. You will have involved your customer at Step 1 by getting their input into your analysis of the changes taking place in the market, your customer, and the pressures on them. They should also be involved throughout the subsequent steps, particularly once you have a set of potential adjustments you can make to the contract to keep it up to date. Bring them into the conversation, get their buy in, and work with them to support any changes you wish to make. You might even get them to invest with you in the changes, and you certainly want them to adjust the contract appropriately to make sure that, by making changes to the way you are delivering, you are not technically breaking the original terms of your contract or specification.

Step 5: Incorporate changes into your Contract Plan.

In *Idea 8*, we introduced the Contract Plan as your overall program and management tool for the changes you intend to make on your contract over its lifecycle. As you identify changes happening over time in the outside world or to your customer, and the things you could do to keep your contract up to date, these should be incorporated into your Contract Plan. As we said in *Idea 8*, your plan will adapt and change over the contract period as circumstances require. External changes may impact your earlier ideas of what is most important—introducing new priorities or making some ideas redundant. Overall, the impact on your Contract Plan will be to ensure the direction is the right one to help your contract remain as up to date at the end of its period as it was at the start.

What are the primary reasons incumbents lose recompetes?

"*They don't learn from their experience during the first contract period, which comes out in the bid, by the way they answer the questions.*"

State Government, USA

Idea 20: Resolve Any Problems Quickly and Completely

Idea Summary:

What:

Always be on the lookout for problems and poor performance on the contract. Resolve these problems as soon as possible. Learn from the issues and show your customer what you have changed as a result.

Section V Improve

Why:

By keeping on top of issues, you will retain a positive relationship with your customer. You will also be able to show at the recompete how you react to problems and what you have learned from them—and how this learning is reflected in your improved solution.

No matter how well and proactively you manage your contract, at some point there is likely to be an issue or problem. Perhaps the original bid was flawed in some respect and your solution isn't delivering either what the customer expected or what was promised. There might be a one-off problem that impacts performance over a short period, or there might be a clash of style or personality with a customer representative or stakeholder. The list of possible problems or issues is potentially endless.

Some issues will be obvious and quickly identified. Others, however, might be more subtle or don't come to your attention immediately. Depending on the openness of your relationship with your customer and end users, you may or may not pick up the signals of disquiet or dissatisfaction.

Always be on the lookout for potential problems. Ideally, you will be able to spot and resolve an issue before it becomes a significant problem.

What you should not do is ignore or deny a problem, particularly if it is brought to you by the customer. Unresolved problems can fester in the mind of the customer and a lack of proactive resolution can severely damage your reputation—even some time after you think the problem has gone away or the customer has stopped talking to you about it (they may just have given up telling you, rather than believing the issue had been resolved). At the recompete, these unresolved issues can cause you real damage, not just in terms of the customer's view of you as you go into the process, but in tainting any claims you make in the recompete about high quality performance.

On the other hand, if you have identified a problem, resolved it, the customer has acknowledged you have done so, and you have clearly learned the lessons; this can be turned into a positive in the recompete, as well as taking you into the process with a more positive customer.

Few customers expect there will be no problems during the course of a contract. What they want is an organization they feel confident will proactively resolve any problems which do occur. If you have proven you are that type of business, with evidence of what you have done, you are actually at an advantage over your challengers, whose reactions to problems will be less clear to the customer.

Also, keeping a clear log of issues that have occurred during the contract (see *Idea 9: Help the Customer Manage Risk*) can give you ammunition to use in your recompete to show you understand, in depth, the requirements and potential risks of the contract. And you can use these to at least imply to the customer that they should check whether your challengers have taken these potential issues into account in their solutions. You will also be able to show how your own solution benefits from the lessons you have learned from the problems you identified and resolved.

What is the most important thing an incumbent can do to improve their chances of winning?

"Acknowledge what they have got wrong in the past."

Private Sector, UK

Idea 21: Know and Use All Available Contract Change Routes

Idea Summary:

What:

As you make changes and improvements to your delivery of the contract, make sure you have official routes to confirm these changes with the customer.

Why:

It may be that this is a route for you to get paid for additional work. Making changes official also means that if there are changes to the customer organization or personnel, there is an official record of changes made to your original proposal and contract to prevent new customer managers questioning why these have been made. At the recompete, the customer also has a record of changes made to ensure their recompete specification reflects the latest reality of the contract and prevents specifications and requirements in the recompete which bear no relation to the realities of the contract.

Section V   Improve

Most of the ideas in the Improve phase of the contract will mean some sort of change to the way you deliver the contract. This might range from increased levels of performance to potentially significant changes addressing new or emerging customer needs, or innovation enabling a step change in performance by delivering some element of the contract in a different way.

While some of these changes will not impact what, how, and to what level you committed to deliver the contract at the start, some inevitably will. At the same time, while some changes will not involve any increased cost to you, others might, and quite rightly you will hope the customer will agree to share the cost or pay for the improvement or new area of service you are delivering (if, as we say in a number of the ideas in this section, these changes are meeting a key customer need).

To make sure your delivery does not get out of step with your contracted service, you need a mechanism to make these changes official and recognized in your contracted terms and conditions and/or the specification for the contract.

You face a number of dangers if you don't do this:

- There is a change of customer representative: if you have made changes to your delivery in agreement with your direct customer representative but have not had these formalized, if this contact changes (and they often do) any new customer manager viewing the contract may not recognize these changes as valid. They could mark you down for performance changes, reduce prices, or demand that you adhere to previous ways of working (i.e., those written in the original contract).

- A customer review of the contract reveals that you are being overpaid or are not delivering as agreed: occasionally customers undertake independent reviews of contracts—or the department may be reviewed. Again, any audit is likely to refer back to the written contract. If you have changed this contract without formalizing the change, then you (and your customer representative) could be criticized.

- The procurement team doesn't recognize at the recompete changes made and doesn't include them in the new specification—meaning the gains you have made are lost in the new specification. There can be dislocation between the operational customer and the procurement team. If improvements, changes, or additional elements of work you have agreed upon with your direct customer have not been formalized, the procurement team may not recognize them or their benefits. They may not take them into account in the recompete specification and leave you with the problem of either having to exclude them from your recompete solution, or (and this is not usually recommended) including them and risk either not being compliant or having added costs versus your competitors.

Understand, Use, or Create Mechanisms for Change

Many contracts will have mechanisms to enable and formalize changes written into them. This might be a change control process, or perhaps a partnering forum which meets regularly to discuss potential changes and agree on them. Make sure you understand the options open to you. Check the contract and discuss with your customer the actual route for changes, their process and approach to changes, and what the customer's attitude is to making changes. Ideally, in your contract you will have a forum or process that will enable you to:

- Hold regular discussions with the customer about the contract and the customer's needs.

- Bring potential ideas to the customer to discuss their merits and understand the degree of interest and support the customer has.

- Test ideas and report back on the results.

- Agree and formalize changes to the contract resulting from your discussions and ideas.

If this type of forum is not part of the contract at the start, suggest to your customer that one is created. It might start with adding items to a standard management review meeting, but ideally you should aim to have this type of meeting separate from the more formal monthly review of performance. This will enable you to make the meeting more open and potentially have other customer stakeholders involved beyond your direct customer contact (such as key department heads, end user representatives, etc.). This will bring more ideas and perspectives to the meeting and widen the range of relationships you have within the customer.

Approach to Formalizing Changes

While you need to make sure you get changes recognized, how you approach this process can make a big difference in how the customer sees your proactivity, flexibility, and commitment to meeting their needs:

- If you treat every change as an opportunity to increase your charges or profit, the customer will quickly see through this and will see any suggestion you make in this light, rather than an attempt by you to provide the service they need. Some changes might deliver you these benefits (and of course, you shouldn't ignore this important commercial reason for having the contract!). But when there is no cost to you for making the change, don't pretend there is. And if there are savings you can make through changes, you should share these with the customer wherever possible—if not directly, then through offering other services or improvements which give the customer a benefit. Your focus should be on delivering improvements (and/or cost savings—depending on what is most important to the customer) that really benefit the customer, not just your bottom line.

- If you become too focused on getting a change signed off before you make any attempt to put it into practice, you will appear inflexible, bureaucratic, and potentially standoffish to the customer. To some degree, the flexibility you can practice will depend on the customer's process for change. Small changes may not require a high level sign off with legal changes to the contract document—simply a letter from an appropriately authorized person in the customer organization might be adequate. Other changes may need more formal and legal processes, senior management sign off and therefore time, to complete. If your customer comes to you urgently needing a change and you insist on following the process before undertaking any work, their problem may have grown too urgent by the time the full process is complete. If you can make the change and are confident you can get it formalized retrospectively, you should do so, perhaps asking for a simple note as an official request and an agreement that the full process will follow. This does involve a degree of trust in your customer following through with payment. However, if you don't trust your customer, you are unlikely to be able to build a strong and positive relationship with them. This type of action would go a long way toward establishing increased trust in both directions.

Collate and Keep All Changes on File

Keep originals and copies of the formal change documents you collect over the contract. They should be kept with the original contract documentation, as they form updates to this. Keep separate copies in your Recompete File (see *Idea 5*). When you get to the recompete, these documents will be useful to convey the full extent of the changes you have brought to the contract.

Link Your Changes to Your Process

As with Continuous Improvement (*Idea 16*), being able to prove at the recompete that you have a clear and working process in place to manage and deliver changes will be a strong tool for you. The changes you have made are evidence of your past performance. The process you used to deliver these changes will go into your solution as a route for delivering more changes in the next contract. Proving to the customer that this is an effective process by showing real examples will give them confidence that you will be able to deliver effective change on the next contract. As you put each change into place, keep a record of how the change came about. Was it:

- Your idea?

- The customer's idea?

- The result of end user feedback?
- The result of an issue that occurred on the contract?
- Generated from another source?

What were the discussions leading to the idea being put in place? How was it tested and signed off, etc.? Having these details around the change and showing how your process enabled it will give both the change and the process (that you are proposing to use in the future to deliver more positive change) credibility. This will earn you more marks in the recompete evaluation than simply listing the change alone.

What are the primary reasons incumbents lose recompetes?

"Constant poor service and delivery coupled with little and no communication between supplier and client, as well as a total failure to adhere to improvement plans and processes set out for them and a blatant attitude that it is their right to win contract extensions/retender."

Private Sector, USA

Idea 22: Constantly Build Customer Relationships and Trust

Idea Summary:

What:

Build relationships with a wide set of stakeholders within the customer. Manage these relationships proactively. Keep an active record of who is who in the customer organization—their needs, expectations, pressures, and goals, as well as your relationship with them.

Why:

Positive customer relationships are the backbone of a successful recompete. By building trust and respect from and with your customer, your contract becomes easier to manage and the customer is more likely to retain you at recompete. However, this process needs to be proactively managed.

Section V   Improve

This might seem like an obvious thing to do, but building relationships within the customer organization can often be an ad hoc effort and restricted to too few stakeholders: usually those directly managing the operational contract from the customer's side.

Having a positive relationship with your customer is, of course, a key goal of any supplier during the contract. It smooths the operation and means there is a greater chance of flexibility from the customer. It is also human nature—those in charge of the contract have to deal with the customer on a daily basis, and even though this is a work relationship, it is always less stressful to get along well with those you are dealing with, rather than not.

When it comes to the recompete, having the customer wanting to retain their relationship with you will be a major advantage. If the customer isn't required to run a formal competition, then they might decide to continue without one, or if there are potential extensions to the contract, you are more likely to get them. You will have a greater opportunity to influence what goes in the recompete, what is specified, how the formal element will be weighted and more opportunity to get insight into what the customer really needs. Even if the evaluation of any formal bids is strictly mechanical and even blind (the markers don't know which supplier's proposal they are marking), if the customer wants you as the supplier for the next contract, there are always ways to give even marginally better marks to you over the competition.

Your relationship with your customer will often be linked to your performance and the changes and improvements you make to the contract:

- The more you perform and make improvements, the happier the customer will be and the better your relationship is likely to become. If improvements relate to strategically important customer needs, you will be seen contributing to these and will gain more attention from senior customer contacts. This relationship and contact is likely to give you better information on where to focus further improvements, and the positive cycle continues.

- Conversely, if you do not perform and do not make improvements, it is likely the customer will not be happy. Your relationship could suffer and they could manage the contract more transactionally and with less flexibility. Your relationships could deteriorate, and you could be excluded from customer strategic discussions or information while they focus on getting you to deliver the basics, perhaps more tightly and referring back more often to the contract or penalty regimes that might apply. In turn, this could reduce your focus on the day-to-day delivery of the written contract with little opportunity to look at wider customer needs.

> *Proposal expert advice:*
>
> *"There are oodles and oodles of reasons that companies win or lose their recompetes. The reason that is fresh in my mind is that a company that I had a brief encounter with lost a large recompete because the agency did not like the people who were working on the current contract. Therefore they lost the recompete. It does not matter what solution you provide in the recompete, the price that you propose or the like. If the customer does not like the people doing the work, you will not be around for very long."*
>
> *Senior Proposal Consultant, USA*

Of course, this is not always the case and the customer starting position will be important, which is why getting the contract right from the start of Mobilization is such a vital initial task, setting the tone for some time to come. Customers also vary in their approaches to supplier management and relationships. Some are collaborative, others more formal and wishing to manage to the letter of the contract. This might be due to the organizational culture of the customer, an individual's own approach or personality, or it could be due to history—previous contractors were poor performers or caused the customer issues (perhaps that is one of the reasons they lost the contract).

Whatever the customer's starting point and approach, building a positive open relationship is your responsibility, not theirs. While it will benefit the customer, it is a necessity for the success of your business and your contract, and needs to be proactively and constantly maintained. Your goal is to create real trust and preference for you as a supplier that will help you deliver the contract and win the recompete.

Build a Wide Set of Relationships

One of the dangers for incumbents at recompete is narrow relationships held within the customer organization. Typically, this means there is a stronger relationship with direct operational customer contacts (those in the customer who directly manage the contract and those who are the key users of the contract services), and less or little relationship with others within the customer—for instance senior management, finance, or procurement teams. This can lead to focus only on the feedback given by, and expressed needs of, this smaller group. Unfortunately, this can lead to two problems:

- During the contract, you are only getting a limited perspective of the customer's total needs and are reacting to this limited perspective in what you do and change on the contract.

- At the recompete, you are relying on this smaller group to get your input as to what is required in the next contract period and what you should be putting in your recompete solution.

In reality, recompetes are rarely devised, run, evaluated, and decided on just by the operational elements within the customer. In fact, in many cases, their input and impact can be minimal. Solicitation processes are when a much wider and typically higher level of management teams become involved in contracts they may have had limited relationship with during their deliver stage. The priorities of the customer in the recompete can be more about change, risk, and value for money offerings than during the contract stage, when the emphasis is more often on quality of delivery and meeting the set specification.

To make sure you have the attention of, preference for, and input from this wider group, you need to be building and maintaining relationships with them during the contract.

One way of getting a view of the influencers and decision makers in your recompete is to look at the contract you won and who within the customer was involved in that process. It's likely your sales or bidding team built relationships with these contacts during that process. Find out from the team who they dealt with and get a handover of those relationships. If you haven't been introduced directly, get that initial introduction in person. Find out their own needs and their views of the contract. Keep in touch with them during the contract and build your own understanding of what they are worrying about and hoping for—in their organization as a whole and their own areas of responsibility, as well as things relating directly to the contract.

Look at ways to build relationships with other stakeholders who are relevant to your contract. If you provide a service to your customer's customers, find ways of building relationships with them. If you deliver services to specific departments within the customer organization or sets of end users, look at how you can build a relationship and set of regular conversations with them as well.

The wider your relationships across the customer and stakeholder group, the more perspectives you will get of what is happening within the customer—the needs you can react to and how you can make a positive difference on the contract through what you do and how you do it. As a result, you will gain a wider set of supporters at the recompete.

Set Up Regular Meetings

Informal and ad hoc chats with different stakeholders are useful for building rapport and perhaps getting informal views and feedback from them. Add to this by setting up, wherever you can, regular, diarised separate meetings with as broad a set of customer stakeholders as you can. These might be monthly or even quarterly, but they should be regular. A diarised meeting will allow you to focus your dialogue with each stakeholder on their needs and how you are—and importantly how you could be—helping them achieve their goals. You don't need to make commitments at these meetings, but you should aim to report to them on what your contract is doing that is relevant to them, together with any measures you have or can develop (see *Idea 11* and *Idea 14*).

Your goal in these meetings is to listen. Draw out the wider context of the stakeholder's drivers, pressures, and needs. These don't need to be directly related to your contract. You are aiming to gain as much context and information as possible about the organization to add to your thinking and analysis of what improvements you could be making to the contract, or extensions of the work you do for the customer. Of course, over time you will need to relate your contract delivery to the stakeholder and at least suggest possible added value, improvements or changes you could be delivering to help them, otherwise they may lose interest in continuing with the meetings. If you find a "hot button" where a key stakeholder need can be, even indirectly, helped by something you could do, you will retain their interest and support, and they will see you as a proactive part of their wider organization's ecosystem.

Keep in touch, as well, with key contacts you have built good relationships with, if and when they move on to other positions. Customer contacts will often move to different departments—some being promoted to more influential positions, others to similar roles elsewhere in the wider organization. Even after they move on, they will often keep in contact with their colleagues and will gain informal information about what is going on in their old departments. If they have moved away from having some formal responsibility for managing your contract, you will often find that they will be more open about what they hear than would have been appropriate when they had direct responsibility. They may also retain some informal influence with their old colleagues and can be excellent coaches for you during the contract and at the recompete.

Keep a Record of Who's Who and Your Interactions with Them

Sales teams are usually good at maintaining records of their contacts and the interactions they have with each prospect and customer. Good sales teams will use databases or Customer Relationship Management (CRM) software systems to keep and allow the sharing of their meetings and details of these contacts. There are many commercial systems available, ranging in cost from a few hundred dollars to several thousand dollars, that collate, organize, and manage this information.

Operators tend not to use these more formal systems as much. On a contract, you are often in daily contact with your key customers. You feel you know them well—and you have formal management meetings with them that are often written up and filed, together with the reports that you are required to generate as part of the contract.

Keeping a simple database of your wider customer stakeholders and writing up your meetings with them will, however, pay back dividends. You can often forget just what was said in a meeting with one of your stakeholders if there was no formal requirement to have a written record of the meeting. Even if there was a record, simply filing it away where it could get lost or where it is not easily accessible can mean you don't pick up on patterns of requests, questions, or expressed needs.

Create a simple database of who your stakeholders are, with some information about their roles, and any other relevant details. Make sure you build up an understanding of their priorities, the pressures they have, their goals, and fears. This will help you manage your interactions with them, as well as adjust the priorities you have for improvements on the contract. Add to this any meetings or other interactions you have with them. These don't have to be detailed formal minutes from every interaction, but you should take five minutes to write up some key notes from your meetings and add them to the relevant part of the database for that stakeholder. These can be used when you are reviewing your Contract Plan (see *Idea 8*) or analyzing your customer's wider needs. Review them briefly before your next meeting with that stakeholder—you might be surprised at what you have forgotten they said.

When you prepare for your recompete, this database will be really valuable. It will help you review how your relationship with each stakeholder has progressed, what they have been most interested in, and how they have reacted to the suggestions and improvements you have made.

Everyone on Your Contract Has Some Relationships with Customer Contacts

You're not the only person who deals with people in the customer organization, or with other stakeholders. Most of your staff and managers will be dealing with individuals or groups of people as part of their day-to-day work. Often these will be contacts you rarely meet yourself. Even if they are relatively low in the customer organization or are individual end users, keeping an understanding of who they are, what their own pressures and priorities are, and what they think about different aspects of your contract can be important.

Encourage (or require) your managers to keep records of their own meetings and interactions on your contact database. Encourage all your staff to keep an eye on the needs of those with whom they are dealing. Proactively get feedback from all of your people on what is happening, what contacts are thinking, and what ideas your staff have to improve things for them. Make sure all your staff understand you are committed to delivering the contract well, understanding and meeting your customer's needs, delivering improvement to the service you give, and retaining a long-term relationship with your customer by winning the recompete.

The same applies to others within your wider organization who deal with the customer. If you have central departments that interact with the customer, even if they are not part of your contract, keep in touch with them to get intelligence they may be picking up. When your senior directors or managers from your business come visiting, make sure they know what you are doing and what you want to know from their (probably more senior) contacts with the customer. Wherever you are able, use all the resources of your company in a coordinated way to build a network of relationships across your customer organization.

Earn Trust

Simply knowing and talking to your customer is not the same as having a positive relationship with them. To earn your customer's respect and trust you have to be consistent; you have to listen and understand what they are saying; you have to be proactive in looking for and delivering ideas and real improvements that meet your customer's important needs, and you need to react to what your customer is telling you in a positive way. Over time, this behavior will build the right relationship with your customer and will mean you have the best opportunity to win your recompete.

Section VI

Mid Term Review

Figure VI.1   The Contract Lifecycle Mid Term Review Stage

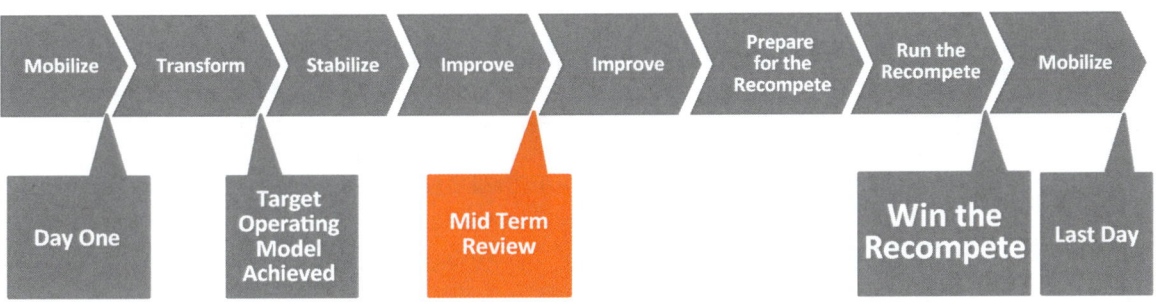

What aspects of incumbents' proposals have been particularly good?

"Knowledge of strategic direction of organizations."

UK

Idea 23: Conduct a Mid Term Review

Idea Summary:

What:

Conducting a Mid Term Review involves using people from outside your contract to review what your achievements have been to date on the contract, how you are performing, what the customer's view of you is, what has changed from the perspective of the customer's needs, and how you should react to this.

Why:

The review sets a marker for progress to date and any changes required in the contract over the next period to ensure it is on track to have delivered as required and to be in the best position for the recompete.

No matter how well you have been managing the contract—delivering to the original specification, making improvements, keeping close to your customer, and adapting to meet their changing needs—there is always a benefit in undertaking a formal contract review using external people to check that everything is performing as well as it possibly could be. It can be too easy for a contract team, focusing on the day-to-day and only having the one contract as a reference, to get into a particular way of working or viewing the contract. Having an external review can help give a new perspective. While it might seem to the contract team to be an unwelcome challenge, a distraction, or even a waste of time, having a clear audit of the overall contract at the halfway point gives you a number of benefits:

- It brings a fresh view of the contract and the customer from people with a different perspective who may see things that have been missed, not challenged, or taken for granted by the contract team.

- It brings an opportunity for the customer to talk to other people in the business and express their opinions of the contract (good or not) and give input into changes they might like to see on the contract. Without this review, these opinions might not be expressed to the contract team, or be taken into account sufficiently to be acted on and could "fester" until the recompete. By then it could be too late to make changes on the existing contract and go into the recompete with a fully satisfied customer.

- It gives the contract team the opportunity to change direction if it is needed (or at least fix any issues identified) early enough in the contract to make sure any changes take effect.

- It helps keep the contract relevant to the customer for the whole period.

- It can be the opportunity to benchmark the contract against other contracts in the company and bring in new ideas—and be the source of good ideas for other contracts.

- The review should also look at opportunities to improve margins on the contract—looking at costs, organic growth opportunities, etc.

- In addition to identifying changes, it can validate the good work already being done, giving the contract team renewed confidence they are doing a good job and the motivation to drive through further improvement in the second half of the contract, while building on the achievements already made.

Section VI   Mid Term Review

At the recompete, the Mid Term Review's outputs and recommendations will mean there has been a chance to update the contract and make it more relevant to the changes in the customer's needs since the start of the contract. You, therefore, go into the recompete on better footing than if the contract and contract team had been left alone.

At the same time, the fact that your business has the processes in place and has taken the trouble to conduct a review focused on ensuring the contract is meeting the customer's needs is another core company process which can be evidenced in the recompete as an example of quality and customer focus.

When Should the Review Take Place?

As the name suggests, you would normally conduct the review halfway through the contract. For longer term contracts (for instance, 12- to 15-year-plus contracts), the review might be converted into a five-year review and take place twice or more over the contract life.

Bring in an External Team to Conduct the Review

Who exactly runs and takes part in the review will depend on your company. Whoever they are, they should be external to the contract team. You need the review to take a fresh view of the contract. As you will see below, the review will look at a range of areas, so the following skills should be included in the team as a minimum:

- Commercial and financial.

- Customer relationship and needs.

- Appropriate subject matter experts, depending on the functions your contract undertakes.

If your company has an internal audit function, this might be the source of some of these skills; they will certainly have the process understanding of undertaking a review. You might also include people from the business development team, as they are likely to have a focus on meeting customer needs and an up-to-date understanding of what customers in the marketplace are expecting.

In some circumstances (for instance on a particularly large or important contract, or if you don't have the capability or capacity available internally), you might decide to use expertise entirely external to the company, either to be part of the team or even to lead the review. This expertise might come from a third party audit consultancy or market research organization.

Whoever you use, there should be a single lead responsible for the review and the final report, together with a team reporting to them for the purposes of the review.

The Size and Extent of the Review Depends on the Size and Complexity of the Contract

The size and extent of the review will depend on the size, and to some degree the length, of the contract. There will be a cost of undertaking the review, so this needs to be taken into consideration as well. Generally, the size and extent of the review will be larger as the size of the contract is larger. The profit margin being made on the contract should be less of a deciding factor; a contract making a low margin could benefit from a review finding ways to improve profitability.

Similarly, you shouldn't assume that a high margin contract wouldn't also benefit from a review. It's often the case that low margin or loss-making contracts are the subject of a lot of management effort and focus to improve profitability, while higher margin contracts are rarely focused on, even though they could be the source of even more margin. Sometimes teams on high margin contracts can get complacent and not be as driven to seek all the potential routes to improvement those under the spotlight on lower margin contracts are often motivated to do.

At the same time, a contract making a high margin might not be meeting the needs of the customer and might be in danger of losing its recompete if the customer is unhappy. Losing a high margin contract at recompete (even if you would have to reduce the margin to win the recompete) can have a big impact on the business' overall profitability, so ensuring high margin contracts are delivering and in the best position to win the recompete should be a priority.

Content of the Review

The goal of the review is to take a complete audit of the contract and customer situation so all relevant aspects of the contract will be covered:

The original contract.

- What was agreed in the original bid and contract?
- Has this been delivered?
- What changes have been agreed to the original contract?
- Have these been formalized and what impact have they had?

Contract profitability.

- What profit is the contract making and how does this compare with the profit expected in the bid?
- What are the reasons for any variations?
- What are the costs on the contract and how do these compare with the expectations in the bid?

Section VI Mid Term Review

- If investments were made at the start of the contract, are these being returned as expected?

Debtors and creditors.

- How are creditors being managed?
- What are the debtor levels and are payments being managed effectively?

Contract performance.

- What are the levels of performance against KPIs? Are these as expected, and what are the reasons for variations?
- What other measures (if any) have been introduced and what is performance against these?
- Is performance improving and if not, why not?
- What continuous improvement processes are in place, are they being used, and what improvements are they generating?

The customer.

- What have been the customer's drivers since the start of the contract, have these changed, and if so, what impact are they having on the contract?
- What is the customer's view of the contract and their level of satisfaction?
- What changes would they like to see? (To get this information, the review team should look at formal satisfaction surveys and also interview key customer contacts.)

Processes and systems.

- What systems and processes are in place on the contract, and are these working effectively? For instance, these might include Health & Safety, HR policies, staff management processes, and complaints systems, but will also review the core contract workflow processes from order through delivery to payment.

Management and staff.

- What is the management structure and is this as per the bid solution?
- Staffing numbers—again, are these as per the bid? If not, why not?
- Staff turnover—is this high, and if so, why and what are the implications or costs?
- Are key HR processes in place for effective management and development of staff and managers?

- Are staff skill levels appropriate?

- What is the level of staff satisfaction and motivation—if this is poor, why? (As with the customer, this might involve a staff satisfaction survey as well as interviews with some staff members.)

Recompete preparation.

- Is there a Recompete File in place?

- Are performance measures, continuous improvement, and added value processes in place and delivering?

- Are improvements, etc., being collated?

- Are customer relationships being effectively managed?

- Is there a clear understanding of the customer's needs, how these are changing, and are changes being put in place to adapt to these needs?

As the review progresses, issues or areas of doubt uncovered should be the focus of further detailed work to understand the causes and impacts as well as potential solutions. The team should meet regularly to review the results to date, compare notes across different areas to see if there are connections, analyze the information, and draw up initial views on the contract and any areas of concern. This might require a revisit of related areas to get a deeper understanding in light of what has been uncovered.

Output of the Review

The review team should produce a formal report covering the results of their investigations into each of the above areas and any other areas that are relevant to the particular contract. This should cover a summary of the work done in the review and the information collected, but should focus on sections covering strengths of the contract and areas of concern. Finally, the report should conclude with recommendations for the contract. These should focus on actions to ensure the contract is performing as required and is making any changes to be in the best possible position to win its recompete. The exact format will depend on the contract, but the following is a possible outline set of sections to be included in the report:

1. An introduction to the contract and customer.

2. The customer's position, changes in requirements since the start of the contract, aspirations, plans, and future requirements.

3. The performance of the contract to date against original requirements and against present customer requirements.

4. The costs and profitability of the contract and the effectiveness of its organization, processes, people, and systems.

5. Strong areas of the contract, particularly those that may have lessons or implications for what could be done on other contracts.

6. Areas of weakness in terms of performance and particularly against the customer's requirements and the perception of the customer.

7. Recommendations for improvements to the contract now and changes over the remaining period of the contract to put it in the best position for the recompete.

The length and level of detail the report goes into will vary with the size and complexity of the contract. If your company has a number of similar contracts and Mid Term Reviews become a standard part of the company's processes, standard templates can be created with standardized marking schemes, or traffic light (red, yellow/amber, green) summaries of different aspects to help comparisons between contracts. But bear in mind that each contract will be different to a greater or lesser extent, and while this standardized template approach might be a useful summary for comparison, the idea is to uncover the causes of issues and recommend specific actions to resolve them, rather than point out that there may be an area of underperformance.

Presenting the Review

Any report is only as good as the actions that come as a result of it. Therefore, the Mid Term Review report should be presented, potentially in different formats and levels of detail, to a number of stakeholders:

- **Senior management above the contract level**. Particularly if there are significant issues and recommendations, senior management action could be required to support the actions that need to take place. In extreme cases, the contract management team may need to be examined. Of course, the other possibility is there are lessons to be learned from good actions or performance on the contract that senior management will want to cross-pollinate into other contracts.

- **The contract management team**. This will be the main target group for the report. The contract management team will be expected to put the recommended actions in place and will need to understand and accept the need for these changes.

- **The customer.** The customer should have been informed of the review and, in most cases, some representatives from the customer organization will have been interviewed as part of the process. The presentation to the customer is likely to be a summary of key points relating to results and recommendations regarding the service they are receiving. The review should have been communicated to the customer as a positive quality review process aimed at auditing and improving the service they receive, so they will be expecting to be told the outcome. The customer also needs to agree and sign off the recommendations relating to the service they are receiving; there is little point in making changes the customer doesn't actually want.

- **Staff.** Staff working on the contract will be aware a review is taking place. As with the customer, some members of the staff may have been involved in the review process, and it is those working on the contract who are likely to be responsible for delivering a number of the recommendations made. It is good management practice to communicate a summary of the review's findings and recommendations to staff across the contract—highlighting good work done as well as changes that have been adopted.

Follow Up

To have a real impact, the recommendations made by the review need to be followed up to make sure they have been put in place and the results monitored. An action plan of how and when each recommendation will be undertaken should be agreed upon with the contract team and a regular review of progress put in place. This might be through an agenda item on regular meetings between the contract management team and senior management, or through a separate update meeting set for a few months after the report has been made—whichever best fits with the normal reporting and management process you have in place for the contract. The key is to make sure the recommendations are followed through and put into action and the results collected and reported.

What do you expect of an incumbent that is different from new bidders?

"I expect them to use their knowledge of our business in an intelligent way, such as giving examples of the work they have done with us to show they care about the company."

Central Government, UK

Section VII

Prepare for the Recompete

Figure VII.1 The Contract Lifecycle Prepare for the Recompete Stage

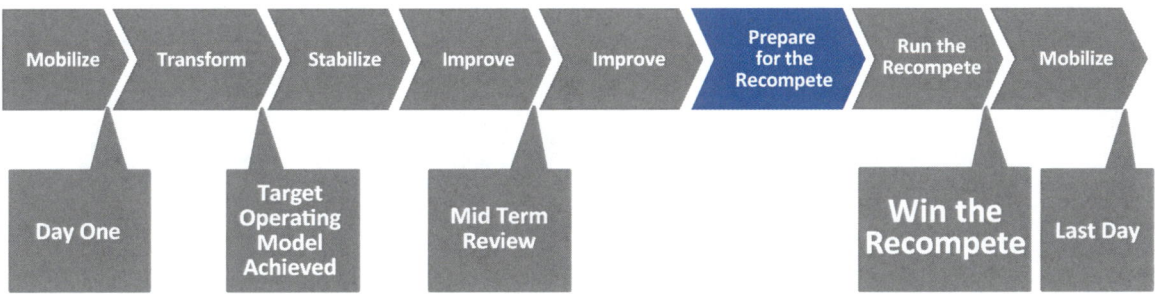

What is the Prepare for the Recompete Stage?

This is the period prior to the customer officially starting the recompete process by publicizing their new solicitation and asking for bidders to come forward. It is the time when you as the incumbent should be:

- Getting your team in place.
- Analyzing what the customer will want in the next contract period.
- Putting together and implementing your strategy for the recompete.
- Collating the information you will need for the recompete.
- Getting your contract into shape for the recompete process.

Your competitors, who will be challenging you to win the next contract period, will also be preparing their own capture strategies, talking to the customer, and putting their own teams and solutions together. As the incumbent, you should have a lot of advantages in preparing for the recompete. But too many incumbents don't use this time effectively, don't create and implement their own comprehensive recompete strategies and capture plans, and therefore go into the recompete less prepared than they should be—and suffer because of it.

Bids tend to be won by the company that has the best relationship with the customer, understands the customer's needs better than the competition (the customer's real long-term and strategic needs as well as those expressed directly in the procurement documentation), and can show that their solution and price meets these needs best. Gaining this information and translating it into a solution, price, and written bid takes time and effort. It usually needs a new look at the customer and contract using people outside the day-to-day contract team—people who will take an objective view and will "get to know the customer all over again." These are usually people from the bid or sales team. Bringing these people into the recompete preparation effort early is an essential part of an effective recompete.

Depending on how your contract has been run up to this point, you may have an easier or more difficult task in collating information on how well the contract has performed. If you have been using the ideas from the previous sections of the Contract Lifecycle, your task should be considerably easier. However, we will assume as we go through the ideas in this section that you don't have this advantage.

Ideas in this Stage:

- **Idea 24: Start Your Recompete Preparations Early**
- **Idea 25: Proactively Manage Contract Extensions**
- **Idea 26: Get the Right Recompete Team in Place**
- **Idea 27: Prepare the Contract Team**
- **Idea 28: Prepare and Implement a Recompete Strategy**
- **Idea 29: Conduct a Contract Review**
- **Idea 30: Run a Recompete Workshop**
- **Idea 31: Reinvigorate Your Customer Relationships**
- **Idea 32: Understand Stakeholder Views on Your Contract and Your Company**
- **Idea 33: Understand the Customer's Next Contract**
- **Idea 34: Analyze How Vulnerable Your Contract Is**
- **Idea 35: Understand Who Will Be Involved in the Recompete**
- **Idea 36: Resolve Existing Contract Issues**
- **Idea 37: Price To Win**
- **Idea 38: Create a Greenfield Solution**

Section VII   Prepare for the Recompete

- Idea 39: Understand Your Competitors
- Idea 40: Create Your New Solution
- Idea 41: Influence Your Customer
- Idea 42: Prepare the Contract

What do you expect of an incumbent that is different from new bidders?

"Insider knowledge, no steep learning curve, lessons learned, suggestions for improvement."

Private Sector, Australia

Idea 24: Start Your Recompete Preparations Early

Idea Summary:

What:

Start your recompete preparations at least six months prior to the beginning of the customer's official recompete process. In most cases, this can mean starting one year to 18 months prior to the end date of the contract.

Why:

Failing to take enough preparation time is one of the biggest mistakes incumbents make. Starting your recompete preparations early gives you time to review the contract, set up a Recompete Strategy, and put in place the actions and changes needed to be fully prepared when the official recompete process starts.

How early is early? It will depend on a number of things, primarily the size and length of your contract and the customer's solicitation timetable. As a general rule of thumb, you should be starting your recompete preparations at least six months before the customer's official solicitation begins and you go into the full recompete phase. You need enough time to complete the following actions:

- Review the contract and your performance to date.

- Fix any issues on the contract that could inhibit the customer from definitely selecting you as the winner.

- Get the full recompete team in place and understanding the contract.

- Get as much intelligence as possible from the customer about their view of you and your performance and their thinking about the next contract and the recompete process.

- Analyze the customer's needs for the next contract period.

- Collate all the information from your delivery of the existing contract into a form you can best use to your advantage in the recompete.

- Prepare your Recompete Strategy.

- Create an outline solution for the next contract period.

- Make any changes to the contract that will show the customer you are able to deliver the next contract.

- Sell to the customer your solution for the next contract and why you are the best supplier to deliver the next contract.

- Generally go into the recompete in a much better position to win than your challengers.

Understand Your Customer's Procurement Timetable

As we've said above, the customer's procurement timetable will be one of the main factors for when you start your recompete preparations. To get a clear understanding of what the timetable is, you should take a number of steps:

1. Different customers will have different processes and timetables for their procurement processes. Generally, private sector customers have shorter timetables than the public sector, although this is not always the case. Public sector customers can also have specific periods of time they are required to give bidders to go through procurements, but again, these can vary depending on the country or type of public sector organization, as well as the specific process they adopt. Look at whether your customer has a legal requirement to recompete and whether there are rules on how they should go about this.

2. Look at the process the customer used for the procurement for your existing contract. This is one potential route the customer will take again. Look also at other procurements your customer is undertaking or has recently completed. These will give you a view of their preferred process now. Remember, trends or even procurement rules may have changed since you won your contract.

3. Work backwards from the last day of your existing contract and take a view of the steps the customer will take and how long each of these steps is likely to take. The table below can be used as a template for this exercise, but make sure

Section VII Prepare for the Recompete

you look at each step carefully for your own contract and customer, as they are likely to be different:

Figure VII.2 Procurement Timetable

Step	Minimum time (weeks)	Maximum time (weeks)	Cumulative weeks from end of contract min (max)	Date
Last day of contract	0	0	0	End Dec 2014
Phase in period	6	12	6 (12)	Mid Nov (Start Oct)
Contract award confirmed	0	0		
Contract negotiations	2	4	8 (16)	Start Nov (Mid Sept)
Preferred bidder announced	0	0		
Final customer evaluation	4	6	12 (20)	Start Oct (Mid Aug)
Final stage of bid submitted	0	0		
Bidders prepare final stage of bid	5	8	17 (28)	Start Sept (Mid June)
Shortlist of bidders announced	0	0		
Customer evaluating initial bids/RFIs	3	5	20 (32)	Mid Aug (End May)
Bidders submit initial RFIs	0	0		
Bidders prepare RFI responses	4	6	24 (38)	End July (Mid April)
Customer releases RFI	0	0		
Bidders submit interest in bidding	2	5	26 (43)	Mid July (end Feb)
Customer requests interested bidders to apply	0	0		

The example timetable above indicates that the customer could be starting the official recompete process any time between six and ten months before the official end of the contract. This is a fairly broad estimate and you should be able to get a tighter range of likely dates.

4. Ask the customer. It might seem an obvious point, but it is surprising how many people fail to just ask the customer what their intentions are. Make sure you are talking to the right people in the customer organization as your operational contact might not know what the procurement team is planning. You should have a broad range of contacts you can trust who will have a good idea when the recompete will start and potentially what the process will entail. If you don't have these relationships, you should be trying to build them now.

Of course, while this is the start of the official recompete process, it is not the start of the work and thinking the customer will be undertaking. Before starting the official process, they will be doing a number of things in the preceding months (or even years), such as:

- Looking at their future needs for the contract within the context of their own strategic needs, pressures, and drivers. What do they need the contract to achieve, and do they even need the work on the contract to continue?

- Deciding whether they want to recompete or give an extension (or even stop the contracted activity or take it back in house!).

- Reviewing the performance of the contract in meeting their requirements to date (probably with a wide set of users, managers, and other stakeholders) and deciding what changes this may imply for the next contract period.

- Deciding on the format of the contract they are likely to procure. Will they want to extend the scope of the contract geographically or in terms of number of activities, break it down into separate lots, measure it differently, or use a different way of paying for the contract or managing it?

- Deciding whether they want to procure alone or partner with other organizations to procure together.

- Putting a budget and team together for the procurement project (depending on its size and importance).

- Potentially employing outside consultants and lawyers to help with the procurement.

- Assessing the risks of the procurement and the contract.

- Doing an assessment of the market to determine what the latest procurement trends are in this particular area, who the potential suppliers are, what the likely level of interest is from these suppliers.

- Talking to potential suppliers (your competitors) with the goal of understanding their offerings and encouraging them to bid so there is a strong competition for the contract, which should lead to the customer getting the best price and solution.

- Setting their own budget and expectation for the cost of the next contract period.

- Writing the specification for the contract.

Section VII   Prepare for the Recompete

- Putting together the solicitation timetable and the process they will use, and getting this signed off and approved by senior management—and potentially other stakeholders.

- Setting the assessment criteria and deciding how they will evaluate bids, who will do this evaluation, and who will make the final decision on the winning bidder.

Part of the reason for making sure you get an early start to your own preparations is to get ahead of these actions and the decisions the customer is making. Ideally, you should be in a position to influence these decisions. At a minimum, if you have the right relationships in the customer organization, you should be in a position to know what decisions are being made and be able to use this early warning to inform your recompete preparations.

Using the relationships you have built up over the contract period will be essential to get an understanding of what the customer's timetable is for the recompete—and therefore when you should be starting your own preparations in earnest.

Example:

The following U.S. Government Accountability Office decision illustrates the importance of building relationships with a wide number of customer contacts outside your immediate customer contract management team—and of being alert to your customer's potential recompete timetable:

In 2010, the Department of Veteran Affairs posted a notice for home healthcare services. Following the closure date for submissions, Bestcare Inc., an incumbent of the existing contract, filed a complaint with the GAO that the customer had not informed them of the recompete, the procurement was not properly publicized and the customer program staff failed to tell Bestcare of the recompete (because they did not know themselves).

The GAO rejected the protest, citing that the customer had actually posted the recompete notice on FedBizOpps (the appropriate site). The fact the customer received 12 bids for the opportunity supports this. They also state there is no requirement for the customer to specifically inform the incumbent that they are recompeting the contract. Crucially, they also point out: "Finally, we also find it unremarkable that the VA program staff were unaware that the RFP had been issued, as contracting actions are not generally undertaken by the program office, but by the agency's contracting office."

> *What is the most important thing an incumbent can do to improve their chances of winning?*
>
> "Use the run up to the tender process to ensure they fully understand the direction of travel of the council and how they can contribute to the wider goals, etc. Undertake an end of contract review to see where they can add further value."
>
> *Local Government, UK*

Idea 25: Proactively Manage Contract Extensions

Idea Summary:

What:

Put together a proactive plan for gaining the maximum time available for extensions to the core of the contract.

Why:

Gaining as many extensions as available on the contract increases the rate of return on your bid and recompete costs. You should proactively work toward gaining contract extensions. You should also use these extensions to put yourself in a better position for the time the recompete does come about by negotiating changes with your customer during the extension period that bring your contract more into line with the requirements the customer is likely to set out in the recompete.

Many contracts are procured for a core contract period plus the option for the customer to grant one or more extensions to the contract length. How many and how long these extensions are will usually (always in public sector contracts) be publicized as part of the initial bid announcement. The process for granting these extensions and the basis on which they can be given will usually form part of the legal contract terms and conditions you agree to when you win the initial contract. If you can get one or all of the extensions to your contract, you will gain in a number of ways:

- ■ The risk of losing the recompete (no matter how well prepared you are, there is always a risk) is put off for a longer period of time—so your income and profit from the contract is extended.

- ■ The costs of your original bid are spread out over a longer period of time, effectively increasing the return on investment from the bid.

Section VII Prepare for the Recompete

- If you depreciated any investment in capital items used on your contract over the core contract period, but can keep using them through the extension periods, your effective profitability on the extension periods is increased.

- Your own cost of running the recompete competition is also put off for a period. If you get extensions on all of your contracts, your overall cost of bidding will be less over a period of years than if you don't get them, as you will be recompeting for each contract less often.

So, unless there are real reasons for not accepting extensions (for instance, you are losing an unsustainable amount of money on the contract you cannot renegotiate at the extension), you should be proactively aiming to get as many extensions as possible from your customer. There are also a number of specific aspects to extensions you should also be considering in regards to your recompete:

Don't Delay Your Recompete Preparations on the Expectation of an Extension

As we've said above, you should be starting your recompete preparations at least six months prior to the start of the official recompete process. That can be 18 months before the end of the contract. Customers won't always confirm you have an extension until closer to the end of your core contract period. Even if you are being given messages from your customer that you will get an extension, don't assume this will happen and delay the start of your recompete preparations because you expect not to need them yet. Things can change at the last minute, or the customer contact you are getting your information from might not be the decision maker or have a full insight into the process.

Expecting to get an extension and then being surprised by an announcement from the customer that the official recompete is starting has happened to more incumbents than it should, and the resulting lack of recompete preparation wastes many of the advantages you should have as the incumbent, putting your successful recompete at risk.

Start your recompete preparations early as per *Idea 24* and others in this section, whether you expect an extension or not. Don't count on an extension until you have the official confirmation, signed by the customer, that the extension has been granted.

Use Extensions to Put in Place Changes Which Will Help Your Recompete

Extensions are often an opportunity to renegotiate elements of the contract. Sometimes the customer will ask for a cost reduction, or perhaps you will ask for a price increase, to cover inflation over the additional period. Usually a compromise is agreed, depending on where the balance of need is regarding the extension and who wants or needs it most.

You can also use the extension as an opportunity to agree on changes to how the contract is delivered, moving it in the direction the customer may be thinking they want for the next contract period. This gives you a chance to test the new way of working and gives you credibility for the recompete by already delivering the new ways of working (and having evidence and examples of working in this new format) for the recompete. If they are now receiving the service they are looking for in the future, it may encourage the customer to postpone the recompete even further and give you more extensions—or if they are able, to do away with the recompete altogether.

Customers can often offer a series of relatively short extensions, for instance, two or three extensions of a single year. You are usually better off getting a single longer extension. Multiple shorter extensions can just extend the uncertainty of how long the contract will last, which can, for instance, unsettle staff, who become unsure of their future. If you can show the transition to the new way of working needs to be in place for a period of time to deliver and confirm its full benefit, you may be able to get this longer single extension, giving you (and your staff) more certainty for a longer time. Having an updated contract delivery in place which is closer to the customer's future needs also means your transition risks and costs for the new contract are likely to be lower—as will the customer's risk of choosing you to deliver the next contract.

A Note on Price

Some contracts can increase their profitability over time from a market competitive margin at the bid to a significantly higher margin in the later stages of the contract. Indeed, this is one of the goals you will most likely have been working toward over the contract period. However, if you are making significantly higher than market rate margins on your contract as the recompete approaches, you face a potentially difficult choice. It is unlikely you will win the recompete if you attempt to retain this margin in your bid (most incumbents who try this, as they feel this is the "right" margin and don't want their margins to fall in the next contract, lose their recompete). But simply making a significant reduction in price in your offer for the next contract by cutting your margins can lead the customer to ask how you have managed this and question whether you were delivering value for money over the previous period (and therefore, whether you will do so during the next contract). This can be difficult to explain in a recompete and can cost you a lot of credibility with the customer.

If you anticipate you might be in this position, you could use the extension periods to start bringing down your price, closer to the market rate, by offering the customer increasing price reductions for longer extension periods. This would mean that by the time you got to the recompete, your margin and price would be closer to the market rate and less likely to be significantly and embarrassingly undercut by your competitors. It also gives you a stronger story to tell the customer in the recompete as to how you have been proactively delivering value for money improvements over (at least) the latter period of the contract.

Of course, this is a difficult commercial decision to take. There is the possibility you still won't win the recompete, in which case you have given away profit now for no future return. However, the other possibility is that, without this offer to reduce margins, you would not get the extensions, therefore losing the additional income over the extension years you might otherwise have gained. And your future income stream from the new contract won at the recompete could also be lost, due to the dissonance the customer experiences when seeing an unexplained steep drop in price from you at the recompete. Only you know what the right balance is for your business and contract circumstances. But do be aware that a number of incumbents have lost recompetes on this point.

What is the most important thing an incumbent can do to improve their chances of winning?

"Leverage their experience and knowledge of the client by paying close attention to the RFP details."

Federal Government, USA

Idea 26: Get the Right Recompete Team in Place

Idea Summary:

What:

The right recompete team mixes the strengths of the contract team, who understand the contract details, with the strengths, challenge, and fresh approach of capture and bid experts and independent subject matter experts.

Why:

It is important to put this team in place early to enable them to build relationships with the customer, understand and challenge the existing contract delivery, and put in place a new solution that fits the customer's needs for the next contract—and does not simply repeat the existing contract solution.

Having the right recompete team in place at the start of the recompete preparation stage will give you the skills mix and capacity to properly prepare for the recompete. The initial team may not include everyone who will work on the later stages when you are responding to the customer official recompete process, but there should be continuity between the two stages.

The exact size and technical skills sets of the team will vary depending on the type of work you deliver, the size of your contract, and its importance to the business overall. But there should be a commitment in your business to assign resources to the recompete early. Most businesses understand the importance of preparation and getting to know new customers before bids for new business come out. While some will simply react to customer published RFI's without work in advance, others refuse to bid most opportunities unless they already know the customer well and feel they know what the customer wants because they see this route as the only one that ensures a high chance of winning.

There can be a tendency not to apply this thinking to existing contracts at recompete, on the assumption you know the customer because you are already delivering the contract. This is a mistake that loses a lot of recompetes. Even if your delivery team knows what the customer wants now, this doesn't mean it is what the customer wants in the future. Putting a recompete team together early and making sure you properly prepare for the recompete are some of the most important factors in increasing your chances of winning.

The ideal mix of team members will include some from the operations side of the contract, combined with others from your sales, capture, or bidding team (depending on how your company is organized).

During the preparation stage, the team will be:

- Getting to know the customer and their needs.

- Creating a Recompete Strategy.

- Building relationships with key customer contacts (members of the recompete team from outside the contract should be building their own relationships with the customer, rather than relying solely on the relationships built up by the contract team).

- Reviewing the contract.

- Identifying what the customer recompete process will be.

- Identifying and influencing, if possible, what will go into the scope and specification of the customer's solicitation.

- Creating an outline solution for the new contract (including an indicative price).

Section VII   Prepare for the Recompete

- Collating the information from the delivery of the contract over its full length to be used in the recompete as evidence of good performance, showing you are the supplier most suited to deliver the next contract period.

- Getting all the preparations in place that will put you ahead of the competition and in the best position to win by the start of the customer's official recompete process.

Include People from the Contract Team

Members from the contract team will bring an understanding of the detail of how the customer works and how the contract delivers at present to the recompete team. They should have a practical knowledge of the workings of the contract and good relationships with the rest of the contract team, as well as the customer. They should also have a good understanding of how to find information about the contract performance from the existing records already held.

> *Proposal expert advice:*
>
> *"It's essential to build on the knowledge and experience of the incumbent delivery team to demonstrate an in depth understanding of the customer's business and services delivered. Offering added value and innovation should be a key win theme, BUT you have to be careful to ensure that innovative ideas are not killed off by the incumbent team. The competition will always be looking to see what fresh angle they can attack with."*
>
> Business Development Manager, Dubai

The recompete team needs substantial time to prepare, and members from the contract need to be able to commit to this. Ideally people working on the recompete team from the contract will be able to spend the majority, if not all, of their time working on the recompete team. This might mean they need to be seconded to the team full time and their contract duties covered elsewhere. However, this needs managing. The more senior the people working on the recompete team, the more important it is they not leave a gap in contract delivery. The last thing you want is for contract performance to drop just as you are approaching the recompete, or your customer to be unhappy because a key team member has disappeared from his day-to-day work. You should be planning well ahead for this—making sure those likely to be put onto the recompete team have clear succession plans in place for people to take on their duties, and the customer isn't put in a position where they feel they are missing a key contract team member.

Bring in Team Members from Outside the Contract

The people allocated to the recompete team from outside the contract will be bringing an objective view to the recompete. They should have the relationship building skills needed to create good relationships quickly with the customer before the official recompete starts, when customer contacts will often feel they must stop talking openly to incumbent teams, as it would be unfair to the competition and could lead to objections later in the process. This skill set will often be found in capture experts within your business. Having at least one capture expert within the team is vital—many businesses put this person in charge of the overall recompete (see below).

The team should bring good research skills to uncover the customer requirements, understand the workings of the contract, and evaluate quickly the likely needs going into the future. They should also bring good analysis and solution development skills. The team should be gathering a significant amount of information about the customer, the contract, the future requirements for the procurement, as well as competitors and their likely approaches. The team will need to analyze all this information and create a winning, costed solution and price.

Put the Right Recompete Team Leader in Place

One person should lead the recompete team and have overall responsibility for ensuring they have enough time and resources to properly prepare for the recompete. Usually this person will be external to the contract. There are good reasons for this, for instance:

- The team leader needs to prioritize the recompete. A senior member of the contract team is unlikely to have the time to cover all the work that needs to be done for recompete preparation as well as ensuring the contract is running effectively.

- The team leader needs to be experienced in running bids and recompetes. Contract team members are less likely to be experienced in running recompete programs or bids.

- The team leader needs to take an objective view of the contract and solution. This is more likely to come from an external person than one involved deeply in the day-to-day running of the existing contract.

Manage the Tensions within the Recompete Team and with the Contract Team

Part of the role of recompete team members from outside the contract team is to take an objective view of the contract, the customer's needs, and what is needed to win the next contract. This will involve challenging all aspects of the existing contract and bringing in ideas of how the solution for the next contract can be different from the existing one. At the same time, the existing contract team is more likely to defend how the existing contract is being delivered and will be thinking along more conservative lines in terms of continuing with many of the good aspects of the way the contract is presently delivered. This will inevitably cause tensions. These tensions shouldn't be avoided, but do need to be managed.

To win your recompete, you will need to draw on the best of what you have delivered to date, but also take a completely "ground up" approach to designing the new solution. Too many incumbents lose because the customer perceives that they are simply offering more of the same, perhaps with some minor changes or improvements and a slightly lower price. Your competitors will be looking to win by bringing in new, innovative, and lower-priced solutions than you are presently delivering. If you, as the incumbent, don't also do this, you will stand too great a chance of losing. Challenge and bringing in new ideas are necessary parts of the process for creating a fresh new solution that meets the needs of the customer in the next contract rather than just repeating the existing solution. Even if the customer is not proposing significant changes to their needs or the specification of the contract, this doesn't mean they will choose more of the same in the solution, especially if they are being offered different options by your competitors.

At the same time, you should draw on the experience of what has worked to date on the contract—and what new ideas might not be feasible or workable. Typically, this is what the contract team will bring to the team.

Everyone on the team wants to win the recompete. The existing contract team should recognize that the challenge that will (should) come from the external team members is aimed at bringing a fresh approach and should not be rejected. At the same time, team members brought in from outside the contract should not ignore the experience of the contract team. Too often, factions can be created within the recompete team with each side stereotyping the other—"the contract team is stuck in its ways," "the external team doesn't know what it takes to actually deliver a solution in practice." Both groups need to understand the other's perspective and work with an open mind to get the best possible solution—and see challenge and argument as a positive part of the process that will lead to this.

What aspects of incumbents' proposals have been particularly poor?

"I have found that I need to guide the incumbent to think outside the box. Some companies have separate bid teams to operations and they don't talk, so the bid is not based on fact, which means having to ask for rework: lack of internal communications."

UK

Idea 27: Prepare the Contract Team

> **Idea Summary:**
>
> **What:**
>
> The contract team needs to be involved in the recompete and all staff need to be motivated to deliver high quality service to the customer. Ensure they understand the process being followed.
>
> **Why:**
>
> Contract teams are less experienced at recompeting than bidders and other business development staff. Ensuring the contract team is prepared for the recompete is an important part of maximizing its contribution and ensuring the contract continues to deliver throughout the recompete period.

The recompete is likely to be a time of uncertainty for the contract team:

- The possibility of losing the recompete to a competitor may unsettle staff, as they could lose their jobs.

- The challenge put forward by the recompete team to existing ways of working might put managers on the defensive.

- The additional workload involved in preparing for and participating in the recompete effort, while keeping the contract delivering to a high quality, can stretch the team.

- Your new solution is likely to involve changes and potentially reductions in staff, which will again potentially unsettle the team.

Keep a balance between overconfidence that the recompete will be won (which can lead to complacency) and maintaining motivation. The contract team, particularly the management team, should be clear that in order to win, it will need to challenge all the existing assumptions from the contract to date. The team should be clear that change is needed and embrace this as an opportunity—otherwise, you risk people going into denial and either not participating positively or taking trenchant positions against any changes put forward.

However, for staff this needs to be tempered. Clearly communicating to staff that you are taking the recompete seriously, are determined to win, and are putting resources, time, and effort into making sure you do win, will give them confidence and help maintain motivation. Staff can also be a source of good information and ideas for improvement, so a degree of involvement in some aspects of recompete preparation will help them feel engaged.

Section VII Prepare for the Recompete

At least some members of the contract management team are likely to be heavily involved in the recompete effort, which will inevitably take up time. Make sure you have planned for this and you have clear succession plans in place. Now is the time when those in the next tier down, identified as having potential, should be ready to step up and take on some of the workload. Planning for and testing the potential for these people to step up by training and giving them opportunities to fill in for some tasks before the recompete preparation process is fully running will also familiarize them, and the customer, with their responsibilities and give both (particularly the customer) confidence delivery will be maintained and the contract is running as normal.

Keep Contract Teams Up to Date with Recompetes in Your Company

Contract management teams are less likely to be experienced rebidders. Some will have experienced recompetes on their previous contracts, but many will not have had significant or regular involvement. Make sure they are aware of the importance of the recompete as part of their role and are equally aware of the processes you use and what you expect of them in the recompete effort.

One way of achieving this is to review recompetes as part of any regular management conferences or meetings. Include a session where managers who have successfully won their recompetes present, with members of the recompete team, the process they went through, what they learned, and their recommendations for other managers. While a degree of choreographing might be needed, these should be open presentations—managers should include issues they faced as well as positive aspects. If there were issues or tensions between the approach of the contract team and the recompete team, these should be aired (though positively). The goal is for contract teams to hear from their peers how they felt about the process, what they learned, and what their own recommendations are to their colleagues, including any learning about how they should be running their contract now to increase their likelihood of winning.

Keeping recompetes as part of the agenda for contract team meetings will help build an awareness of what to expect and an understanding of the importance of the recompete process as part of the contract lifecycle.

The recompete workshop (see *Idea 30*) will also help kick off the preparation of the contract team at the start of the recompete preparation process and make sure they are ready for the effort ahead.

> ***What do you expect of an incumbent that is different from new bidders?***
>
> *"1. Cultural alignment. If they cannot achieve that after a period of incumbency then all is lost! 2. A clear view about what the client should do differently to help the bidder operate the new contract more successfully.*
> *3. Clarity about the SLAs, KPIs and labor loadings, etc."*
>
> *Private Sector, UK*

Idea 28: Prepare and Implement a Recompete Strategy

Idea Summary:

What:

The Recompete Strategy is the overall plan of action for preparing for and winning your recompete. Some companies relate this to a capture plan, and this can encompass many of the actions required for a Recompete Strategy.

Why:

Creating, implementing and adapting as needed a clear Recompete Strategy drives and gives an overall direction to the actions required to win your recompete.

Your Recompete Strategy will encompass your approach and plan for winning your recompete. Creating and implementing your strategy is normally the responsibility of your recompete team leader, although for particularly large or important recompetes for the company, it may be the responsibility of senior management. Depending on how your company uses the terminology, you might equate the Recompete Strategy to the capture plan for a new bid. However, many people use the term "capture plan" to mean the relationship building, information gathering, and influencing elements of a new bid effort.

The Recompete Strategy also includes other actions such as potentially making changes to the existing contract operations. So for our purposes, the overall Recompete Strategy takes in a wider set of actions and elements than you may realize when referring to capture plans, although there is a significant overlap and if you do follow capture plan processes in your business for new bids, you can translate these easily into many areas of the Recompete Strategy.

Most of the ideas in the rest of the "Prepare for the Recompete" stage, as well as the next stage on "Run the Recompete," form part of the overall Recompete

Section VII Prepare for the Recompete

Strategy, so in this idea, we will only outline the stages and breadth of the strategy and leave the details to the other idea descriptions.

What Does the Recompete Strategy Encompass?

Your Recompete Strategy should cover:

- A range of actions.
- An overall approach.
- A set of resources to be used.
- An overall program plan and timetable and a specific timetable for each action.
- Responsibilities for actions.
- A budget.
- Governance and reviews to make sure you are on course.
- A clear objective which all of the above are designed to achieve—winning your recompete.

Proposal expert advice

A key factor in both winning and losing recompetes is the strength of the incumbent delivery team. Losses can be attributed to delivery teams being complacent, thinking that because they are doing a "good" job then the customer will want to retain them, whatever the price and without striving to apply any innovation—looking at alternative approaches to increase performance and/or reduce costs. Incumbent teams can also over-interpret the RFP requirements based on maintaining current practices rather than bidding to the stated requirements. The flip side is that incumbent teams can be the biggest strength in winning a recompete—they are in a unique position to understand the customer's requirements, prove capability, shape the RFP and investigate innovative approaches. Most importantly, the work on the recompete can be started at a much earlier stage than the competition—arguably from Day 1 of the contract. In order to improve on the recompete successes, company management needs to ensure that significant effort is placed on the recompete—checking that a recompete plan is put in place long before the RFP is released, supporting the incumbent delivery team accordingly and by robustly challenging all aspects of the proposed technical and commercial proposal."

Business Development Manager, Dubai

What Actions Should Be Included in the Recompete Strategy?

The main actions in your strategy will include:

- Review your existing contract.
- Build relationships with the customer.
- Understand the customer's needs.
- Influence your customer's approach to the recompete.
- Analyze your competitors and their likely approaches.
- Understand the price it will take to win.
- Build a solution to win.
- Prepare the contract for the recompete.
- Run the recompete process.
- Plan the implementation of the new contract.

The previous actions are generally in chronological order, but of course, many of them will overlap and some will continue throughout the whole recompete preparation and recompete running stages. The exact schedules will depend on how long this overall period is and the size and complexity of your contract, as well as the level of change the customer requires in the recompete. Your budget for the recompete will depend on the same factors as well as your own company approach to how much is invested in business development efforts and the profit return you expect from the new contract period.

Make sure your budget is sufficient to complete a full recompete effort—recompetes should be allocated at least as much time, resource, and budget as a new bid of equivalent value. Too many incumbents work on the basis that, as they are almost definitely going to win anyway and the recompete effort can be run primarily by the existing contract team (which, as you will see from *Idea 26,* is not the best approach) whose time is already paid for by the contract, only a minimal budget is required.

Section VII   Prepare for the Recompete

Idea 29: Run a Contract Review

> **Idea Summary:**
>
> **What:**
>
> The Contract Review collates information from the whole contract period to feed into your Recompete Strategy, your new solution, and your proposal. The review should take place early in your recompete preparations and be conducted by people independent of the contract team.
>
> **Why:**
>
> Reviewing the contract early in the "Prepare for the Recompete" stage gives the recompete team a clear and objective view of what has happened on the contract to date and the information available to them for use in the recompete. The review will also identify unavailable areas of information that need further investigation to uncover or start collecting while there is still time.
>
> **Key Steps:**
>
> 1. Review the original procurement and bid.
>
> 2. Review your original implementation.
>
> 3. Review the changes made to the contract.
>
> 4. Review volumes of work across the contract period.
>
> 5. Review performance across the contract period.
>
> 6. Review issues and how they have been resolved.
>
> 7. Review added value, innovation, accreditations, and other achievements.
>
> 8. Review key processes used on the contract.
>
> 9. Collect any other relevant material.

One of the first steps the recompete team should take is to review the existing contract. Start from the beginning of the contract and work through the whole contract period. The goal is to give the recompete team a full picture of the contract to date, create a solid understanding of the contract as a basis for the recompete, and assess what information on the contract's performance to date is available for the recompete—or might need collecting.

Step 1: Review the original procurement and bid.

Go back to the original (or previous) customer procurement, the bid your company put in, and the contract that was signed. Hopefully, the records for this are still available, though they may take some searching out. Look at:

- How the customer procured the contract.
- The process they used.
- What their specification was.
- How they evaluated the bids.
- Who the competitors were.
- What was in your bid.
- Why you won.

While you should not assume the customer will repeat the same process, or will specify the same requirements, understanding how they procured last time may give some insight into how the customer works and what they look for in a bid. It will also help you understand why you won and the expectations you set in your bid.

Look at the terms and conditions of the signed contract. Understanding this in detail may again give you some indication (though not a guarantee) of what the customer is looking for in the contractual terms. It should also give you a comparison, together with your original bid, to test whether you have actually delivered what you promised.

Step 2: Review your original implementation.

How well did your original implementation go:

- What were the plans you put in your bid for transformation?
- What went well?
- What issues did you face?
- Was your transformation a success?
- What lessons did you learn?
- What was the customer's view of your transition and do you have anything on this in writing?

Section VII Prepare for the Recompete

Showing you are capable of delivering a strong and successful transformation will be an essential part of your recompete. Understanding the potential pitfalls will give you ammunition to show why you are the lowest risk supplier for the transformation next time and why your competitors may be higher risk. Gathering this information will give you a head start in your recompete.

Step 3: Review the changes made to the contract.

Review the changes made to the contract since its start:

- How much has the contract changed?
- What changes have been made and in what areas?
- Who instigated the changes—the customer or your team?
- What impact have the changes had?
- Who benefitted from the changes—particularly, did the customer?
- Was there a consistent forum set up to look at potential changes and was this effective?
- Were there changes the customer wanted but were rejected or not put in place?
- Has the contract team been proactively putting forward change options?
- Have all the changes been properly documented and signed off into the contract?
- What, if any, pattern is there to the changes which might give you a view of the direction the contract is taking and the potential changes in the recompete the customer might want to make?

Understanding the level and type of change on the contract will give you a view of how flexible and dynamic the contract (and your contract team) has been, as well as the reasons and direction of change the customer has sought—a narrative or story for the contract. Being able to collate these changes will give you more ammunition to use in your recompete as evidence you have been a flexible, proactive contractor which has consistently met your customer's changing requirements.

Step 4: Review volumes of work across the contract period.

What has changed in the volumes of work (the demand) you have delivered over the contract period?

Analyze the levels and mix of volume of work, number of orders, number of end users serviced, etc., and how this has changed over the period of contract. Look at the information on two levels:

- What is the larger pattern and direction of growth, reduction, or changing form of demand?

- What are the details? How does demand fluctuate over the short term—are there daily, weekly, or seasonal cycles or other patterns or fluctuations correlating with specific customer issues? What are the peaks and trough levels and what are the reasons behind these fluctuations?

Analyze these volume levels against a range of other factors to understand efficiency ratios (volume per member of staff, for instance). This will help give a base for calculating costs and resources for your new solution (although only a base—you should always be looking for new and more efficient means of delivery).

Understanding the direction of demand will give you insight into the likely levels of demand going forward into the next contract, both to help your solution and anticipate the customer's recompete requirements.

Knowing the detail of fluctuations will also help you with your solution. These are areas where your competitors may not have information. You can use this to reinforce your own arguments in the recompete for why your solution is most appropriate for the customer and potentially cast doubt in the customer's mind whether competitors' solutions meet their needs. For instance, knowing that demand is particularly high on a Tuesday afternoon and the problems not meeting this demand could create for the customer can be used to show why you have put staff rosters in to cover this (with evidence over the period of the contract)—and if competitors have not covered this surge, the problems this could cause. In some cases, the customer may not be explicitly aware of these details and may not include the information in their general documents and briefings for bidders, which can put you at an even greater advantage.

Step 5: Review performance across the contract period.

Pull together the historical information about contract performance from the start of the contract:

- Is there a complete and official record of performance throughout the contract?

- What performance measures have been used?

- What levels of performance were required in the contract, if specified?

- How well has the contract performed against these measures?

- Have there been fluctuations?

- What are the reasons for any underperformance or fluctuations?

- Have new performance measures been introduced: if so, why and by whom?

- What reports are available (for instance, monthly customer reports) showing performance?

- What record of customer feedback on performance is available—what does it say? Are there good (or bad) comments you can use in the recompete or need reviewing?

- How much has performance increased (assuming it has) over the period of the contract and what are the reasons for this?

Ideally, you will be able to source this information easily (see *Idea 5: Set up a Recompete File*). Often however, particularly on a long-term contract, the information is more difficult to find or is incomplete. Collate as much as possible and piece together a complete picture of performance over the contract period. If full information isn't immediately available, keep looking throughout the recompete preparation period. Not only will this information be useful for your new solution, it will be good evidence to use in your recompete.

Step 6: Review issues and how they have been resolved.

Every contract has issues at some point. They might be issues the customer experienced which have led to changes in demand or specification, or issues of performance the contract has experienced. They may have been one-off (a flood, for instance), or they may have repeated or even been long-term problems. Understanding what issues have occurred on the contract will give you a sense of the potential difficulties you might face in the future. More importantly, if there have been issues, the customer will remember them, and this might impact their view of you as a contractor. What is most important is how the issues were resolved.

If issues were identified early, clearly communicated with the customer and resolved quickly to the customer's satisfaction—particularly if the issue was not a fault of your contract team, this will be a significant positive story you can use in the recompete. Collecting the evidence of what happened—the potential or actual impact, the resolution, and customer reaction—will give you positive input into your recompete to show you are a flexible, proactive supplier.

If issues were caused, or contributed to, by your team or some element of your delivery and reoccurred or were not quickly resolved, you need to understand the issues and the reasons in detail. They could still have a negative impact on the customer's perception of you. Perhaps the problem was never fully resolved to the customer's satisfaction—in which case, see *Idea 36*. Even if the issues have been resolved, you will need to carefully review the impact on the customer's attitude towards you as a supplier (see *Idea 32*) and attempt to resolve any problems during the recompete preparation stage. Ultimately, you will need to take these issues into account in your recompete, potentially accepting that problems have occurred, and showing the changes you have made or will make to ensure they don't recur in the next contract period. Your competitors will be seeking out these issues in their own Capture Planning research and may use them against you in their own bids. You can't ignore them or assume they are in the past and forgotten by the customer.

Step 7: Review added value, innovations, accreditations, and other achievements.

What other added value have you delivered to the customer over the period of the contract and are there other initiatives, accreditations, commendations, etc., you have received during the contract?

Search out any other good examples of performance, actions, awards, or initiatives over the contract period. You should capture as many as possible at this stage. You are particularly looking for evidence of customer commendations, letters of thanks from end users or other stakeholders you can use as evidence of your proactive, customer focused approach over the contract period.

A table collating these, or short stories or vignettes describing them, can be powerful pieces of evidence you can add to the recompete. Understanding the extent of the evidence available early in the recompete preparation process gives you time to use them to best effect. Always look at the impact on the customer these positive actions have delivered; this is the key outcome you should be demonstrating to the customer (and, of course, the main area they will be interested in).

Step 8: Review the key processes used on the contract.

Review the management processes used on the contract and how effective these have been, for instance:

- Communication and regular management review processes with the customer.
- Partnering processes and forums.
- Stakeholder meetings, satisfaction surveys, complaints processes.
- Quality processes.
- Health and Safety processes.
- Staff development and communication processes.
- Continuous improvement processes.
- Audit processes—both internal and external.

Look particularly for evidence that these processes have been used proactively to deliver change, improvement, and initiatives on the contract and for the customer and have not just been bureaucratic exercises with little or no impact. Showing a clear relationship between established processes you have in place on the contract and resulting improvements will be a very positive aspect you can use in your recompete. It will show how you have been able to proactively create positive change on the contract—and how these processes will continue to be used during the next contract to deliver more improvements.

Step 9: Collect any other relevant information.

Depending on the type of work done on the contract, there will be a range of other historical information you can use for the recompete or to develop your new solution. The list could include changes in staff costs, use of technology, product specifications, supplier details and their performance; the list will depend on the contract.

Sources of Information

As we have said, your main source of information for all of the above areas is likely to be documentation such as management reports, meeting notes, etc., collected during the course of the contract. If you run accredited quality processes, you may well find these encompass many of the areas covered. As they require regular evidence to be written down to show that the processes are being followed, they may include a range of useful information. If you conducted a Target Operating Model Review (see *Idea 7*) or a Mid Term Review (see *Idea 23*), these will provide excellent summaries of how the contract was working and progress made at these times.

But these sources might not tell the whole story. Not all contract information or initiatives are formally reported or documented, and even those that are can be misfiled or lost.

The contract management team and staff will not only guide you to the right documentation, they can themselves be a useful source of information. Interview key members of the team, either individually or in groups, to pull out information on the contract. A set of interviews with consistent questions can elicit a lot of useful information that can be followed up and evidenced as part of the contract review or later in the recompete preparation process.

Collating and Using the Information Gathered from the Contract Review

Your review will collect a lot of data and information. The steps above give you a way of sorting this into areas of interest, but as you progress, you will find other uses for the information. Make sure the information you collate is filed in a coherent format so it can easily be found and referred to later.

Analyze and turn the data into summary formats you can use for the recompete or for input into your new solution. This might involve:

- Creating summary outlines of particular areas of the bid together with clear references back to the source information for evidence.

- Creating lists of information that collect together a particular set of information from throughout the contract (for instance, all the items of added value).

- Creating tables or diagrams summarizing key information (for instance, performance against a particular KPI throughout the contract on a single graph).

Create a final report or presentation that summarizes the data found. Present this to the recompete team and the contract team to ensure the recompete team knows the information available and the contract team can comment on and add to what you have found. The full set of information will be a significant part of your source material as you move forward to creating your solution and writing your recompete. For more on this, see *Idea 47: Use the Information You Have Gathered*.

What aspects of incumbents' proposals have been particularly poor?

"Not caring to complete the proposal in accordance with the requirements, assuming that they don't have to comply, assuming the recompete is a formality."

State Government, USA

Idea 30: Run a Recompete Preparation Workshop

Idea Summary:

What:

A Recompete Preparation Workshop attended by key members of the contract team and run early in the recompete preparation stage helps collect information relevant for the recompete.

Why:

The workshop gives the team an understanding of the recompete process and pressures and identifies areas where more work is required.

Section VII Prepare for the Recompete

Key Agenda Items:

1. Introductions

2. The Recompete Timetable

3. Customer Recompete Team

4. Contract Performance

5. Customer Future Needs

6. Competitors

7. SWOT

8. Win Themes

9. Key Actions

Running a recompete workshop at the start of preparation for the recompete, with the contract management team and those from the contract on the recompete team, will give the attendees a quick introduction to the recompete process and what it will entail. The workshop will also help the recompete lead gain information from the contract team about a range of areas from the contract as a kickoff to the contract review. Most of the sections in the workshop will relate to separate reviews or research the recompete team will be undertaking separately as part of the wider recompete preparation process (see some of the other ideas in this section). The workshop can be used as a kickoff for these reviews to get initial input and information from the contract team that you can expand and follow up on later.

By the end of the workshop, the recompete lead should have an understanding of the contract team's view of the recompete and a view of their thoughts on key areas. You will also have a set of actions for the contract team; for instance, sourcing information for the contract review. Below, we set out an agenda and detailed description of a sample recompete workshop. Most of the sections cover areas we deal with in more detail in ideas later in this stage.

How Long Should the Review Take?

Depending on the size of the contract, the review can usually be run in a half or a full day. A white board and flip charts should be available, and ideally someone to take notes and record the outcome of each part of the agenda.

Suggested Agenda

Item	Subject	Timing (minutes)
1	Introduction	5–10
2	The recompete timetable	15–20
3	The customer recompete team	20–30
4	Contract performance	30–40
5	Customer future needs	30
6	Competitors	15–20
7	SWOT	40
8	Win Themes	20
9	Key Actions	15
Total time		3–4 hours plus breaks

1. Introduction (Timing: 5–10 minutes)

This should be a short introduction to outline the purpose of the day, the agenda, how the workshop will be run, and the outcomes the workshop should produce. Usually, the contract team will know each other, so introductions should not be required, although if the recompete lead is not familiar with the contract team attendees, a short introduction of their roles may be useful.

2. Recompete Timetable (Timing: 15–20 minutes)

The goal of this session: To understand the likely recompete timetable and where the customer is in this. The contract team may be inexperienced at recompeting and may not be aware of the different stages the recompete goes through. In this case, the outcome will be an understanding of this timetable and the key work required before each step. The goal will be to establish its equivalent for the contract in question.

Section VII Prepare for the Recompete

Figure VII.3   Bid Process with Key Stages and Events

Activity or point in the process	Potential length of time	Count back from last day of the contract (weeks)
Last day of the existing contract		
Phase in of the new contract/contractor		
Final negotiations		
Chosen contractor confirmed		
Stand still period		
Chosen contractor published		
Customer evaluating final bids		
Final bids delivery date		
Contractors preparing final bids		
Final stage documents published to shortlisted contractors (e.g., RFP)		
Customer evaluating initial bids (RFI) and choosing shortlist		
Initial bids delivery date		
Contractors preparing initial bids		
Initial bid documents published		
Period for contractors to express interest		
Customer publicizes recompete		
Customer deciding evaluation process and preparing documentation		
Customer agreeing on the breadth of the new contract and its form		
Customer deciding on the requirements of the new contract		

The table above is an example bid process with key stages and events. This will vary from sector to sector, so before you start the workshop, create your own table which fits the usual process used for the type of contract you are covering in the workshop. The output of this session in the workshop will give you a view of the process this customer has used in the past; it may not tell you what they will actually use this time.

Begin by identifying the last day of the contract—i.e. the day prior to the new contract starting. Write this up on the whiteboard.

Ask the team what they believe the previous stage of the recompete would be (this will be the phase-in period of the new contract). Ask the contract team the likely time this period will take. For reference, it may be useful to ask how long this period was in the original contract. Put this timing onto the whiteboard and estimate the actual date this period will start.

Ask the team to identify the event that initiates the phase-in period (usually this will be contract signature), and the process prior to this (usually negotiation). Again ask how long this is likely to take, and once an estimate of this is established, write the date of the beginning of contract negotiations on the whiteboard.

Work back in this way through the recompete process, with key events, deadlines, and estimated dates for these being added to the whiteboard until the period when the customer is deciding on their requirements for the new contract is established. This will be considerably closer to the time of the workshop than was perhaps anticipated by the contract team (in a number of cases, it may be prior to the date of the workshop itself) and will often create a sense of urgency and perhaps unease that the recompete is already happening. This can be used to create focus for the rest of the session and the actions that emerge.

3. The Customer Recompete Team (Timing 20–30 minutes)

The goal of this session: To understand who within the customer is likely to be involved in different stages of the recompete process, and the level of relationship the contract team and/or the wider business has with these contacts. (For more on this subject, see *Idea 35*.)

Referring back to the recompete timetable, start with the period of the customer deciding on their requirements for the new contract. Ask the team who from the customer organization is likely to be involved in this process. Some prompting may be required from your own experience of the type of role or department that may get involved at each stage. Once a list is created of the individuals or departments involved in this stage, ask the contract team what the present level of relationship is with these individuals/departments and who has the lead from the contract in this relationship.

Work forward through the process, repeating these questions of who will be involved from the customer, what the level of relationship is, and who holds this relationship. Particular questions should be asked of the following:

- Who will be involved in deciding the shape and specification of the next contract period?
- Who will prepare the recompete documentation?
- Who will run the overall process?
- Who will evaluate the responses to each stage of the recompete?
- Who will recommend a winner for the recompete?
- Who will make the final decision on the winner?

Section VII   Prepare for the Recompete

The answers to this session can be built into a table along the following lines (only some stages are illustrated below):

Stage	Who will be involved (name and department/position)	Level of relationship (don't know them, know them a little, know them well)	What is their attitude toward us? Range from +3 (very positive) to -3 (very negative). Particularly if negative, give reason	Who holds the relationship
Deciding on breadth of contract				
Writing spec				
Managing process				
ITT evaluation				
Recommend winner				
Final decision				

Depending on the level of relationships with, and knowledge of, the contract team, there may be a number of blank spaces on the table. If the table is not well populated, one of the key actions for the contract team will be to work with the recompete lead to use the contacts they do have to fill in the gaps. Remember that external consultants may fill some of the roles listed. (Building relationships with these contacts will also be the focus of *Idea 31*.)

Next, add in those who may have some influence on the recompete decision and who presently deal directly with the contract; for instance, the customer contract manager and others with whom the contract may deal directly or deliver services to department managers in the customer, key end user groups, etc.

4. Contract Performance (timing 30–40 minutes)

The goal of this session: To establish the present and historical performance of the contract, both overall, against KPIs and in the eyes of the customer. In particular, identify any issues or problems which have occurred, but also examples of high performance, added value, and achievements—particularly as recognized by the customer. To save time and enhance the value of this session, the contract team should have previously been asked to bring records of previous performance.

Successes/strengths	Issues/areas for improvement/cost saving

First, ask the team about the general level of performance on the contract and any areas where performance is higher than expected and lower than expected by the customer.

Ask the team for the key KPIs that the customer requires and for performance against these over the contract period.

Check with the team whether there is a clear history of performance reports available over the contract period. Review these with the team, particularly focusing on improvements in performance and how these were achieved. List on the whiteboard.

Performance improvements/innovations	How achieved

Ask if there have been barriers to improving performance—break these down into barriers within the contract and barriers on the customer side. Again, list these in two columns on the whiteboard. Breaking down these barriers may be a route to gaining improved performance over the coming months or in the next contract period.

Section VII Prepare for the Recompete

Barriers to improvement/cost saving internal	Barriers to improvement/cost saving external

Ask the team about any customer commendations the contract has received—do they retain proof or copies of these? List on the whiteboard.

Ask the team about added value delivered on the contract. If this is not a common term used in the business, it may require explanation (see *Idea 15*). If lists are not already available, get the team to go through the contract period and think of times they may have delivered examples of added value and list these on the whiteboard.

Depending on the depth of the performance, added value, and improvement data that has been made available by the team—or that they have easy access to—there may be a number of actions that come out of this section for the team to find and collate a history of contract performance, etc. Set these actions for specific members of the team.

5. Customer Future Needs (Timing 30 minutes)

The goal of this session: To gain an understanding of the team's views on the customer's needs and drivers, how they have changed over the contract period, how they may change over the future period, and what impact this may have on the recompete through changes to the scope of the new contract.

You will need to create four columns on the whiteboard.

Changes to customer—external and internal	Impact on customer priorities	Impact on needs for the contract	What have we done/should we do to help

Begin by asking the team for a list of the key things that have changed in the customer's market or sector over the contract period. List in the first column. In the second column, list how these have impacted the customer and their needs. Include the changes that have happened in the supply industry—new types of contract, new technologies, etc. If the team are struggling, go through PESTLE (Political, Economic, Social, Technology, Legal and Environmental changes), asking about each element to pull out changes.

Next, ask about changes within the customer, and again how these have impacted the customer's needs and priorities. List below the items in the first and second columns.

In the third column, list against each of the items already on the whiteboard any impacts these changes have had on the customer's wishes or priorities regarding the contract and what, if any, changes they may have asked for in the contract.

If the contract deals with end users—in the form of the customer's customer—then repeat the above for end users.

In the fourth column, list any changes or improvements to the delivery of the contract that have resulted from these changes in need.

Move on to looking at the future and repeat the exercise, first listing what the team sees as future changes in drivers for the customer, then how these may impact the customer's needs. Next to these, list the potential impacts of the customer's needs of the contract—for instance, how the customer may change the scope and specification of the contract at the recompete. Finally, brainstorm how the contract could be required to change to address these needs.

At the end of this session, there should be an initial view both of how the contract has reacted to changes in the customer's needs, and a view of future customer needs and potential further changes required to the contract to meet these at the recompete.

6. Competitors (timing 15–20 minutes)

The goal of this session: To gain a sense of the likely competitors for the recompete, whether they have contact with the customer, and the team's views on how the competitors may address the recompete. See *Idea 39* for more on this.

First, ask the team to give their view of the likely competitors for the recompete and list these on the whiteboard. Then ask the team if they know of any contract that each competitor might have with the customer (for instance, do any of the competitors have contracts with the customer elsewhere, or perform different contracts for the customer).

Section VII Prepare for the Recompete

Competitor	Customer contact	Strengths	Weaknesses	Approach

Then ask the team for their views of the likely approach each competitor may take to the recompete and what strengths each could bring. In some cases, the contract team may have little wider knowledge of the competitors for the recompete, however in others, they can be a strong source of information.

Any information gleaned should be added to other information you have on the competition and will help form a view on how the competition can best be beaten at recompete.

7. SWOT (Timing: 40 minutes)

The goal of this section: Based on the above information, but taking any other relevant factors into account, create a set of Strengths, Weaknesses, Opportunities, and Threats (SWOT) for the contract at the upcoming recompete.

To get a set of starting points to this session, once the basics of a SWOT analysis have been explained to the team, split the team into two or three groups (depending on the size of the group) and ask them to spend 15 minutes separately listing their views of the strengths, weaknesses, opportunities, and threats for you as the incumbent contract at the recompete.

Bring the teams back together and get each to contribute their findings and put a consolidated SWOT on the whiteboard.

These will obviously vary depending on the contract and situation. Spend 15 minutes exploring the issues raised and going into more detail about any specific areas that appear to be of importance. Look, particularly, at how weaknesses may be overcome and threats avoided, but also at how strengths can be used in the recompete and how opportunities may be exploited.

8. Win Themes (Timing 20 minutes)

The goal of this session: To get from the team its view on the potential win themes for the recompete, but also to ensure the team understands the concept of win themes and how they will be important to the recompete success. See *Idea 51* for more on win themes (as well as Discriminators, Differentiators, and Benefits).

Begin by outlining the key features of win themes. Then briefly review some of the outcomes from the earlier sessions—particularly customer needs, contract performance, competitors, and the SWOT. These may provide a view of where some of the win themes may originate.

Break the team into two or three groups and give the groups 10 minutes to separately list the key win themes they see for winning the recompete.

Bring the teams back together and ask them to briefly explain their win themes and list on the whiteboard. Then group these win themes so that similar ideas are joined up.

Figure VII.4   Win Theme Matrix

	Win Theme Development	
Benefits based on our company capabilities		
Benefits being delivered in our solution		
	Other competitors can deliver	**Unique to our business/solution**

Now, work through the list of win themes given and place them, in discussion with the team, into the appropriate box in Figure VII.4. This process may require a degree of challenge to ensure only those that are really unique to the business or contract are placed in these boxes. For those that do go into these boxes, particularly those in the "Unique to our business/solution" "Benefits being delivered in the our solution" box, test how these can be evidenced from data or examples from the work being done on the contract and how they can be put in place if not already being delivered on the contract.

Emphasize that a benefit is only something that positively meets a need that the customer has. If it doesn't meet an important customer need, then it is a feature.

At the end of this session, you will hopefully have a set of win themes, some of which may be of use on the recompete. It is likely there will be others that have not been identified through this process and will need to be worked through as the Green Field solution is developed (see *Idea 38*) and the solution as a whole (see *Idea 40*) is put together. There can be a tendency for existing contract teams, especially at this early stage of the recompete, to focus more on incremental or already existing work rather than radical new ideas. However, this is not always the case, and good ideas do come from these sessions.

9. Key Actions (Timing 15 minutes)

As the workshop has progressed, a number of actions are likely to have emerged. These may include: a need to source or find further existing information on past contract performance, a need to go back through the contract and identify added value initiatives, work to find which customer contacts are likely to be involved in the recompete, or projects to be set up to overcome areas of underperformance or perceived weaknesses on the contract.

Summarize these actions and allocate them to people on the team as appropriate, agreeing timescales for completion, and outcomes required. A date for further review of these actions and their results may also need to be set.

Once this list is completed, the workshop is complete. The final action is to write up the outcomes of each session, copy them as appropriate to the team, and feed into the recompete process.

Output from the Workshop and Next Actions

The workshop and its outputs are an introduction for a recompete team to the contract recompete. It will give the recompete contract team an understanding of the position and the task ahead. It will also give the recompete lead a sense of the relationships held by the contract team and a first view of the contract history and information that may be available to them for the recompete. It will also help highlight any issues needing resolution or information to be found or reviewed further.

The actions from the workshop must be followed up and momentum created for the recompete effort. There is a real danger that if this is simply an isolated session, further work will not be completed and the recompete effort will lose vital momentum.

What aspects of incumbents' proposals have been particularly poor?

"A very lax approach to retender, as their thinking was that they already have it in the bag and take it or leave it attitude regarding the price of the contract."

Private sector, UK

Idea 31: Reinvigorate Your Customer Relationships

> **Idea Summary:**
>
> **What:**
>
> Reinvigorate your customer relationships. Use your recompete team to build a wider range of relationships than the contract team already holds so you are not restricted by the perspective these contacts have. If you use capture teams and capture planning processes, this is a very similar idea and you should follow capture techniques.
>
> **Why:**
>
> The goal is build fresh relationships with your customer to gain a wider understanding of their needs, gain information on the recompete, and ensure you have the customer on your side through the recompete period.

The recompete team should take the approach that no matter how well you think you know them, you need to get to know the customer all over again.

As the incumbent, you will already have a number of customer relationships. Your contract team will have been building relationships throughout the contract, and hopefully others in your business, including senior managers, will also have built relationships with their counterparts in the customer organization. As you enter the recompete preparation phase, you need to analyze these relationships and make sure you have the right breadth, level, and depth of relationships with those within the customer who will be involved in the recompete. This relates directly to the capture process you use for new bids, and you may well have established processes and learning for working through the capture plan. If so, apply them with equal vigor to the recompete.

We are not about to rewrite what is a broad and well-established set of literature and processes for sales approaches. If you need to understand this in more detail, there are many books and training courses on the subject. More likely, you already have the skills in your business. Everything you would apply to a new sales approach, you should also apply to the recompete. It's surprising how many companies don't do this, on the assumption that because they are the incumbent, they already have all the relationships they need, when in fact, they don't.

You will often be wrong to assume you already have the type and number of relationships you need for the recompete; often the relationships built during the operational phase of the contract are not those you need for an effective capture exercise. During the contract phase, your team will have focused on the relationships relevant to running the contract. Typically, these are mid level operational

Section VII   Prepare for the Recompete

customer contacts. For the recompete, a different set of influencers and decision makers within the customer are usually involved; for instance, senior finance and procurement management and, potentially, those at the most senior levels in the organization.

Your operational contacts, while always useful, might not have the final say in what the customer is deciding at key stages of the customer solicitation process; for instance, what the range of activities involved will be, the importance of price vs. quality in the decision making process, or the final decision on the winner. In fact, relying on operational customer contacts can mislead you; they may have their own views on what is needed for the next contract (such as a higher level of resources or quality) not shared by the real decision makers. A good capture team will build these wider relationships with the real decision makers and influencers. They will also want to find, ideally amongst this group, one or more coaches—people who actively prefer your company and solution to the competition and are willing to give you the information and feedback you need to win (within the strictures of the solicitation rules and the legal and organizational policies of the customer organization). If you only listen and talk to your operational customer (who might exaggerate their own involvement and influence on the direction of the solicitation), you could fail to influence the real decisions being made about the recompete and could make decisions based on their thoughts and recommendations to you, sending you and your solution in the wrong direction.

> *Proposal expert advice*
>
> *A strong capture effort must lead recompetes the same way it does bidding on new businesses. Strong capture professionals look forward, assess the current competitive landscape and influence the proposal effort with their knowledge and vision. Strong capture pros also assess your resources (what you're planning to offer the customer) and identify the gaps between the customer's future vision and what you currently provide. You may be surprised by this gap analysis, but it's critical to a winning bid. Past performance can be used to support claims about what you'll do in the future, but keep those succinct and targeted. Your best bet for clarity is a capture pro who hasn't been immersed in the current work. This person will have the necessary objectivity to see the situation as it looks to the customer.*
>
> *Proposal Consultant, USA*

This is another reason for starting recompete preparation early. For the recompete team (or capture team, if you are using this process) to build meaningful relationships with the right people in the customer organization, you will need time. Start before the customer is so close to the official recompete process they feel they should not be talking too openly with their incumbent about the recompete, as it could cause competitive issues for the solicitation process (particularly an issue in the government sector). If you leave it too close to the recompete to have new people from your business engaging with the customer (and you should definitely be focusing on having people from outside the contract team building these new relationships so you get a new and broader set of perspectives), they will also perceive this as only being done for the purposes of the recompete—and may not be receptive to your approaches.

The purposes of building a range of relationships with the right people in the customer organization (and in other relevant stakeholders) are:

- To gain a positive view of you as a company within the customer organization so you are preferred as the supplier for the next contract period.

- To get a better understanding of how the customer perceives your company and how the contract has delivered.

- To get information on the customer's needs, now and for the next contract.

- To get information about the customer's solicitation process.

- To influence the customer regarding how they run the solicitation and what they include in it, so your company and solution have an advantage over your competitors.

- To test your ideas for the recompete at various stages and get feedback from the customer about their preference (or not) for these ideas.

- To build a set of coaches to help gather information from, and pass on information to, and if possible, influence the recompete decision makers.

The contacts you form as part of your relationship building and capture campaign will be needed to get the information for a number of the other ideas in this stage. Starting early and putting a well managed effort into relationship building, rather than assuming you don't need to work hard on it, can make the difference between these ideas being effective or not, and between success and failure for your recompete.

One final note on this area: Over the period of the contract, some of your contacts in the customer organization will have moved on to other roles. Some will have left the customer, but others will have moved to other (potentially more senior) roles in the wider organization, which means they have less direct contact with your contract. Particularly if they were positive toward you in their previous role, now is the time to reconnect with them. They may have insight into the customer's solicitation plans. As they now have less direct responsibility for your

Section VII   Prepare for the Recompete

contract, they may be more objective and open in their communication with you than they felt they could be previously. They might even have some influence on those directly involved in the customer solicitation process.

> *What are the primary reasons incumbents lose recompetes?*
>
> *"Failure to evidence the work they have done and making assumptions that we "just know" what they can do."*
>
> — Federal Government, USA

Idea 32: Understand Stakeholder Views of Your Contract and Your Company

Idea Summary:

What:

Research the views of all the major customer stakeholders toward your contract and company. Identify any areas where they are not entirely happy.

Why:

Use the information to focus relationship-building efforts, make changes to your contract delivery now and inform your solution for the recompete.

What Do Your Key Stakeholders Really Think of You?

One of the possible dangers for incumbents is a misplaced sense that the customer is positive towards them and wants them to win the recompete. This might be true of some of the people in the customer organization—or it might not—but are all the stakeholders that you deal with, and particularly those who could have influence over the result of the recompete, absolutely happy with every aspect of your work and your company? Are you certain they will demonstrate loyalty to you in the recompete and positively act to ensure you are the winner?

Now is the time to look carefully, openly, and objectively at whether this is the case, and if it isn't, to do something about it.

Your goal should not just be to confirm that the customer likes you. You want to know what each key stakeholder, or stakeholder group, really thinks of you—including the things they don't like and what they think could be improved.

In addition to your key customer contacts, you should be seeking the views of any group that could have an influence on the recompete and those groups whose opinions you could potentially use in the recompete (either to inform your new solution or to use for evidence of your good performance); for instance, end users.

Depending on the numbers of people in different groups, you can either directly ask individuals, or use survey tools for larger groups.

Some of those you should be asking are:

- Your direct customer contacts.

- Senior customer managers who will have input or influence on the recompete.

- Any customer end users you deal with as part of the work you deliver.

- Customer staff who come into contact with, or are the recipients of, the work you do.

- Potentially members of you own supply chain.

The people bought into the recompete team from outside the contract are well placed to get this sort of feedback, as they will initially be seen as more objective by the customer and, as newcomers, are in a better position early in their relationship building with the customer to ask these types of questions. For a completely objective view, employ an outside research agency to ask the questions that will elicit what can be difficult answers. More and more companies are taking this approach and you should look seriously at getting a professional research business to undertake this work.

For wider surveys of groups of stakeholders, you will be looking for levels of satisfaction with various aspects of the work you deliver. For individuals, you will be asking questions such as:

- What is your view of our contract and business overall?

- What are the good points of what we deliver?

- What do you like about the contract/company?

- What don't you like about the contract/company?

- What about what we deliver could be improved?

- What issues have you had in the past with the work done, and were these issues resolved well?

- What could we be doing to make things even better from your point of view?

Section VII Prepare for the Recompete

If you have been conducting regular surveys over the period of the contract, you should already have some useful information from end users (see *Idea 14*). If so, make sure these are up to date and you can use the information gathered over time to show you have improved satisfaction levels and how you achieved this.

Ideally, you should also be getting a view of what your customer thinks of potential competitors versus yourself. For instance, do they see them as more innovative than you? (For more on this, see *Idea 41*.) However, your main focus should be aimed at understanding key stakeholders' attitudes towards your own contract and company.

Remember, this is not an exercise to confirm your popularity. The goal is to clearly and objectively understand the real views and perceptions of your customer and stakeholders. The review should be completely objective and, if needed, as hard hitting as possible. You are looking for any reservations your stakeholders may have, no matter how small or indirectly phrased. Watering down, ignoring, or explaining away any issues for internal political reasons or to soothe egos and feelings will work against you in your recompete efforts. Verge on being paranoid in seeking out potential problems; don't assume that just because you have thought all is well, that it actually is. This is your last real opportunity to discover the truth and do something about it.

Once you have the information, focus on what you can do to improve your standing with your customer and stakeholders. What are their reservations or issues with you? Focus on resolving these and doing the things that will instill the most positive attitudes toward you amongst all those who will have influence in the recompete.

Idea 33: Understand the Customer's Next Contract

Idea Summary:

What:

Review what changes the customer is looking for in the next contract period—and how these will impact the recompete.

Why:

Understanding early what changes the customer is likely to make in the recompete for the next contract is important in creating your new solution. It will also help you make any changes needed to the existing contract as the recompete approaches to show you can deliver to these new requirements.

Key Steps:

1. Review the wider market.

2. Review the supply side of your market.

3. Review your customer's internal changes and drivers.

4. Collate your findings.

5. Draw up a list of the most likely changes to the next contract.

6. Check with your customer and use to build your new solution.

What will your customer's next contract look like? What changes will they be looking for, and therefore, what will the recompete look like and expect of you?

Before you can effectively start work on your next solution and influencing of the customer's recompete, you need to understand what the customer is looking for in the next contract. Too many incumbents fail to win their recompete because they have assumed the customer is looking for more of what they are already getting. Even if you have been performing extremely well in your existing contract and your customer is happy with your performance, that doesn't mean they don't want or need to change to reflect their future requirements.

Your present contract is likely to have been procured several years ago, and the customer will have been deciding what that contract required even before then. For the coming recompete, they will also be looking some years into the future to anticipate what they will need throughout the contract period. Even for a three-year contract, the time between the customer's last review of what they needed and the time period they are anticipating could be six years or more, during which time a lot can change.

Your reinvigoration of customer relationships and your capture plan will enable you to ask the relevant questions of your customer contacts. You should also review the trends in the wider market and your customer's strategic direction and drivers.

If you have been regularly reviewing your customer's environment and their needs as part of your Contract Plan (for instance, using the processes suggested in *Ideas 15, 16* and *17: Added Value, Continuous Improvement, and Innovation* or *Idea 19: Keep Your Contract Up to Date*), you will already have a process in place and a database of the needs, and changes in these needs, throughout the contract history. Even if you do have this background, you should update your information at the start of the recompete preparation stage by conducting a more up-to-date review. If you haven't been conducting this type of review, now is the time to start.

Section VII Prepare for the Recompete

Step 1: Review the wider market.

What are the macro trends impacting your customer and, therefore, their future needs and the recompete?

Review:

- Wider political changes. Particularly in the government sector, changes in government or policy at federal, state, or even district levels could bring a new direction or approach to outsourcing—what are these changes and how might they impact your customer?

- Economic changes. The present economic problems mean both government and many private sector customers are facing significant budget reductions. Price is becoming more important in their decisions, but the scope and size of the customer organization may also be shrinking.

- Social changes. What are the changes impacting your customer and their needs and requirements from social changes? These could be changes in the form and expectations of their own customers or end users, or changes in the demographics of their end users (age, wealth, location for instance). What impact could these changes bring?

- Technology changes. What impacts are advances in technology having on your customer and its market or sector? What new technology, or uses of technology, might be impacting now and in the future that will be reflected in the next contract?

- Legal changes. Have there been changes in legislation that could impact the recompete or the next contract or solution? Changes, for instance, in employment law, data protection, or myriad changes specific to your sector or service?

- Environmental changes. While there may not be specific environmental changes that will impact the contract, awareness of environmental issues, relevant legislation, or guidance is increasing and may have a greater impact on the customer, their expectations, and potential solutions.

Step 2: Review the supply side of your market.

Understand the changes in contracting trends and your competition. Remember, if the customer changes the contract significantly—for instance, combining it with another contract with different services—you may find a different group of potential competitors would be interested in the combined opportunity.

Review:

- Changes in your direct competitor environment—new entrants, mergers, new approaches, who is particularly successful or cost aggressive.

- Trends in contracts—what types of contracts are being procured and won:
  - Are they shorter or longer in length?
  - Are contracts broadening in scope?
  - Are measurement regimes and payment or penalty mechanisms changing?
  - Is up front investment being required?
  - What are the trends in margin?
  - What are the trends in price vs. quality weighting?

- What new approaches or solutions are being introduced by your competitors—will these change how your customer awards the contract or what you will be competing against?

Don't assume your customer is working in a vacuum. They will be aware of what is happening on the supply side of the market and what the trends are in contracting. They are likely to be in contact with your competitors, who will have been approaching them for some time as part of their own capture plans and attempting to influence your customer to prefer their own business, putting forward their own options, strengths, and suggestions as to what is possible and preferable. Your customer is likely to be proactively researching the market, talking to colleagues or contacts in other organizations, and potential bidders, and is likely to be approaching some in order to guarantee the best possible competition (from your customer's perspective) for the forthcoming solicitation.

If you aren't fully aware of the potential options and external influences the customer has from the supply side of your market, you could be unpleasantly surprised when the format or specification of the recompete favors a way of delivery where a competitor has an advantage over you, or you find one of your competitors has built a strong relationship with key contacts in your customer organization.

Step 3: Review your customer's internal changes and drivers.

Your customer will be reacting to the external drivers it faces and the environment it finds itself in, and proactively driving its own agenda to achieve its strategic and tactical goals and objectives.

Section VII   Prepare for the Recompete

Understanding what these goals and objectives are, and what the customer's plans and priorities are for achieving them, gives you the context within which your recompete will be set. This will help you design a solution that helps the customer achieve their key goals, and fits with the strategies and programs they put in place to deliver these goals. It will also enable you, in your recompete, to show your broader understanding of the customer's needs and illustrate why the different parts of your solution enable their delivery.

Look at:

- Your customer's published goals and objectives.
- The strategies and programs they have put in place to deliver these objectives.
- How these relate to the particular part of the customer.
- How the contract activities contribute to these goals and strategies.
- What changes to the contract would result from these strategies and programs.
- What changes to the contract would be likely to improve the impact it can have on these same strategies.

Review what the trends have been over the existing contract period:

- What changes has the customer put in place internally?
- What changes have there been on your contract—and which of these have been requested by the customer?
- Have there been changes the customer has discussed, but have not been put in place?
- What other changes have you seen or heard of?

All these changes together will help build a picture of the trend and direction of change in your customer to help indicate what the future may hold.

Step 4: Ask the customer.

This might seem obvious, but it can be overlooked. Ask your customer contacts what they expect and want to see in the next contract period and what changes they expect to see in the recompete. Find out why they want these changes or think they will happen; this will relate back to their wider goals. Of course, you could discover problems or frustrations your contacts have had with the existing contract (its structure, as well as possibly, your delivery), all of which will be useful information.

Step 5: Collate your findings.

The tools and tables you used to understand your customer's environment and needs to create your Contract Plan (*Idea 8*), and then to improve and adapt your contract over its life (*Ideas 15, 16, 17* and *19*), can be reused for collating the information you have gathered from your review. Each area you have examined will have an impact on the contract and recompete, either directly or indirectly:

Figure VII.5   Drivers and Pressures on the Customer and Contract

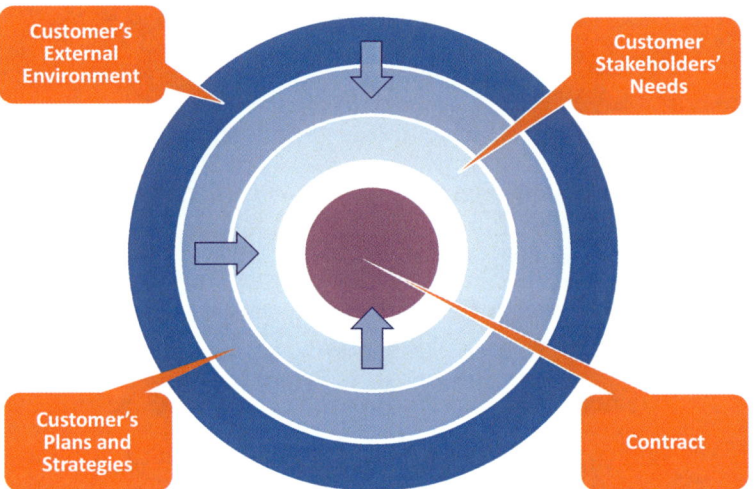

As Figure VII.5 illustrates, the external environment will impact inward to the customer drivers, their strategies, and then to your contract. List the drivers you have identified in each area and compare how each impacts the next level. For instance, how would a change in the economy impact the customer, what would this do to their goals and objectives, and how in turn would this filter down to the needs of the departments and stakeholders you deal with directly and, therefore, what they want from your contract?

Section VII Prepare for the Recompete

Figure VII.6   Sources of Impact on the Contract

External Drivers			
Area	Driver	Impact	Importance 1=low to 5=high
Political			
Economic			
Social			
Technology			
Legal			
Environmental			
Competitive			
Other			

Customer Aims and Strategies		
Customer Goal or Strategy	Impact on Areas Relevant to Contract	Importance 1=low to 5=high

Stakeholder Needs Analysis			
Stakeholder	Key Needs	Impact on Contract	Importance 1=low to 5=high

Step 6: Draw up a list of the most likely changes to the next contract.

From your list of likely changes in the wider environment and your customer's drivers and needs, you should now be able to infer what the likely changes are to the contract in the next term, and what you will be facing at the recompete. What type and level of change will these bring? How radical are the changes likely to be, and what do you need to do to put yourself in the best position to win?

Draw up a list of what the changes you have identified could mean in terms of changes in the contract.

Don't downplay the potential changes based on an assumption that things are already working well on the contract now. Even if they are, and your immediate customer contacts are happy, the influence of others in the customer organization at the recompete will mean that change is more likely than not. The biggest danger for you, as the incumbent, is not accepting and embracing these changes, and to be seen by your customer as complacent or not innovative.

Figure VII.7   Table of Drivers and Potential Changes in the Recompete

Driver	Potential impact on the customer & their needs	Potential impact on the next contract	Changes required to deliver a winning solution
Customer budget being reduced by 20%	Reduced cost of work	Price will be more important than quality	Can we offer reduced quality of work to reduce price? What efficiencies can be driven into processes to reduce costs?
	Reduced customer staff	Volumes of work will be reduced	Contract volumes and staff can be reduced Can we automate elements to reduce requirements on customer staff?
	Economies of scale more important	Potential to combine all existing Regional Lots into a single procurement	Need to expand operations to cover wider regions—or partner with contractor strong in regions we don't cover

Step 7: Check with your customer and use to build your solution.

The process of gathering, analyzing, and using potential changes for the next contract will be an iterative one. As you gain more insight into the customer's goals, check your understanding with your customer contacts. As you start to develop your own thinking and solution (see *Idea 40*), test elements of this against what you understand about your customer's goals, and again test directly with your customer contacts to make sure they see and approve of the connection and positive impact your ideas will have.

What are the primary reasons incumbents lose recompetes?

"Complacency—they assume and rely on the train of thought that I already know about them, who they are, what they do, etc., and they lose sight of the fact that companies bidding to be new entrants will be aggressively competitive."

Public Sector, UK

Section VII **Prepare for the Recompete** 205

Idea 34: Analyze How Vulnerable Your Contract Is

> **Idea Summary:**
>
> **What:**
>
> Review the risk areas for your contract and assess what level of risk you have, in each area, of losing your recompete.
>
> **Why:**
>
> Understanding how vulnerable your contract is to being beaten by competitors at the recompete, and where those vulnerabilities lie, will help you focus resources and efforts on strengthening the right areas.
>
> **Key Steps:**
>
> 1. Decide which are the key risks to your contract.
>
> 2. Review your contract's position for each factor.
>
> 3. Collate your answers.
>
> 4. Decide on priorities and actions.

You should never be complacent and assume that you will win your recompete easily. But how vulnerable is your contract to losing at recompete and what are the specific reasons for that vulnerability? Understanding the level and detailed reasons for potential vulnerability can help you focus resources and efforts to improve your chances of winning.

You can review your contract's potential vulnerability at any point in the contract; for instance, you might do so at the Mid Term Review (see *Idea 23*). But undertaking a full review of vulnerability at the start of your recompete preparation phase will give you a sense of areas to focus on, and the level of resource you need to overcome the danger.

Step 1: Decide which are the key risk factors for your contract.

Look at a range of factors which will impact your chances of winning the recompete such as:

- Level and quality of relationship with key customer contacts.

- Performance on the contract.

- Issues faced on the contract.

- How much improvement you have delivered on the contract.
- How much added value you have delivered on the contract.
- Customer and end user satisfaction.
- Availability of contract information for use in the recompete.
- The level of competition you are likely to face.
- Customer attitude towards your contract; for instance, does your customer trust you?
- The potential amount of change the customer may introduce at the recompete.
- Your knowledge of the likely recompete process and customer requirements.
- Uniqueness and relevance to key customer needs of any product or service you provide (your differentiators or discriminators).
- How prepared you are for the recompete.
- The availability of recompete resources available.
- How long you have until the recompete.

You may have other specific factors relevant to your own market or industry to add to this list. It's better to look at more factors rather than fewer; you are less likely to miss something important

Step 2: Review your contract's position for each factor.

Use a number of sources to gauge your position. Ask management and staff on the contract (for instance, as part of a recompete workshop—see *Idea 29*), review reports (for instance, as part of your contract review—see *Idea 28*) and get customer input (for instance, as part of *Idea 31*).

Step 3: Collate your answers.

Look at each factor objectively. You should go into some detail in understanding each one. The result of your analysis should be collated into a detailed report showing the areas that are most vulnerable and your source for this view. You can summarize your findings in a simple matrix such as the one that follows:

Section VII Prepare for the Recompete

Figure VII.8   Example Contract Vulnerability Matrix

	🟢	🟡	🟠
Level and quality of customer relationships	●		
Performance on the contract		●	
Issues on the contract			●
Improvement delivered		●	
Added Value and innovation delivered			●
Customer and end user satisfaction levels		●	
Customer attitude to the contract		●	
Availability of contract information	●		
Level of likely competition	●		
Level of changes likely in the recompete			●
Knowledge of likely recompete process & specification	●		
Uniqueness of product/service	●		
Level of preparedness for recompete		●	
Resources available for recompete	●		
Time to recompete		●	

Step 4: Decide on priorities and actions.

Your summary will give you a clearer sense of the overall vulnerability of the contract and the specific areas which need work. Now decide what actions you can take to reduce these vulnerabilities. You may decide to weight the different areas, depending on how you see their relative importance to your recompete. Move any areas that are particular weaknesses (for instance, in the red in our matrix above) into at least neutral territory, as any real weakness will work against you in the recompete. You should assume your competitor's research means they are aware of the weakness and will work to exploit it in their own bids.

Your actions should be included in your Recompete Strategy with a target for how and to what extent you will reduce the weakness or improve the strength of each area.

Again, you might summarize this in an addition to your matrix:

	🟢	🟡	🟠	Actions
Level and quality of customer relationships	●			
Performance on the contract		●		
Issues on the contract			●	Resolve longstanding issues
Improvement delivered		●		Focus on improvement
Added Value and innovation delivered			●	Introduce latest product version
Customer and end user satisfaction levels		●		Focus on service
Customer attitude to the contract		●		Show improvements
Availability of contract information	●			
Level of likely competition	●			
Level of changes likely in the recompete			●	
Knowledge of likely recompete process & specification	●			
Uniqueness of product/service	●			
Level of preparedness for recompete		●		
Resources available for recompete	●			
Time to recompete		●		

Of course, the earlier you undertake your vulnerability assessment, the more time you will have to make changes to reduce your weaknesses and improve your strengths; another reason to start your recompete preparations early.

Wider Use of Contract Vulnerability Assessments

You don't need to wait until your recompete to undertake a contract vulnerability assessment. You can put in place a program conducting similar reviews of all your contracts. By summarizing the strengths and weaknesses of each contract across your portfolio, you will find any common issues across a range of contracts. This could give you the information (and motivation) to undertake a wider set of actions across the business to put in place portfolio-wide improvements or changes that will have a positive impact across your contracts—and help improve your overall future recompete success rates.

Section VII   Prepare for the Recompete

> *What do you expect of an incumbent that is different from new bidders?*
>
> "I expect the bidder to understand that it is fair game and not expect that they have the contract."
>
> State Government, USA

Idea 35: Understand Who Will Be Involved in the Recompete

Idea Summary:

What:

Build a map of the people who will make decisions and have influence at each stage of the customer's procurement process and identify what their views, needs, and preferences are.

Why:

Understanding who will be involved from the customer in the recompete at each stage, and what their priorities and preferences are, will help you understand and influence what will go into the procurement process and what you need to do in your recompete and new solution to meet these customer preferences and needs.

To focus your efforts in building the right customer relationships and putting your capture plan into action, you need to understand exactly who, from your customer organization, will be involved in different aspects of their procurement (your recompete) process.

This should be one of the early tasks you complete during recompete preparation.

As we discussed, when looking at the customer's recompete timetable in *Idea 24*, a lot of preparation and decision making will be done well before the recompete is publicized to the market and the official recompete competition starts. You need to understand and influence what goes into the procurement and how it is formatted. By the time you are being evaluated, decisions on what is to be evaluated, the weightings of each factor, and how the scoring is given will already have been decided.

Start by finding out who will be involved in these early stages and then move on to those who will be involved in the latter stages. Some people will be involved from the start, while others will only be involved in particular stages.

The stages and particular activities you are interested in will include:

- Who is involved in the decision to give an extension or go to procurement.

- Who decides who else will be involved in the procurement and who will take responsibility for what.

- Who is involved in the process of deciding the breadth and requirements of the new contract—this includes both the strategic elements (what the contract needs to achieve, the general breadth of the contract, etc.) and the detail—and writing the detailed specifications.

- Who is involved in researching the supplier market and the latest potential forms of procurement.

- Who is involved in the process the recompete will follow; for instance, the number of stages the solicitation will go through, the schedules, whether it is run through electronic portal or is more paper based, and how the customer will funnel the number of bidders down at each stage.

- Who is administering the process and responsible for its successful completion to time and budget.

- Who is involved in deciding what questions are asked, what the weighting of different questions are in the marking scheme, how each answer will be scored.

- Who is involved in the financial and commercial elements; for instance, deciding on models for pricing, how supplier risk is taken into account, whether securities will be required from bidders, and what the terms and conditions of the new contract to be signed by the winner will be.

- Who will be evaluating each stage of the bidders submissions.

- Who will be collating the scores for each bidder and who will be involved in recommending which bidders go through each stage and who the final winner will be.

- Who will be involved in making or ratifying the final decision.

For each stage and part of the process, different people will fulfill different roles:

- There will usually be one person or occasionally a group (a board or committee) who are the final decision makers.

- Those who have some influence over the decisions being made—either through influencing those making the decision (perhaps by making formal recommendations, through personal influence, or through some form of lobbying) or through the role they take in the process (marking the submissions for instance).

- Those who do the work, for instance, write the specifications. These are usually also people with a greater or lesser degree of influence over what form that work takes (e.g. what the specification says).

- Those who are informed, through whatever means, about what is happening; again, these people may or may not have influence.

Not all of these people will be part of the customer organization. For example, customers often use consultants to help with, or even run parts of, the solicitation process. These consultants might take any of the roles above (with the probable exception of final decision making) and can have a very significant influence on the form the solicitation takes. They may be procurement consultants, financial specialists for helping create or audit financial models; they could be lawyers ensuring that the process is legal and will not be challenged, or involved in drawing up the final contractual terms; or they could be subject matter experts for particular aspects of the work being contracted.

Discovering the Process and Who Will Be Involved

There are a number of ways to find out what the likely process will be and who will be involved in what roles:

- Look at the rules, guidelines, or policies the customer has on procurements. Government customers are generally fixed to certain procurement rules or processes set at national or regional levels. For instance, in the U.S. government and its agencies, procurement is regulated by FAR (Federal Acquisition Regulation) and its clauses. Private sector companies are not bound by these rules, but will often have a set of published policies in place.

- Look at how the contract was bid last time—what process was used and who was involved. This is not a definite predictor of your next recompete, but will give you a starting point.

- Look at other recent procurements by the customer—again, what process was used and who was involved.

- Ask your customer contacts. Depending on the level of relationship you have with them and their own influence within the organization, they may be able to tell you what the process will be, what the customer will be emphasizing, and who will be involved.

- Look at consultant's past work and their own websites and publicity. If you can find out which consultants are likely to be used, research their past projects and how they publicize their own services. Different consultancies often have their own particular methods they take from procurement to procurement. Your company may have had dealings with them on other bids and may even have relationships with and experience of particular consultants within the consultancy organization.

Draw Up a List of Who Will Be Involved and What You Know about Them

As part of the recompete workshop in *Idea 29*, you would have asked you contract team for their understanding of the people involved in the customer procurement and completed as much as possible of the table below:

Figure VII.9   Attitudes and Relationships of Customer Recompete Decision Makers

Stage	Who will be involved (name and department/position)	Level of relationship (don't know them, know them a little, know them well)	What is their attitude toward us? Range from +3 (very positive) to -3 (very negative). Particularly if negative, give reason	Who holds the relationship
Deciding on breadth of contract				
Writing spec				
Managing process				
ITT evaluation				
Recommend winner				
Final decision				

Section VII Prepare for the Recompete

You can expand this analysis of the key players by determining what their key drivers are, what they want to achieve in the recompete, and their present view of the contract and your company regarding the recompete. Then add to this analysis a view of what you would like or need their view to be, and how you will go about changing their view. Keep the analysis dynamic by regularly reviewing your progress towards achieving this change. Finally, review what each key player's importance is to your recompete success and, therefore, the level of focus required on them:

Figure VII.10   Recompete Stakeholder's Drivers and Views

Stakeholder	Key drivers for recompete	Present view of contract and us	Desired view	Actions to move to desired view	Progress	Level of importance to recompete (1-5)

Ideally, you will have all stakeholders perceiving you in a very positive way—seeing your contract and company in a positive light and wanting you as the successful bidder who will help them achieve their goals. Failing this, you may need to prioritize: aim to have key people positive towards you and no one against you (see *Idea 41: Influence Your Customer*).

You should also be identifying those within this grouping who will be the best people to feed information to about your solution; who is most likely to be a source of reliable information about the recompete and what the customer is doing or thinking, and who can be relied on to act in your favor, perhaps by persuading others of the value of your business and solution to the customer organization.

This analysis and your progress toward achieving preference for you in the minds (and actions) of key individuals will be an ongoing process throughout the recompete preparation stage and through to the end of the recompete process. It will help focus and drive your capture plan and actions.

> *What aspects of incumbents' proposals have been particularly poor?*
>
> "The number one problem is when suppliers put no effort whatsoever into the bid and expect to win on the basis of 'well you know what we can do because we have been doing it'."
>
> *Federal Government, USA*

Idea 36: Resolve Existing Contract Issues

Idea Summary:

What:

Use the information you have from your relationships with the customer and satisfaction research to identify and resolve both specific and general issues the customer may have with you or the contract while there is time to show the improvement and resolution before the official recompete begins.

Why:

If the customer perceives that there are unresolved issues on the contract as you go into the recompete, they may feel you are unresponsive to their needs and expectations. This could impact their view of you as a preferred choice for the next contract. It will also make it difficult for you to talk about high quality work, customer focus, and flexibility in your proposal if the customer perceives you have not resolved existing problems.

As you approach the recompete, make sure any areas causing issues for the customer are quickly resolved. While customers can have long memories, the more recent performance of the contract will be foremost in their minds when they are deciding on the supplier for the next contract. If you go into the recompete with unresolved issues, particularly if these have been a point of contention with individuals in the customer organization for some time, these will work against you. The customer will feel that you are not responsive to their needs, are not focused on them, and could potentially continue with the issues unresolved into the next contract if they choose you. Any arguments or statements you make in your recompete, claiming you are responsive, etc., will be met with this negative experience and will not only be discounted, but the dissonance between statement and perception could impact how the whole of your recompete is received.

Section VII Prepare for the Recompete

If you start resolving these issues early in your recompete preparations, you have a chance to show a good period of delivery where they are no longer present—and the impression you have only changed at the last minute to look good for the recompete will at least be partially diminished.

Your early analysis of the contract history and position (see *Idea 28: Conduct a Contract Review*) should highlight some of the potential issues faced during the contract. Your review of customer perceptions and satisfaction (see *Idea 31*) and your reinvigoration of customer relationships (*Idea 30*) should also give you a clearer idea of any problems customer contacts and stakeholders might have with how the contract is being delivered.

The issues you find could cover a range of areas, but there are generally two types:

- Specific delivery issues
- General approach issues

Specific Delivery Issues

These can range from a particular aspect of performance that has not been attained, or a way of delivering a specific element of your service which doesn't fit with how the customer would prefer it. It could be something as simple as faulty invoicing.

These delivery issues can often, with the right resource and focus, be resolved relatively quickly. Look carefully at the cost of doing so, but see this cost as an investment in your future contract with the customer. If there is an additional cost to resolving the problem or an ongoing cost to meeting the higher level of performance, you may decide, for the remaining period of the contract, this investment is worthwhile. Your new solution should, of course, aim to permanently resolve the issue in the next contract.

As with all changes and improvement, find a measure that can be used to demonstrate the resolution is working and get confirmation from the customer that they see the issue as solved.

General Approach Issues

General approach issues that customer contacts or stakeholders have with you can be more difficult to define, but significantly more damaging. They can be issues such as:

- The customer doesn't feel they can fully trust you.
- They don't feel you are customer focused enough.

- They feel you have been complacent over the period of the contract.

- They feel you don't understand, or care about, their business and their real needs.

- They feel you have been focusing on your own profitability rather than delivering improvements, cost reductions, or change for them.

It's less likely that customer contacts will express these sentiments bluntly or clearly face to face. Low levels of scores from survey questions asking about trust and customer focus will, of course, give a sense that there is an issue. However, you may have to infer from other comments and actions implying these types of issues and test carefully to confirm whether a suspicion is true or not.

Resolving these types of problems is difficult to do directly. You need to identify which actions or characteristics of your management of the contract have led to customers having these perceptions of you. Resolving these underlying problems and finding ways to demonstrate the positive characteristic missing (trustworthiness, for instance) will help start the process of changing perceptions. But negative perceptions can take time to be reversed and require more than a one-off action—they need consistency.

You may need to take brutal steps if you believe these negative perceptions will not be resolved easily. This could involve a change of management on the contract to bring the opportunity for a fresh start. Such a move needs to be handled sensitively and after careful analysis; for instance, is the management team, or members of it, part of the problem or the only people the customer personally trusts, and the issue is with the wider company approach?

No matter how difficult to analyze or resolve, these issues with your company or contract approach must not be ignored. Unless you can reduce their impact or reverse them in the mind of the customer, they will impact your recompete and potentially undermine even the best and most appropriately priced solution and offer.

What aspects of incumbents' proposals have been particularly poor?

"Making broad assumptions on how well they are performing. Failure to look at and take on board industry trends and innovations."

Private Sector, UK

Idea 37: Price To Win

> **Idea Summary:**
>
> **What:**
>
> Rather than cost and price your bid once you have created your solution, reverse the process: Understand the price most likely to win the recompete first, then create a solution that works within that price. Review the customer's likely budget, competitor's likely pricing, how important price will be in the evaluation of the recompete and the customer's preferred pricing formats and attitude to risk.
>
> **Why:**
>
> With price becoming increasingly important in recompete decisions, leaving costing and pricing until last in how you put your bid together could lead to you being beaten by the competition. Even if you don't follow the process completely, going through the exercise will challenge you to take a fresh look at your price and solution and help you avoid a common incumbent failing of only making minor adjustments to the solution and small cuts to the price in the recompete.

A common mistake incumbents can make is to see the price they put forward in the recompete for the new contract as simply a variation of the existing contract—perhaps a reduced margin plus some further cuts in cost to give the customer apparent value for money compared to the existing contract.

Even if you take a more ground up approach to your new solution (see *Idea 39*), it is still common practice in many businesses to put a price to your bid only after you have costed this solution, then decided what margin you will put on top.

The Price To Win approach reverses this process. It challenges you to come up with what you believe will be the winning price first, and then create your solution to meet this price. In doing so, it encourages you to treat cost as an independent variable. So rather than cost simply being dependent on what you have put in your solution (you add up all the costs of the different parts of the solution you have created and that is your total cost), you see cost as something you set first—then your solution is designed to meet that cost.

While it may seem counter-intuitive, it is a particularly useful exercise for you as the incumbent because you are likely to be under more internal pressure to base your price for the next contract on what you are already delivering.

The Price To Win approach is becoming more well known in many sectors and there are now books, training courses and consultants to help you understand the process and undertake a Price To Win exercise.

Rather than attempting to take you through the whole process in detail, we will outline some of the key concepts of the Price To Win approach, as well as some other price considerations, and encourage you to undertake a Price To Win exercise as part of your recompete preparations either yourself (preferably using a team separate to the core recompete team) or using a consultant. Even if you don't take a complete Price To Win approach, the exercise is part of the necessary approach you should be taking as the incumbent to challenge all your existing concepts about how the contract should be delivered in the next period. It will help you avoid the mistake made by many incumbents of starting your recompete from your existing contract and making insufficient changes or innovations to meet your customer's needs.

Understand Your Customer's Budget and Expectations

As part of their planning for the next contract period, your customer will be setting their own budget for the services or products you are supplying within the contract. As in all organizations, there will be challenge to the existing costs and, particularly in a climate of reduced budgets and pressures on costs, senior management will be challenging the relevant departments to reduce the cost of these services. This might be in the context of further challenge to improve quality, but it may acknowledge that value for money is the important measure, or even recognize that quality or volumes may need to be reduced to meet these cost challenges. These costs will become a part of the business plan going forward for your customer's organization, and therefore set the price they are willing, or able, to pay for the next contract.

As part of your recompete preparations, do all you can to find out the budget the customer has set for the next contract period. Ask your contacts and review published plans, accounts, budgets, and minutes of meetings. You should also look at the trends in your customer organization in other areas. What is happening to budgets and spending in other parts of the customer organization? What are they basing contract decisions on for other contracts? If other contracts are being decided on the basis of lowest price and the budgets are being cut by 20%, unless in exceptional circumstances, expect your contract to face a similar challenge.

Review Your Competitor's Pricing Approaches

The procurement means your customer will be faced with a choice between your own bid and price, and those of your competitors. Only the most naive incumbent would assume the customer will choose them no matter how low the competition's prices are. Even if you believe the customer is loyal to you, is highly impressed by your performance over the existing contract, and your operational customer contacts are saying they definitely don't want to change, this apparent resolve will be seriously tested by a competitor offering significant price savings over your own. Equally, don't assume your competitors will only be able to offer a lower price by cutting quality so far, the customer would be crazy to accept it. Your competitors might be able to offer an innovative approach which reduces their costs dramatically while maintaining quality. Or, perhaps, your customer is under pressure to accept lower quality if the price is right.

Research your likely competitors for the recompete:

- What prices are they putting forward for other bids?

- What is their success rate?

- What new offerings are they bringing to the market and what is their cost base?

- Who are they partnering with and what advantages might this bring them in terms of costs?

- What is their attitude to winning new business—how aggressive are they and at what margins are they prepared to bid?

Pull together as much research as you can on your competitor's likely approaches and prices. Your business development department will most likely have a review of recent bids which might be of use. Estimate what their likely price for the next contract will be. How does this compare with the customer's expectations and budget? How does it compare with your existing price for the contract?

At an extremely simple level, understanding your customer's budget and your competitor's likely pricing will give you a price, or more likely a price range, within which you can start to work as a target price for your solution. However, there are a range of other factors to take into account which can have a sometimes dramatic effect on how you price and your chances of putting in a winning price solution for your recompete:

Understand How Your Customer Will Evaluate Price Versus Other Factors

Review how important price will be in the evaluation of your recompete as opposed to other factors. At its most simple, understand the relative weighting of price versus quality aspects of the solution. For instance, how you approach the development of your solution will be very different if price only comprises 20% of the total marks given by the customer, rather than 80% of total marks. But there are other ways the customer might evaluate bids which will increase the importance of price. For example:

- If the customer takes a Lowest Price Technically Acceptable (LPTA) approach to evaluation, then any added quality you build into your solution over the benchmark levels of performance or quality the customer sets will be wasted, and will work against you if there are any additional costs associated with delivering that additional quality.

- What reduction in scores will the customer give to higher priced bids versus the lowest price bid? For instance, compare the following two options:
  - In option 1, the lowest price bid gets 100% of the available pricing evaluation score and a bid that is 5% higher gets 5% lower marks, one that is 7% gets 7% lower marks, etc.
  - In option 2, the lowest price gets 100%, the second lowest gets 80%, the third 60%, the fourth 40%, etc.

  The difference between the two marking approaches of being 1% more expensive than the cheapest bidder would vary between losing 1% of the available marks and losing 20% (or 40% if another competitor was only 0.5% more expensive than the cheapest, for instance) of the marks available. Knowing this could put a significantly higher premium on putting in a solution that is the lowest price.

- Will the customer evaluate the quality aspects of the lowest price bidder and then only move onto the next lowest price bidder if the first bidders quality is not acceptable?

There are many other ways an apparently subtle or even procedural approach taken by the customer to evaluating price could have a major impact on the relative importance of price to your chances of winning your recompete. Knowing what approach the customer will take before you start your solution development will help you decide the approach to take in pricing your solution.

Review Pricing Options

Beyond the evaluation criteria we have examined above, there is a wide range of ways your customer might ask for pricing, and how you can price the contract to best meet your customer's needs and your company's particular strengths and approach (and mitigate against your competitor's strengths). Analyzing these before you get to the official recompete stage will allow you to influence the customer in how they approach their pricing preferences and evaluation in their procurement, as well as giving you important information about how you might structure not just your pricing, but also your overall solution.

Section VII   Prepare for the Recompete

For example, will your customer prefer:

- A cost plus approach.
- A fixed price approach.
- A price per item.
- Volume discount.
- Consistent pricing throughout the contract.
- Reducing prices over the contract period.
- Upfront investment (and whether the customer will pay for this or expect it to be recouped over the contract period).
- Capital expenditure costs versus operational expenditure costs.
- Lifecycle replacement costs included, separate or variable.
- Variable or consistent pricing against a range of volumes or other variables.
- Pricing against a bill of materials (and if so, what is the expected mix of spend).*
- Regular price benchmarking during the contract.
- Input based pricing.
- Output based pricing.
- Payment by Results (if so, what results and what % of total pricing to be put at risk?).

Note on Bill of Material (BoM) pricing. As the incumbent, you should have a clearer understanding of the relative use of different items of a bill of materials pricing schedule. For instance, in a housing refurbishment contract, you have two items to price on a BoM schedule, such as replacing a faucet and replacing a kitchen sink unit. If you have complete records of what you have done on your contract, you will know, for example, that very few sink units are replaced, but many faucets. If you have done your research and also know the customer will give each equal marking, then pricing kitchen sink replacement low will give you more marks in the evaluation at a low cost. You can make this up by a marginally higher price on faucet replacement for which you know there will be a higher volume. Be careful, of course, to ensure you also have a clear view of the likely future volumes over the next contract period. If you have already replaced all the taps in the housing estate during your existing contract, but the sink units have now reached the end of their life, you could have a problem.

- Will the customer expect to see separate prices for different parts of your contract delivery or an overall price?

- Will they want to see your pricing of G&A, overheads, and profit separately or is this included?

- Will they pay separately for the implementation and, if so, will this be based on milestone payments?

- Will they take into account "total cost of ownership," such as the added costs to them of how the service might be delivered, or alternatively, savings you might be able to help them make in other areas of their business not directly included in the contract price?

- Will they take into account cashable savings you can offer them in their wider business and non-cashable savings (for instance, a cashable saving being a reduced cost they can take immediately and "cash" it versus a non-cashable saving being a potential saving, such as the ability to reduce their staffing in another department, which they may not choose to take as a saving but reallocate those staff to other valuable work)?

- What is the cost of money to the customer and the availability of cash versus cash cost and availability to you? For instance, if the customer is cash rich or has yearly budgets, would they be willing to pay you early for a reduction in price? Or if they have low cost of capital and high available capital budgets, would they pay for any capital expenditure rather than you significantly reducing your price? Alternatively, if the reverse is true, would extended payment terms or offers of provision of capital expenditure within the contract be of more value to the customer?

These are just a sample of the many options open to the customer and yourself. Understanding how the customer will prefer and mark the pricing formats put forward by bidders and how they will assess the total price over the contract period will give you an opportunity to build your pricing models early and test these for the best overall price or pricing options you can offer the customer to fit their financial needs. It will also give you the opportunity to influence the customer's approach to pricing evaluation to best fit your own strengths or counteract those of your competitors.

Assess the Customer's Approach to Risk and Reward

Risk

We will talk in *Idea 54* about how you can use the relatively low risk you, as the incumbent, should represent to the customer as their chosen supplier for the next contract.

Section VII Prepare for the Recompete

In this section, we are referring to the ways the customer will allocate risk between themselves and the supplier and how they will reward you for improvements or other elements of high quality provision.

One of the benefits for many customers of outsourcing is that it enables them to pass appropriate risks on to their supplier. These might be risks of quality provision, volume variation, cost variation, or other aspects of the particular function outsourced. These risks are usually fully costed by bidders who assess the likelihood and potential impact of these risks in their pricing.

But some risks can actually cost the customer more than it would be worth if the customer retained the risk themselves. This can happen, for example, if:

- The risk—or more specifically, the consequence of the risk to the supplier—is particularly severe (especially in relation to the value of the contract).

- The risk is outside the control of the supplier (such as the impact of changes in the wider economy); or

- The risk is particularly difficult to quantify either in its likelihood or impact (this can sometimes be because the customer has not clearly set out the risk, or the details of the contract or work involved, sufficiently enough for the suppliers to be able to understand it).

In these cases, the supplier will often cost the risk with a significant premium to cover the potential losses it would incur if the risk happened. And if the event or issue doesn't occur (which can often happen if the risk is low in likelihood but high in impact), it means the customer has paid this premium throughout the contract and not had the "benefit" of being protected from it by the contractor. In effect, the customer has paid for an insurance policy with an inflated premium for an event that has not occurred. And in the case where the cost is imposed on the supplier by the customer if the risk occurs—either in high levels of damages, penalties, or termination of the contract—it is potentially the customer who has set the premium higher than was necessary.

In addition, different bidding companies are likely to price risk differently. Some may assess the risk or impact lower than others or have a higher appetite for risk. Some may feel that they have a solution that mitigates, and therefore reduces, the risk. Some may have a broader portfolio of business than others across which they assess, or feel they can absorb the impact of the risk, more easily than other perhaps smaller companies, for which the impact of the risk occurring could have significant financial impact for the whole business. Some may simply not have recognized the extent of the risk.

As the incumbent, your experience gives you a better understanding of the risks on the existing contract. Although you should recognize the new contract may have different risks or change the likelihood of risks occurring, you are potentially in a better position to assess where each risk should best sit to give the customer the best value for money.

Factoring in risk effectively, understanding the likely approach competitors will take to risk in their pricing, and working with the customer to put risk in the right place and at the right level, should give you a clear opportunity to understand the risk element to add to core prices—and develop a solution which reduces the remaining risks.

Reward

How you are rewarded for the contract can also have an impact on your pricing:

- Is there a bonus for overperformance?
- Is there a pain share mechanism?
- Is there a gain share mechanism encouraging the supplier to deliver improvements?
- Is the pricing mechanism clear and fair?
- How are penalties for underperformance applied? For instance, is there a chance to get the performance right before penalties are automatically imposed; do penalties ratchet up; are they applied to a small or wide range of performance aspects; what is the level of penalties; is there an open and fair mitigation or resolution process in cases where the supplier believes penalties have been improperly applied; is performance on which penalties are imposed entirely within the control of the supplier or not?
- Are payment terms reasonable?

Again, all of these factors may impact how you price the contract. Knowing what these reward processes are likely to be will help you understand what premium, or perhaps discount, to put against your core costs for the contract, and also impact how you design your solution.

Summarizing Your Price To Win

All of the factors we have summarized above will have an impact on the price which will win the contract:

- The customer's budget sets a maximum price level.

- Your competitors' prices are what you will need to beat.

- How the customer evaluates and weights price in the bid will determine its importance versus quality or other delivery aspects.

- The options you have for how you price the contract through its life and in other respects will impact the total value of the contract and the lifetime cost to the customer.

- The risks the customer places on the suppliers will need to be factored in to your overall price.

- The rewards (or penalties) system the customer puts in place will impact your ability to deliver a consistent or increasing margin over the contract period.

All of these factors can also have an impact, if you know or can estimate them with some degree of confidence prior to completing your solution design, on what your solution will look like—for instance, the level of quality delivered, the flexibility across a range of volumes, or the over-engineering to reduce penalties or avoid risks.

So before you start (or at least in parallel with) developing your solution, spend as much time as you can in:

- Understanding these likely aspects of pricing as early as possible.

- Setting a target price range and modeling price options.

- Influencing the customer's own approach.

This will help you design a solution with the best chance of having a winning price.

What are the primary reasons incumbents lose recompetes?

"Complacency when it comes to cost. Not realizing there is competition out there."

Private Sector, USA

Idea 38: Create a Green Field Solution

> **Idea Summary:**
>
> **What:**
>
> Get an independent team to build a new solution for the recompete from the ground up, based only on the customer's likely requirements for the next contract, with no reference to how you are presently delivering the contract.
>
> **Why:**
>
> The Green Field solution will help you challenge your existing assumptions based on how you are delivering the contract now, and help you deliver a truly innovative solution. Even if the Green Field solution is not what you finally propose, the challenge will help you overcome the incumbent tendency to focus on the existing contract provision in the recompete and not fully fit it to the customer's needs for the next contract.
>
> **Key Steps:**
>
> 1. Collate the information you need.
>
> 2. Put the right people on the team.
>
> 3. Develop the Green Field solution.
>
> 4. Present the Green Field solution to the recompete team.

There is a great temptation as the incumbent to base your new solution on how you are delivering your existing contract. After all:

- It is working well.

- The customer likes it.

- It will take less time, cost, and effort to write and price for the recompete.

- It will minimize transition time, cost, and risk.

- The customer might not be making major changes to their requirements.

"Make some minor changes and tweaks to cut costs, a small reduction in margin (which we can make back later), and the customer will have a proven solution that delivers some improved elements and at least a part of the cost savings they are looking for from

Section VII Prepare for the Recompete

a trusted and known supplier. If we do that, then focus on the risk to the customer of changing to a new supplier, we are going to win."

This (partly) made up quote might be an exaggeration, but the principle of basing your new solution on your existing contract is a common approach for incumbents—although one which loses a lot of recompetes. Often, the influence of the existing contract is more subtle:

- Assumptions on costs for the new solution are based on existing costs.

- The supply chain being used is not fully tested.

- The basic process of delivery of different functions is not challenged sufficiently.

- Whether some functions are still needed at all is not challenged sufficiently.

- The management structure on the contract (or indeed the management team) is not challenged.

- Existing technology is preferred as proven—especially if the cost or risk of introducing new technology is overestimated versus the benefits it would deliver to the customer.

- Speed of delivery or levels of performance are seen as areas to be evolved rather than seeking ways to deliver a step change.

- Staff numbers, costs, skill levels, or even specific individuals (with experience, capabilities, or good relationships with the customer) are seen as a benchmark that can only be changed marginally.

- Aspects of delivery or performance that operational customers have expressed a liking for are seen as essential, even if their replacement or reduction could offer significant savings.

Even when the customer is expected to significantly change the contract—geographically, in the number, type, or breadth of services required, or the specification of services and products—the core delivery model and cost base of the existing contract is still used by too many incumbents as the basis for thinking about the new solution.

The dangers of this type of thinking are:

- Your customer is expecting a new solution that will be right for their future contract, not what was right for the past. If you don't show real innovation, the customer is likely to see you as being complacent.

- If the customer has changed the specification and other aspects of the contract, it is likely they have reviewed their needs and decided they will benefit from a different type of contract. They are unlikely to be looking for the same type of solution.

- Your competitors will be offering new and different approaches to the customer and claiming these offer significant benefits. They may also be implying (explicitly or implicitly) that your existing approach is outdated, expensive, and not delivering the performance or value for money the customer should be expecting. Don't confirm this by offering more of the same, justified by arguments that add up to how it has been good over the past period and therefore is right for the future. At best, you will appear to be defensive. At worst, arrogant and out of touch.

Create a Solution from the Ground Up

The Green Field approach deliberately ignores everything you are presently doing on your contract. Using the Green Field approach, you build a new solution from the ground up based on what you know of the customer; their organization, goals, and needs and the latest technology, processes, and approaches available or in the market or can be developed. You are not building your solution based in any way on what you already have in place. You are building from scratch, hence the term Green Field.

The solution you create using the Green Field approach will not necessarily be the final solution you put forward in your recompete. You can use it in a number of ways:

- As a template for your final solution.

- As an alternative solution to include in your recompete.

- As a basis for challenging all aspects of the main solution you build, which may be partially based on aspects of your current contract.

- As a route to encourage more innovative and "outside the box" thinking by the recompete team.

Eventually very little, if any, of the Green Field solution may end up in your final solution. But the thinking and challenge process involved in putting it together and the alternative to existing assumptions of what is right for the customer and possible for you as a company will help open the minds and thinking of the recompete team. It will also counter the often natural default approach as the incumbent of starting from the point of your existing contract.

Section VII   Prepare for the Recompete

Building Your Green Field Solution

The amount of time and resource you put into creating your Green Field solution will, of course, depend on the size and importance of your recompete. Take into account as well the level of change you expect the customer to be requiring in their procurement—the greater the level of change, the more you will need to be innovative. Even if you do not expect significant change, you should still take the Green Field exercise seriously. As we have said above, just because the customer isn't changing their specification, that doesn't mean they will be expecting you to deliver the same solution you are delivering now. It may be that the extent of your work on a Green Field solution for a small contract is only one day. For a major contract, however, the process could take several weeks. This is one of the reasons for conducting the exercise during recompete preparation rather than during the recompete writing period—you may not have time to create and use the Green Field solution to properly challenge assumptions and impact your solution when you are also in the process of writing the recompete documents. However extensive the resources and time allocated to the Green Field solution, take the following steps:

Step 1: Collate the information you need.

The more information the team has, the more comprehensive its solution will be.

Focus on the following types of information:

- The market and wider environment within which the customer is working.
- The drivers and pressures on the customer.
- The customer's strategic goals and plans.
- The needs the customer has expressed for the future and the future of the contract.
- Similar information for all the customer's relevant stakeholders (e.g., the customer's end users, customers, staff, etc.).
- Information on who will be involved from the customer side in the solicitation, together with any existing knowledge of their preferences and priorities.
- Information on the wider supplier side—what the latest technology or solutions are, what the latest wins are for your company and competitors, and what new solutions have been put in place or suggested.
- Information on the type of services or products the customer has said will be included in the new contract.

If there is time available, the team may decide to do their own research: reading industry magazines, researching the customer themselves, attending industry conferences or exhibitions, etc.

Do not, at this stage, include information on the existing contract. Even if the team has some awareness of the contract, it should be focused on building a solution that has no preconceptions based on existing delivery.

Wherever possible, make sure that the information provided is "source" information. Data is better than summary reports, and the source of any information should be clear to the team. Try to avoid any information based on assumptions. If there are any assumptions, make it very clear this is the case, whose assumptions they are, and the basis for them. Again, the focus of the team is to create something new and not based on existing preconceptions. If they are fed information as fact that is actually based on existing assumptions, their thinking will be restricted.

Give the team time to absorb the information before commencing with the development of the Green Field solution. Ideally, they should have the information at least a week prior to beginning their work.

Step 2: Put the right people on the team.

The exact size and composition of the team creating the Green Field solution will depend on the size of the contract and the specific type of work it encompasses. Your goal should be to create a balance of skills and experience between subject matter experts and those who can bring a completely new perspective, but will not necessarily have an in-depth understanding of the technical aspects of the services or products involved.

Avoid including people from the existing contract at this stage. Although it might mean the Green Field solution lacks insight into the specifics of the contract, this is partly the point of the exercise: If they are to create a truly alternative option, the team should be unaffected by the existing thinking and assumptions of what has worked best on the contract to date.

> *Proposal expert advice*
>
> *Certainly engage existing operational contract teams in seeking out recompete solutions and engaging in an advance strategy for improving customer relations and ensuring existing targets are delivered BUT avoid letting the existing operational contract teams dictate the recompete solution. Sometimes they are too close to the existing contract and may stifle some change aspects.*
>
> *Senior Contract Manager*, UK

Make sure you include people with commercial and finance skills and perspectives—the Green Field solution should not just be an operational model. Taking a clean sheet of paper to how the contract could be costed and priced, the potential payment mechanisms, investment approaches, or contractual arrangements that could be used can bring as much valuable innovation and advantage as changing how the operations are delivered.

You can include members of the recompete team. But if they have been working on the preparation for the recompete, they could bring with them some of the assumptions picked up from their review and investigation into the contract. Make sure they consciously set these aside when taking the Green Field approach. Using members of the recompete team does bring advantages. While other members of the team are likely to go back to their day jobs after the exercise is complete, the recompete team members will be able to take into the rest of the recompete process the challenge and ideas these other members of the team have bought through their Green Field thinking.

For some contracts, you might decide to bring in team members external to your business; for instance, industry experts, trusted consultants, or others who have a wider experience of the market, or the technical elements of the services and products involved in the contract.

Step 3: Develop the Green Field solution.

As we have said, the amount of time and resource you put into your Green Field approach will vary with the importance to you of the recompete. If this is a "must win" recompete for a major contract, then the Green Field team could be working on an alternative approach for several weeks in parallel to your core recompete team, building a detailed and fully-costed solution capable of being presented to your customer alongside your main solution. For other recompetes, you may decide a single day is sufficient (or all your recompete budget can afford) to create a set of outline ideas bringing enough challenge to the recompete and contract team to stimulate their thinking. For the purposes of this idea, we will take the latter approach, although the sequence and principles apply to a more in-depth effort.

- For a single day exercise, appoint a facilitator who will take the team through the process and make sure the main aspects of the contract are properly covered and the ideas captured and recorded. The facilitator could be one of the team, but you will usually get more value from using someone who will focus only on the facilitation aspects of the day and not try to mix facilitation and contribution.

- Start by agreeing on the customer's key drivers from the information the team has previously been given (see Step 1). Write these up and prioritize which the team sees as most important to a successful new solution and what it should deliver to the customer.

- Even with good preparation, the information the team has will be incomplete in some way. This means there will be a number of questions the team asks in this and the other sections of the day which can't be answered immediately. Record and "park" these separately—perhaps on a flip chart, if you are using one. This will avoid the team spending too much time on unknowns. This list can be used later, if the team is to meet again, to find the answers for this subsequent session. It can also be used as part of the challenge to the recompete and contract team—do they know the answers to the questions posed? And if not, what will be the impact of the missing information on developing their own solution?

- Next, review the different stakeholders on the customer side, including wider stakeholders such as end users. List their priorities and how important these might be to the winning solution.

- Brainstorm the different aspects of a potential solution, bearing in mind the overall drivers and needs of the customer and stakeholders already identified. Work through the different aspects of the potential contract:

  - What overall model could be used for delivery?

  - What would each aspect of the service or product delivery look like?

  - What financial and contractual arrangements would best meet the customer's needs?

  - How could performance be maximized?

  - How could costs be minimized?

  - How could technology be used to deliver both high performance and low cost?

  As with all brainstorming sessions, the emphasis is on ideas, not why they won't work.

- Next, the team should work through the brainstormed ideas and decide which have most merit in meeting the customer's needs and creating a winning solution. The preferred ideas in each area can then be pulled together to see if they create a coherent solution for the overall contract. This should take the majority of the time in the day. Further ideas will probably emerge as the exercise progresses. They can either be added to the initial brainstorming list or added to the solution as the team sees best.

- Finally, a summary of the complete solution can be created. For each aspect, there should be a link back to the needs and information the team was given so that the reasoning behind the idea is clear.

Step 4: Present the Green Field solution to the recompete team.

This should take place separately from the day or time when the solution was created. The presentation can also be an opportunity for the Green Field team to be exposed to the way the existing contract is being delivered and any thinking on a core solution the recompete team has been working on. Potentially, the teams can present to each other.

Following the presentation, the teams should discuss the merits of the Green Field solution. There can be a tendency for the recompete team (particularly contract team members) to reject elements of the Green Field solution as unworkable, quoting their superior knowledge of the contract and customer. While healthy debate shouldn't be avoided, there should be open discussion about why the ideas could have merit, rather than simply shutting them down as unworkable. The goal of the whole team (Green Field and Recompete) is to ensure that the final solution is based on a clear understanding of the customer's future needs and avoids the trap of basing it too much on present or past assumptions from the contract. The Green Field team should have a remit to challenge assumptions behind the existing solution, and those holding them must be prepared to properly justify why these assumptions are held.

At the end of this session, the recompete team will hopefully have a number of new ideas for the solution. How much of the Green Field solution is incorporated into the final recompete solution will vary, depending on the situation. In some cases, it may completely change the original thinking of the recompete team. In others, some ideas may influence aspects of the final solution. Sometimes the Green Field solution will form the basis for an additional alternative offer the team put forward to the customer alongside their core offer (see *Idea 53*). It is rare for nothing from the Green Field exercise to have any positive impact on the thinking of the recompete team and the innovative and winning nature of the recompete solution.

What is the most important thing an incumbent can do to improve their chances of winning?

> *"Analyze in detail future requirements and improvements required and not reflect on past performance against a past specs."*
>
> *Local Government, UK*

Idea 39: Understand Your Competitors

> **Idea Summary:**
>
> **What:**
>
> Review your likely competitors. Draw up a SWOT and a likely solution for each of them. Review the potential threats these solutions could have to your own proposal and likelihood of winning the recompete and adjust your proposal accordingly.
>
> **Why:**
>
> Too many incumbents feel the competition cannot put in a solution as good as their own, or feel the competition stands little chance of winning, as the customer prefers the incumbent. Taking the competition seriously helps drive a better solution and ensures you don't take the recompete win for granted.
>
> **Key Steps:**
>
> 1. List your likely competitors.
>
> 2. Create a SWOT for each competitor.
>
> 3. Create an outline solution and approach each competitor may take.
>
> 4. Present each outline solution to the recompete team.
>
> 5. Incorporate the competitors' challenges.

Just as you are preparing your recompete, your competitors will be preparing their efforts to oust you from the contract. They will be running their own capture plans, talking with the customer, getting the best understanding possible of your present solution and its potential weaknesses, and influencing the customer to prefer their own solutions and incorporate their ideas into the procurement.

Too many incumbents don't take proper account of their competitors in recompetes. They feel they are too well positioned through their incumbency for the customer to possibly pick anyone else for the next contract. Or they believe competitors cannot possibly understand the contract or customer needs well enough to put forward a winning solution. It is a mistake too many incumbents end up regretting when they find they have lost the recompete.

Section VII   Prepare for the Recompete

Take the threat from your competitors seriously. Spend time reviewing who the likely competitors will be, what their approaches and strengths will be, and what weaknesses they will attack in your own record of delivery on the contract and future bid. Your competitors are not stupid. Don't treat them as such. As part of your recompete preparations, you should review who your competitors are likely to be, what their approaches will be, and how you will overcome their attack.

Step 1: List your likely competitors.

You will usually have a core set of competitors you compete against time and again. This is the core of your initial list. However, you should not ignore new entrants or local competitors.

The more your customer is likely to change or broaden the scope of the contract at recompete, the more you will be likely to face a different set of competitors. For instance:

- If the contract is being expanded geographically, will this bring in competitors presently delivering in these new geographical areas—and will they also see themselves as incumbents if they are already delivering for the customer in these regions?

- Similarly, if the contract expands to include new disciplines, will the present providers of this work for the customer become competitors for the wider bid? Or will new competitors usually focused on these different disciplines see the wider contract as an opportunity to expand?

- If the contract is now significantly larger than before, will this attract larger competitors who might not have competed so strongly for the previous smaller contract?

- Alternatively, if the contract is broken down into separate parts, does this benefit smaller or specialist contractors who would not have had the size or breadth of skills to bid for the whole contract before?

- Will the new contract mean new alliances or consortia of competitors will come together and be able to offer different capabilities?

- What will it mean for your supply chain—could one or more of them now be able to bid directly for the contract?

Step 2: Create a SWOT for each competitor.

Allocate teams to look at each competitor. The teams might be small (even just one person) but they should each focus on creating two strengths, weaknesses, opportunities, and threats matrices for their chosen competitor regarding your contract and bidding for it: the first matrix to focus on the competitors' SWOT regarding the contract, the second to focus on how that competitor sees your own SWOT.

Unlike the Green Field exercise in *Idea 38*, make sure each team has full access to your own delivery structure, performance on, and review of your contract; you should work on the assumption your competitors have this information anyway.

You may have people in your business who have previously worked for some of your competitors. If so, get them to take on the exercise using their inside knowledge, putting themselves in the position of their old employers. If the recompete is important enough and you have the budget, you might also bring in outsiders with knowledge of your competitors to conduct the exercise. Another source of potential "competitor teams" could be from your business' sales and bidding teams. They will be more likely to have faced your competitors recently in other bids and will perhaps have a better, more up to date, and objective view of the competitions' abilities.

Encourage each team to act and think of themselves as the competitor. They should get into the role to the point of referring to the competitor as "we" (not "they") and really focus on what "we" will do to win the contract and beat the incumbent. Not only can this help overcome a degree of stereotyping of your competitors, it can add to the motivation of each team to come up with more aggressive approaches and be more critical of your own strengths and weaknesses in the recompete.

Step 3: Create an outline solution and approach each competitor may take.

Next, get each of your "competitor teams" to take a view on what "their" approach as the competitor will be to winning the bid. This might be influenced by knowledge of other bids where your company has faced your competitor, any insider knowledge from previous experience, or employment by the competitor, as well as the SWOTS already completed in Step 2. If you have completed a Price To Win analysis (see *Idea 37*), add this information into the exercise.

The team should outline:

- The key elements of "their" bid.
- How they would attack the incumbent.
- What their pricing structure would be.
- Any innovation they would bring.
- Which customer needs they would focus on.
- Who in the customer they would be talking to.
- What benefits they would be telling the customer their approach will bring.

Depending on the size of the teams you have put in place and the time given to complete the exercise, this might be a simple outline or a more detailed report.

Step 4: Present each competitor's outline solution to the recompete team.

Set up a meeting where each "competitor team" presents their SWOTs and outline bid to the recompete team. Still in role, the team should discuss the relative merits of their approach and complete a Q&A with the recompete team.

Step 5: Incorporate the competitors' challenges.

Once the competitor presentations are completed, the recompete team, together with the "competitor teams" (now out of role), should review the risks presented by each competitor. The exercise will have generated a number of alternative ideas for the solution and how the customer's needs might be approached. The best of these should be reviewed with a view to potentially incorporating them into the recompete solution. Finally, the team should look at how they can react to the challenges the competition presents:

- What messages might be put to the customer to counter any ideas the competition might be presenting which would benefit the competition?

- What weaknesses has the exercise exposed in your contract or approach which need resolving?

- How will you counter potential competitor approaches in your recompete submission?

While this exercise is unlikely to be a detailed and completely accurate insight into how your competitors will finally approach the recompete, it should stimulate additional challenge to the recompete team and bring new ideas as well as exposing potential weaknesses in the existing contract approach. It should also help overcome the tendency of some teams to downplay the threat from the competition or negatively stereotype the competition.

The core of your recompete effort should still be to put forward a solution focused on meeting your customer's needs in the best possible way. The customer should remain the focus of your attention, not the competition. But ignoring or underestimating the competition is a danger, leading to complacency and failing to drive toward this best possible solution. Always keep in mind that there are real challengers out there and they are putting a lot of effort into beating you.

> **Example:**
>
> *The following decision by the U.S. Government Accountability Office (GAO) illustrates the danger of assuming your solution will automatically be the best:*
>
> *In November 2012, the GAO published their decision regarding a protest by A&T Systems Inc. A&T, the incumbent for a telecommunications and engineering support services contract for the Department of the Army protested the award of the recompete to a competitor. Amongst A&T's reasons for the protest was their assertion that the winner's proposal should have been found technically unacceptable because its staffing plan was inadequate to perform the required work. GAO quote A&T as saying in their protest that only its proposal "featured the absolute lowest staffing composition and corresponding price still capable of satisfying all the Solicitation requirements" and that it is "not feasible for <the winners>, or any offeror's, proposal to satisfy the Solicitation's criteria for technical acceptability with less staff than proposed by A&T."*
>
> *The GAO commented that, while this may be the incumbent's belief, it is the contracting agency which has the primary responsibility for determining its legitimate needs and whether an offered service will satisfy those needs and "a protester's mere disagreement with the evaluation does not show it lacked a reasonable basis."*
>
> *The GAO rejected A&T's protest.*

What is the most important thing an incumbent can do to improve their chances of winning?

> *"Don't sit on their laurels, be honest about current levels of performance, look carefully at competitors' likely offerings."*
>
> *Central Government*

Idea 40: Create Your New Solution

> **Idea Summary:**
>
> **What:**
>
> During the recompete preparation stage, create an outline solution for the next contract.

Section VII Prepare for the Recompete

Why:

Creating a solution early gives you time to test the solution with your customer prior to the official recompete start, saves time during the recompete stage, and enables you to influence the customer towards your new solution. It also enables you to put in place now elements of the new solution you wish to show the customer you can deliver.

Creating as much as possible of your solution during the recompete preparation phase will give you a real head start when the customer's official recompete process starts. While you may not have complete detail of the customer's final specification, your preparation work to date should give you as clear an understanding as possible of the key elements of the procurement requirements. You may have to adapt some parts of your solution when the final documentation is released, but you will be ahead of where you would have been if you had not created a solution now.

Creating a detailed solution now, including costings, pricing mechanism, and commercial elements will also help you in other ways:

- It will reduce the time taken up creating the solution in the recompete stage, giving you more time to focus on producing your response to the customer and arguments for winning the recompete.

- The more change the customer is likely to impose in their solicitation for the new contract compared to your existing contract, the more important starting your solution early will be. For instance, you might need to find partners to cover geographic or technical areas where you have no presence or capability. You may need to review and change your supply chain; for instance, researching potential suppliers of new technology; or find staff with the requisite skills to deliver the new type of work. All of these actions take time. Finding the right partner, agreeing to work together, building a relationship, agreeing on workshare, and creating the appropriate contractual arrangement can take months, as can convincing the customer you are the ideal partnership for the new contract. Similarly, gaining a clear understanding of a new process or work function can also be time consuming. You will find this difficult if you are writing your bid at the same time.

- Having a solution prior to the official recompete starting will give you a template from which you can present and test your ideas with the customer, get their response and input, and potentially help you refine them further.

- Your template solution also gives you a basis to influence the customer in how they specify their recompete procurement to give you a greater advantage over your competitors (see *Idea 41*).

- Having clarity of what changes you will need to make to the existing contract gives you the opportunity to prepare for these changes and potentially put some of these changes in place early. This will both help give you a reference point to show the customer you are able to deliver the improvements you are proposing, and reduce the time, cost, and risk of this transformation in the next contract period—giving you a further edge for the recompete (see *Idea 42*).

The exact approach you take to creating a solution will depend on your own company processes and the type of market you are in. Generally, it will follow similar processes to the way you produce solutions for new contracts.

However, there are some areas where the creation of a solution for your recompete should have a particular focus:

Your Customer's Future Strategic Goals and Needs

The customer will be writing a detailed specification for the new contract, talking to new potential suppliers, perhaps running bidder events, and distributing information to help all bidders understand their business and needs. Your competitors will be researching the customer and talking to them as part of their capture efforts to learn more about them.

But you have the unique advantage of having worked with the customer over the period of the past contract and building a range of relationships with people within the customer organization. You should know the customer's real organizational goals, strategy, and needs better than any of your competitors. And you should have a clearer understanding of how the work of the contract can help the customer achieve these goals and deliver their strategies. During the contract, you have hopefully been reviewing the customer's market and environment; the drivers these place on them; their goals, strategies, and programs of work; their priorities and the progress they have made (for instance, see *Ideas 15, 16, 17* and *19*). During your recompete preparations you will have analyzed your customer's future goals and how these will impact what they want from the contract (see *Ideas 29* and *33*, for example).

Now you can use all of this knowledge and experience to design a solution that fits with these goals and objectives as they will apply in the next contract period. Because you are the incumbent, the customer expects you to have a better understanding of their organization. They expect you to be able to submit a solution which will demonstrably help achieve these wider goals. In your recompete submission, you will be able to explain how your solution will link to their needs for the future and why it will be the most effective way to achieve them.

Section VII   Prepare for the Recompete

As you start to develop your solution, always have a clear list in hand of what the customer's key organizational goals are and the strategies in place to achieve them. These are the starting point. You then look at how you can help them achieve these goals. This shapes what your solution will look like.

Figure VII.11   Linking Customer Strategic Goals to Your Solution

Customer strategic goal	Customer strategy/ program to achieve	How can we help achieve the goals and strategies	Element of our solution that relates to this

Don't follow this sequence in reverse at the start of your solution design process. There can be a real temptation to decide what your solution will be, then see how you can fit it to the customer's needs. You are unlikely to deliver a solution that is really based on your customer's needs by following this route. At best, you will have tweaked the edges of your solution to fit some elements of the customer's goals. At worst, you will simply leave it to the writing team to attempt to explain how your standard solution (or the solution you are already delivering on the contract) is right for the customer. Our experience shows the customer will see through this approach.

Later in the process, once your solution is more defined, you can use the reverse sequence as a check to ensure that, as you have progressed and added new elements or changes to your solution, each of them has a link to your customer's wider needs.

Changes in the Breadth and Type of Work Involved in the New Contract

We have already mentioned in several places the real likelihood that your customer will take the opportunity presented by the end of your existing contract and the start of a new contract to make significant changes to the breadth, specification, and other aspects of the work involved. No matter how flexible and innovative you may have been on the contract to date, there will have been changes in the customer's environment, organization, thinking, or strategies that the contract they and you signed several years ago has not enabled them to put into practice fully. The customer will be looking ahead to what their needs are likely to be over the coming years and designing their new contract requirements to fit. They may also be reacting to changes in legislation, procurement best practice, or supply side changes. If the previous and next contracts are five years in length, then the customer is making changes covering a ten-year timeframe. Not much remains the same over this length of time, and the changes in your next contract's requirements could be radical. For instance, the customer could:

- Change the geography covered by the contract; they could either break the existing areas into smaller regions or increase the scale to cover a wider region, potentially even worldwide.

- Break up the disciplines contained in the existing contract into different contracts. Or they could extend the contract to cover a wider range of disciplines, or perhaps combine the contract with other contracts (potentially already run by other incumbents).

- Segment the end users being served by the existing contract and procure separate contracts for each type of user, particularly if each has a sufficiently different need to warrant a different level or type of service.

- Change the measurement and payment for the contract from an input- to an output- or outcome-based model.

- Change the technology required on the contract to fit their own changed technology base or processes, or what they know is available in the market.

- Change the relative importance of different factors in the delivery of the contract; for instance, increasing the importance of the environmental impact of solutions or the importance of end user satisfaction in how they evaluate the bidders solutions.

- Require bidders to invest up front in capital expenditure to add new infrastructure or upgrade existing infrastructure.

- Change the relative importance of price versus quality in how they will evaluate the contract. Particularly if price is made more important, this might mean adding a requirement to reduce levels of service and find new ways of delivering at a lower price (although the customer would still ideally want more quality for less price).

These are just some of the potential changes. There are, of course, many more variations specific to your own industry or sector.

These changes will have a big impact on your solution design:

- Can you deliver these changes yourself or do you need partners to cover geographies or disciplines where you have no coverage or experience? If so:
  - Who are the best partners to team up with?
  - How will you contract with them?
  - How will you share the work, the risks, and the rewards?
  - How will you work together to design a coherent solution?

- Even if you can deliver the new solution yourself, what effect are the changes required by the customer going to have on your solution? For instance, does an increase in geographical area covered mean:
  - A "site by site" solution is better than a regionally based solution, or a solution with mobile resources?
  - Are there opportunities for centralizing certain elements of your solution such as help centers or warehousing?
  - What management structure is most appropriate?

Again, the options are as varied as the changes the customer may have made and the specifics of your product or service.

However, the impact is likely to mean simply expanding on the existing solution you have in place, or adding new elements to the existing core solution model, will not be the only, or best, route to creating a new solution which best meets the new requirements the customer needs.

Working through these changes and their implications early means you have time to explore all the options available and put the building blocks of your solution in place (such as agreements with the best partners) ahead of the recompete process officially starting.

Incorporating Your Green Field Solution

If you have created a Green Field solution (see *Idea 38*), now is the time to take the learning from this and incorporate those elements from the Green Field work into your solution design. If you have chosen to take the Green Field solution forward further in parallel to your core solution, then continue with this process as described in *Idea 38*.

Take the Competitions' Approaches into Account

If you have completed a review of your competitors' likely approaches (see *Idea 39*), take any good ideas from this analysis as potential additions to your thinking about your solution.

This element of solution design should, however, be treated with some caution. While there may be good ideas that can be incorporated into your solution, just defending against your competitors' should not become the core focus of your solution. Your focus should always remain on your best route to meeting your customer's needs. Maintaining this focus on the customer is a much surer way to beat your competitors.

End Users Perspective

Your contract is almost certainly going to have end users of some type. These might be sections of the customer's staff, or perhaps the customer's own customer base.

Clearly understanding the needs of these end user groups (and those who interact with other elements of your contract delivery) and incorporating ways to better meet their needs into your solution can be a decisive route to a winning bid.

If the stakeholders and end users are the same groups you have been interacting with in your existing contract, you should have good insight into their needs and what their levels of satisfaction are with your existing service (see, for instance, *Idea 14*). This will be information your competitors do not have. If you can design your solution, taking the needs of these different stakeholders into account, and can evidence how you will be delivering a better service to them, you will be at a real advantage over your competitors. Even if the customer specifies the level or type of service required in their recompete documentation, understanding how you can achieve this more effectively and efficiently will be a major advantage.

If you are going to be asked to work with new end users as part of the new contract, spend time understanding their needs. Don't assume they are the same as the end users with whom you presently deal. If you have established customer survey processes, these will be useful; but remember, people will only answer the questions you ask. If you have a new group of stakeholders to survey, using the same questions as you ask existing groups may not get you the information you need (for instance, they might have a particular need you don't ask a question about because you have used an existing survey focused on another group's specific requirements).

Just as with your customer, you should not assume the end users' needs over the past contract period will be the same in the next period. Trends and expectations change and the circumstances of end users change. If your contract has an emphasis on delivery to end users, research what these changes are likely to be over the next contract period. For instance, what will be the social and economic changes impacting on the group, how will their interaction with the customer and you change; in other words, will they increasingly prefer online interactions?

If you run user groups, use these to ask what changes the users are likely to see in the future, along with what they would like to see in the service they receive in the future. Or run specific forums where you ask these questions of users or staff as part of your recompete preparations. In some cases, merely the fact that you have taken the effort to ask can positively dispose towards you those end users and involved staff, and this might have some positive impact on the recompete later in the process. And as you communicate your new solution to the customer, having the evidence from your research to back up your solution will give your submission increased credence and weight with the customer. In some instances, you might even be able to show you know more about your customer's end users than your customer does.

Innovations and Changes in Process/Best Practice

Look outside your own contract to see what the latest thinking and practice is in the marketplace:

- What solutions are winning contracts?

- What solutions are winning awards or are being put forward as good practice for the industry or related industries?

- What are your business development teams seeing as the most up-to-date solutions and what are the most forward-thinking customers your company deals with looking for?

- What is being talked about or exhibited at industry conferences?

- What new technologies are available and being put to effective use?

- What new ideas for contracting models are being written about in industry magazines and what new innovations are being featured?

While you may not take on all of the latest (and perhaps unproven) technologies and processes in your solution, you should at least be exposing your team to the latest and most up to date ideas. They will certainly help avoid the trap of seeing the next contract only in terms of your existing solution, and there may be ideas you can test now and include in your new solution.

Learning from the Existing Contract

We have emphasized in the headings above the need to bring new thinking into the design of your solution and not just rely on the existing solution or assumptions. But, of course, there will be a lot of experience you can bring from your existing contract to your solution. This will generally cover two areas—the customer and your own solution. Both need to be approached with the caveat that, while they applied in the last contract, all of them need to be challenged before you can be sure they will also apply in the next period. Some examples of learning include:

For the customer:

- What aspects of the customer's requirements are specific to them and need to be included in your thinking for the next solution?

- What is the pattern of demand and how does this impact the solution—for instance, are there yearly, monthly, weekly, daily, or even hourly cycles or surges in demand that need to be taken into account?

- What are the customer's processes and how do they impact a solution?

- What are the specific requirements of individual customer stakeholders?

- What other customer preferences do you need to take into account?

For your solution:

- What has worked particularly well in your delivery and should be retained or improved on in your next solution?

- What issues have you had with delivery or costs that need to be rectified in the solution?

- What processes do you have in place in your contract which perhaps have successfully delivered continuous improvement that you should also put into your new solution?

- What do you understand about the costs of your existing solution that you can use in your new solution?

- What innovations or improvements did you consider or suggest during the contract which did not get final approval to go ahead, but might now be feasible in a new contract setting?

Ideas for Improvement from Staff

Your contract staff are a potential source of ideas for the new solution. As they are delivering the contract and working directly with end users, staff are likely to have a number of ideas of how things could be improved. Hopefully you will have been encouraging their input throughout the contract. You should do so again now, either formally in groups or forums or individually. Staff will most likely be nervous about the impending recompete. Involving them will also help their motivation in a period when you need the highest levels of performance to keep your customer happy.

Partners and Supply Chain

Your existing partners and supply chain should not be a given for the next contract. Review and refresh your existing set of partners and suppliers:

- Are you getting the best deal possible from them for the new contract?

- Are there other suppliers or partners better placed to deliver what is required for the next contract?

- Should you be looking to create exclusivity deals with any of your suppliers to preclude your competition from using them?

- Are any of your partners or supply chain potentially going to favor a competitor, or even become a competitor by bidding for the contract directly?

You should also look to your partners and supply chain for their ideas and possible innovations you can use in your solution. They may have access to, or knowledge of, similar contracts where things are delivered differently. They may also have access to new products or services which could enhance your solution. Talk to them and get them involved in thinking about what they can contribute to your next contract.

Financial and Commercial Options

Your new solution is not just about the operational aspects of delivery. How you organize your financial solution could be key to your overall offering to the customer (see *Idea 37: Price To Win*). Whether you are creating your solution to a specific price envelope or have the potential to price your contract to be more attractive to your customer—for instance, spreading the return of investments you make over the contract period, creating gain share mechanisms, etc.—ensuring the financial and commercial aspects of your solution are considered at the start and are an integral part of your thinking throughout the development of the solution will be crucial. Don't just leave the finance team to add up the costs of your solution at the end of the process.

Working through other aspects of your potential solution, such as creating an outcome-based payment mechanism or anticipating the costs needed to cover a penalty regime for non performance the customer may be putting in place, will also be crucial. For instance, what is the most economical level of performance based on a particular penalty regime? It might cost you significantly more to put in place a solution that garners no penalties through 100% performance than it would to deliver 98% and take the cost of penalties for the remaining 2%, assuming the customer would accept this reduced level of performance for the reduced price it would allow you to deliver.

Transformation and Implementation

Part of your thinking in developing your solution should be how you will successfully complete the transformation from your existing contract to the new solution. As the incumbent, you should be the lowest risk bidder in terms of having the ability to put the new contract in place on time, within budget, and without a dip in performance along the way. You should reinforce this by thinking through every aspect of the changes that will be needed to put your new solution in place, and all the advantages you can turn into benefits for the customer in this transformation:

- How will you further reduce the risks?

- How can you make the transition faster than competitors so the customer gets the benefits faster?

- How can you make it cheaper for the customer than your competitors can?

We will return to this in *Ideas 42, 54* and *57*. However, for the purposes of solution design, think through how you can implement the new solution and ensure your solution includes a clearly thought out and comprehensive plan and process for achieving the change.

What aspects of incumbents' proposals have been particularly poor?

"They submit the exact same bid they submitted for the first contract without regard to spec changes."

State Government, USA

Idea 41: Influence Your Customer

> **Idea Summary:**
>
> **What:**
>
> Use the relationships you have built with key customer stakeholders to influence what they put into the recompete and how they view your potential solution versus those of your competitors.
>
> **Why:**
>
> Influencing the customer now means they are more likely to put together a solicitation approach and specification which will be more realistic and enable a workable, profitable new contract. In addition, you can put forward options more likely to favor your own solution. Waiting until the recompete has officially started reduces the options you and the customer have to change the key decisions being made now about the core elements of the solicitation.

While you are preparing for your recompete, your customer is also preparing their solicitation process. Our advice has been to start your recompete preparations at least six months prior to the official start of the recompete process—more, if your contract is large or is longer than four to five years. The main reason for starting preparations early is to put yourself in the strongest position possible by the time the recompete starts officially (see *Idea 40*, for instance). You will also have time to influence your customer's thinking about their solicitation (your recompete) before they have made all the major decisions about when they will run the solicitation, what they will be asking of bidders, and how they will evaluate the responses.

Once the official solicitation starts, there is little room to change these key elements, which could make a significant impact on your chances of success. And the customer will often feel they cannot be so open with you during the official solicitation process, due to problems this would cause with maintaining a competitive level playing field for all bidders, so you will have less opportunity to talk openly and freely with them.

Different customers will have different levels of openness to your approaches. In some cases, you might have such a good relationship with the customer that they ask you to help write aspects of the new specification. But however little you may think you are able to influence the customer, having a clear strategy for how and to what end you will be aiming to influence them is an important part of any Recompete Strategy.

Of course, you are already influencing the customer in some respects; how you are performing on the contract, the type of relationship you have with customer stakeholders over the period of the contract, changes and improvements you have suggested and implemented, or problems and issues you have encountered; all have some influence on the customer.

They are also likely to have some influence on the customer's solicitation. For instance, if the customer has felt for some time that the cost of the service they are receiving is higher than their budgets will allow in the future, they are more likely to make price an important factor in the recompete and may specify lower levels of service to help achieve this. There is also the possibility they are dissatisfied with the level of service you have been delivering and are running the recompete to give themselves an opportunity to get a better service, either from you or another supplier.

An important question to ask yourself, and of course the customer, is why they are running the recompete now and what they want to change as a result of it.

What Outcomes Might You Aim for?

At different points in the process, you might have different goals for influencing your customer. But, in general, the goals would be to:

- Avoid a recompete completely.

- Get an extension to the contract.

- Influence the customer's perception of you and your capabilities versus their needs and their perceptions of the competition.

- Have the shape, contents, or process of the recompete better fitted to your company and offering and/or less suited to the competition.

- Ensure the solicitation process is not overly onerous to you (or the customer) in terms of the time and investment required to complete it.

- Ensure the next contract is workable and profitable.

Let's look briefly at each of these, in turn:

Avoid a recompete completely.

This might not be possible with government customers, but with many private sector customers, there are no regulations forcing them to recompete the contract at regular periods. Show the customer you are delivering the most efficient and effective contract possible; are acting as a partner; bringing new ideas; delivering at a price they can be confident is market rate; and being so flexible they are able to achieve the changes they need without going to recompete. If the customer is happy they are getting the best deal already, they may decide the cost and work of running a competition is not necessary.

Get an extension to the contract period.

We have discussed extensions in *Idea 25*. In all but exceptional circumstances (you are losing money on the contract, for instance), getting the maximum number and length of extensions to the contract will be beneficial to you. If you can influence the customer to grant these extensions, you will have gained additional years of income from the contract and return from your investment in the original bid. You will also have put off the risk of losing the contract.

The customer can also gain from postponing the cost of the solicitation. They face some element of risk if they bring in a new contractor or change the form of the contract—the new form may not be as successful as they hope, and there is also the risk of failure in implementing the new contract. They will be factoring this into their thinking and comparing it to the potential benefits of the new contract and the competition created by the solicitation, driving bidders to offer new ways of working and a better value for money solution.

What benefits can you offer the customer in return for granting an extension to the contract? A price reduction is one potential offer. But you might also, by understanding their goals for the next contract, be able to offer changes to how you are delivering the contract now that would meet some of these needs. This might be enough for them to postpone the recompete. Perhaps you can offer to work with them to test out new ways of working so they have a clearer idea of their impact and effectiveness before they go out to procure them, thus reducing the potential risks of not getting the procurement right. This also gives you the benefit of having tested the new procedures the customer is asking for and the ability to reference your delivery and flexibility in your recompete.

Change the customer's perception of you, their needs, and the competition.

The customer will have a set of needs, requirements, and priorities for the next contract. Hopefully, you already have a good understanding of what these are and the relative importance or priority of each versus the others. Some requirements will be "must haves," others may be "nice to have." Ideally, you will be able to list the requirements the customer has in order and with a sense of relative priority.

For instance, on a scale of 1 to 10, where 10 is most important or "must have":

Priority	Requirement
10	Requirement 1
9	Requirement 2
8	
7	
6	Requirement 3
5	Requirement 4
4	
3	Requirement 5
2	
1	Requirement 6

These requirements and relative priorities are important to know. What is also important is how the customer perceives your abilities and offerings versus these priorities. For instance, if the customer's must have requirement (Requirement 1 above) is speed of delivery, but they perceive your speed of delivery to be weak, you have a potential problem. This will be exacerbated if you also find the customer perceives one or more of your competitor's capabilities to be very high in this important area. Similarly, if the customer perceives one of your capabilities (for instance, end user communications) to be very high, and you yourself see this as a key strength but it is actually low in their list of priorities (for instance, Requirement 6 in the table), then pushing this strength in your bid will have little positive benefit for you.

Hopefully, you will have, or be planning to, run a survey of your key stakeholders' attitudes towards you (see *Idea 32*). This should give you a good sense of their perceptions of your relative strengths. Your relationship building and capture effort should also get as accurate a picture as possible of the customer's relative priorities (remembering that different stakeholders within the customer will most likely have different priorities and you need to understand the relative influence each stakeholder will have on other stakeholders and on the final decisions being made).

Section VII   Prepare for the Recompete

From the information you have gained, map the customer's priorities and perceptions of your relative strengths on a matrix like the one below:

Figure VII.12   Priorities vs. Perception Matrix

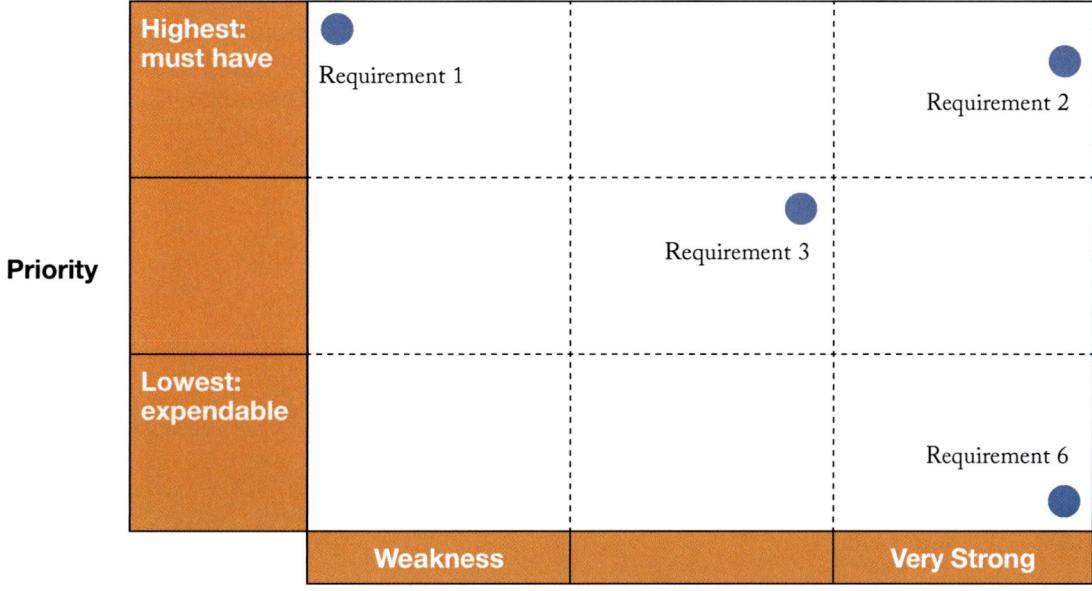

In this example, we have used some of the requirements from the list in the table above and mapped these onto some assumed customer perceptions of your own relative strengths in these areas. Remember, these are priorities for the next contract, which could be different from the priorities the customer had or has for your existing contract. For this example:

- In Requirement 1: you would have a significant issue—the customer perceives you are weak in their most important priority area.

- In Requirement 2: you are in a good position—this is a priority area for the customer and they perceive you to be very strong in this area.

- In Requirement 3: you are in a fair position—it is a medium level priority for them and they see you as having medium strength.

- In Requirement 6: you have another issue—it is seen as a major strength of your offering by the customer. But they see it as a very low priority, one that is unlikely to influence the outcome of the recompete.

This helps you prioritize your own influencing tasks. For Requirement 1, you need to change the customer's perception of your strength in this area. Understand who within the customer sees this area as a weakness and why. Look at how you can improve your performance in this area over the final months of the contract, prior to the official start of the recompete. Perhaps it is seen as a weakness because you have little chance to demonstrate it on the existing contract, but it will become more important on the next contract. Do you have other contracts where you deliver this requirement in a more vital role and can you take the customer to see these contracts?

You could attempt to reduce the relative importance of Requirement 1 to the customer. However, this is usually more difficult to do. If you can't improve the customer's perception of your strengths in this area, can you increase their view of the importance of other requirements so Requirement 1, while not decreasing in absolute importance, at least has rivals for the most important requirement where you do have strengths?

For Requirement 6, your task is different; rather than change the customer's perception of your capability, you need to increase their view of its importance to them. Understand why they see it as expendable for the next contract: Will the specification or breadth of the contract change to make it less relevant? Are there aspects of the requirement the customer is unaware of, perhaps its impact on end users? Can you demonstrate to the customer the real impact of reducing the delivery of Requirement 6?

For all these tasks, be aware of who within the customer organization holds these views. Do all the stakeholders hold similar views? Do some hold views more favorable to your position? Can you get close to and work with these contacts to influence others, or do you need to directly address those with views negative to your preferred position?

Take into account the customer's views of your competitors' relative strengths. If, for instance, one of your key competitors is seen as very strong in Requirement 1, understand why this is the case. Can you "ghost" their perceived strength, or should you look at how they are delivering and match this?

Section VII Prepare for the Recompete

The arrows below show how you are trying to move the customer's relative priorities versus perceptions:

Figure VII.13 **Priorities vs. Perception Matrix—Actions**

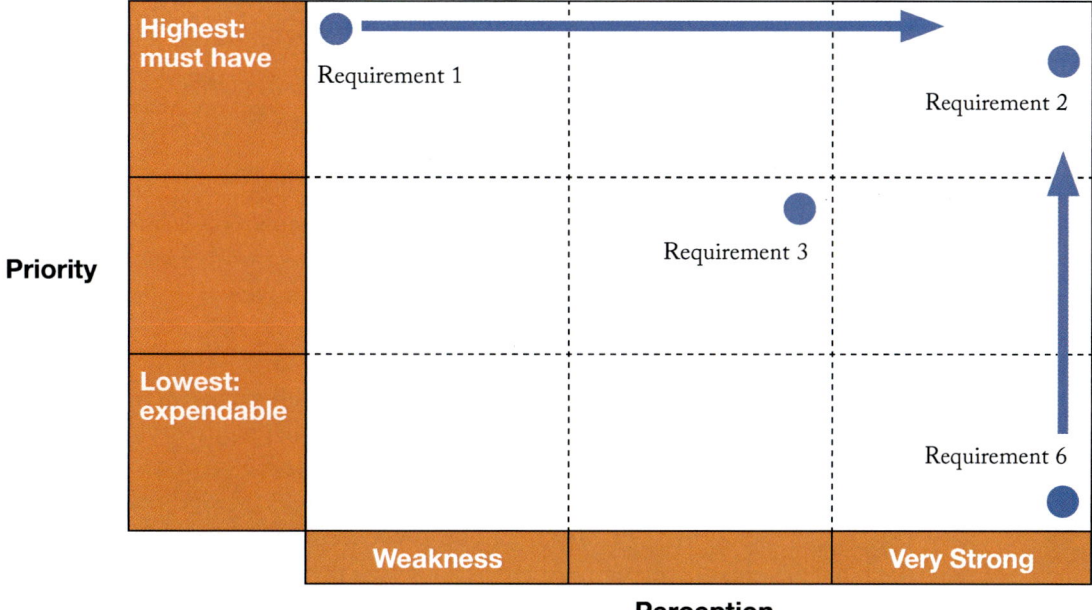

Impact the shape, content, or process of the recompete.

This is related to the section above, but covers a wider set of areas and is more directly related to what goes into the written official procurement process.

As you gain a clearer understanding of what your customer may be planning for the recompete, compare it with what would help or hinder your chances of winning. For example:

- Are there particular disciplines or services that could be included to give you an advantage over your competitors?

- Would a shorter recompete process suit you better?

- Would you be able to put together a stronger bid if the customer solicitation asked for outcome-based solutions rather than an input-based solution?

- Are there specific elements of your offering which give you a strong advantage over the competition (for instance, a type of software application) you want to ensure the customer includes in the specification for the recompete?

- Are there costs or activities associated with the contract you want to ensure the customer is aware of and includes in the specification, so you are not at a disadvantage by costing them in when competitors may not do so, as they were not in the specification?

- Are the requirements the customer is putting into the solicitation for winning the contract different from those required for running the contract? For example, are they planning to make the decision for the winner based on an evaluation of costs that will not be part of the contract, or not to the same mix?

- Would a greater emphasis on quality be better for you than a focus on price?

This last point is particularly important for an increasing number of contracts. When budgets are tight for customers, they can change the way they procure to reflect this by increasing the emphasis at the recompete on price versus quality. This can happen in all sectors and all countries, however in the U.S., it has been enshrined in a specific type of procurement. Currently in the U.S., the government is increasingly moving away from Best Value procurement, where price is only one factor in their decision, and a strong quality score and/or a strong past performance from a bidder can mean they win the contract even if they have not put in the lowest price. This type of procurement is being replaced by Lowest Price Technically Acceptable (LPTA) procurements for many contracts—particularly where the customer feels the risk of failure is low and believes they would gain no benefit from a solution offering more than the specified level of service or product (or they believe that getting the lowest price outweighs any such benefit). In this type of procurement, the customer specifies what they want and bidders can only be scored a pass or fail on each of the specified areas (including past performance). The customer then chooses the bidder with the lowest price who has passed all the other criteria.

For bidders, this means there is no value in putting any additional offering, innovation, or services into their solution above the level which will achieve a pass mark. In fact, if they do, and this increases their costs, it puts them at a major disadvantage, as they will no longer be the lowest price bidder and will lose. For you as the incumbent, having your customer move to an LPTA type procurement at the recompete will have a significant impact:

- It will mean your past performance will not give you higher marks than the competition (as long as they get a pass mark, they are deemed equivalent to you, no matter how well you have performed on the contract).

- It will mean there is no value in putting additional levels of service into your proposal.

Section VII   Prepare for the Recompete

- It will mean the experience of your staff, if it is above the levels required in the specification, is of no advantage to you (in fact, if the level of experience your staff have makes them more expensive than staff with only the required level—which is the level at which your competitors will bid—it puts you at a major disadvantage).

- It means you will have to lower your margins, overheads, and all costs to the minimum possible to be at a lower cost than your competitors in order to win.

Unless you are absolutely convinced your experience on the contract means you are able to deliver the specified levels of service or product at a lower cost than all competitors, you will most likely want to avoid moving from an existing contract based on Best Value to one based on LPTA.

If you believe your customer is planning to move toward a form of recompete that would disadvantage you, the time to try to influence them away from doing so is before they make that decision. By the time the solicitation is publicized to the market, it will be too late, in most cases, to change their minds. If the customer is planning to move to an LPTA type of competition, your main route to influencing the customer will be to convince them either:

- There are real risks of failure to the contract if the customer picks the wrong contractor, and the impact of that failure to them would be severe; or

- The technical and quality aspects of a decision in the recompete are so important, they should use the Best Value approach, where they will be able to give a range of marks to past performance and technical aspects of the bids and be able to choose the bidder offering the best mix of quality and innovative new ideas at a reasonable (though not necessarily the lowest) price—not just the cheapest bidder offering the minimum quality set by the customer in the specification.

The specific risks and areas of technical or quality aspects most important to the customer will vary from contract to contract. But your previous performance on, and knowledge of, the contract should help you identify what will be most important to the customer. How you have performed on the contract will also make a difference:

- If you have kept close to your customer and understand their strategic needs and how these have changed over the period of the contract, you could use this information to identify areas where they could suffer if not deciding the next contract on Best Value terms.

- If you have used your Contract Plan (see *Idea 8*) to transform the services delivered on the contract, you will be able to show the benefits of a contractor bringing flexibility and proactive change throughout the contract, compared to one simply delivering the contracted specification.

- If you have delivered improving performance, added value, and innovation and have kept the contract up to date through changes to meet the customer's most important changing needs (all parts of your Contract Plan), and have the measures to show this improvement and the impact on the customer, you will be able to use this evidence to back up your assertions.

- If you have worked closely with the customer on identifying and managing risks, you will understand the risks involved in the contract and the potential impact these could have on the customer, and use these examples to illustrate the dangers of the contract being delivered to a tight budget with perhaps the "wrong" contractor.

- If you have built strong, positive relationships with a range of decision makers and influencers, you will be able to use these relationships to get your message across.

- But, of course, if you have done little or none of the above, you will find it difficult to justify why the customer shouldn't use LPTA to find the cheapest supplier of the services they specify; after all, you might have shown them there is limited value in doing anything else.

Ideally, you will be able to persuade the customer to use a Best Value approach. If you fail, your backup to reduce the potential damage an LPTA type procurement may cause will be to ensure the specifications set are as high as possible and to include all the cost areas needed to deliver the contract (see *Idea 52*). For example, if your staff have five years' experience and a certain level of skills or qualifications, make sure this is the level required in the specification. If the customer only asks for two years' experience or a lower level of qualification, your competitors will find it easier to source these capabilities at a lower cost than your existing staff. To match this, you will be forced to either change your staff for those with a lower skill set, or ask your staff to take a pay cut, otherwise your staff costs will be more expensive and you risk losing the recompete.

Ensure the solicitation process is not overly onerous.

Bids cost money, time, and resources to complete. The more complex and lengthy the solicitation process, the more effort you, your competitors, and the customer have to put towards it. This can be driven by the number of stages the solicitation goes through, the complexity and detail of the specification, or the quality of the effort the customer applies to the project.

In particular, you do not want the process to be flawed in such a way that it would be open to challenge by a competitor who bids, but loses. This would cost both you and your customer time and money and delay your opportunity to put the new contract in place and secure its future income. While in some cases, this delay can mean you gain additional extensions to the contract while the challenge is being worked through (and hopefully rejected), this is rarely of benefit to you, due to the uncertainty it brings to the operation, and of course, the possibility the customer could be required to rerun the procurement.

For new bids, most bidders prefer a relatively short and straightforward solicitation process. Usually, this would also be the case for you, as the incumbent. However, you may want to balance this against the benefits you might gain from a more detailed and comprehensive process, which would mean your superior knowledge of the customer, their needs, and the details of the operation give you an advantage over your competitors.

In some areas, you might know the details of the contract and the services delivered even better than your customer. Using this knowledge to ensure the customer does not overlook a key aspect of the contract in their deliberations could help both you and the customer.

Ensure the next contract is workable and profitable.

There are occasions when the customer, through their process and the specification they include within it for the next contract, make the running of that contract inefficient or even unworkable. This can mean the winning contractor is put in a position where they cannot successfully deliver the core needs the customer actually has for the work, and/or find it impossible to make a profit on the contract.

Don't confuse this with the situation where the customer has rightly asked the contractor to work harder for their money (perhaps because they saw the abnormally high profits made in the last contract). Or where the bidder has mistakenly mispriced the contract or put in a solution they then find is not deliverable in practice. The first is absolutely the right approach for the customer to take. The second, while it could be attributed to a poor decision by the customer on the realism of the bidder's pricing, is ultimately the fault of the bidder concerned.

The situation we are covering here is where the customer has, usually unwittingly, put something in their specification or commercial requirements for the contract that does not work in practice in the contract. For instance:

- The customer puts in place a performance measurement regime forcing the contractor to spend more time focusing on meeting the KPIs (and the customer spends too much time and resources monitoring the KPIs) than delivering the customer's actual requirements (in this case, the customer has usually put in too many KPIs).

- A form of payment mechanism, particularly a penalty regime, which means the contractor is penalized for performance that is actually acceptable, or over-penalized for small errors or underperformance. This could lead the contractor to focus more effort on mitigating penalties than delivering performance.

- The customer does not properly estimate or cover for changes in demand or volumes over time in the contract and has no clear provision for making appropriate changes to the contract when these occur.

As the incumbent contractor, you should be in a better position to spot these potential problems early and guide the customer away from them. After all, you don't want to be in a position where you have won your recompete but then can't profitably deliver the next contract.

Align Your Own and Your Customer's Benefits

To successfully influence the customer in their thinking and decisions about their procurement, you must be able to align the benefits you will gain from the changes you are seeking to benefits the customer will also gain (beyond just keeping you as their supplier). If the customer is going to be disadvantaged by any changes you intend to influence the customer to make, you will most likely fail (and perhaps you should). If this is the case, focus instead on redesigning your offering and solution to make it more competitive and something that gives the customer real advantage.

Look at the potential changes you will be seeking. Work out what the benefit is to the customer of this change and make sure you and the recompete team have agreed and are clear on these benefits before talking to the customer. The influencing process then becomes a part of your capture plan and effort.

Change	Benefit to the customer	Benefit to you

There are many circumstances where the benefits to you will align with benefits to the customer. For instance, you will not want a contract with design flaws stemming from the solicitation process making it unprofitable, and even the most price conscious customer is unlikely to want a contractor working for them who is losing money. They will understand the drivers the contractor will be facing to cut their own costs and the focus on returning to profit will inevitably have some impact on performance or proactive service improvement.

Section VII   Prepare for the Recompete

This is important to get right. If you don't focus on the benefits to the customer of the changes you are proposing, you will simply come across as a supplier who is trying to avoid the recompete or fix it for their own purposes. If the customer feels this is what you are doing, not only will they be unlikely to listen to you, it will also damage their perception of you as having a partnering approach, being customer focused, and the contractor best suited to work with them in the future.

Talk to the Right Customer Stakeholders

To influence customer decision making, you need to be talking to those stakeholders in the customer's organization who can make or influence these decisions.

This is where the work you have already been doing mapping out who in the customer organization (and beyond) will be involved in the recompete decision (see *Idea 35*), and your work on reinvigorating your relationships with the customer (see *Idea 31*), will help you target the right messages to the right people.

Take a consultative approach, focusing on the customer's requirements and goals, making suggestions with clear customer benefits, as we have said above. You won't always succeed in getting all the changes you might hope, but you may well get some. And, done properly, your approach will have reinforced your position as a trusted advisor to the customer.

What aspects of incumbents' proposals have been particularly poor?

"Where they simply haven't put the effort in. They assume because they already have a contract they will win. There is also sometimes a tendency to go for "business as usual" with no ideas or innovation. Complacency is a killer."

Private Sector, UK

Idea 42: Prepare the Contract

Idea Summary:

What:

Using the information you have gathered during the recompete preparation stage and the outline solution you have put together for the recompete, look at how you can make changes now to your existing contract which align to the new contract.

Why:

There is a concern that the customer perceives you only in light of your existing delivery. If you are able to make changes now, they will show your customer you are able to deliver key aspects of the new contract requirements. Making the changes now also helps gather evidence and statistics for the recompete on how you are delivering the new aspects of the contract. It also means you will need to make fewer changes as part of your transition to the new contract, which you can use to show the customer this transition will be lower risk, faster, and cheaper than competitors' solutions.

We have already covered some aspects of preparing the contract and contract team for the recompete in *Idea 27: Prepare the Contract Team* and *Idea 36: Resolve Existing Contract Issues*. Now that you have a clearer idea of what the customer will be asking for in the recompete for the next contract (see *Idea 33*) and have designed your solution for the next period (see *Idea 40*), you will have a much clearer view of the changes needed to get from your existing service to the delivery the customer wants and you are proposing in the recompete.

You now have the opportunity (because hopefully you started your recompete preparations early enough) to begin making some of these changes before the official recompete process commences.

There are a number of benefits to taking this route:

- Particularly if the customer is asking for a product, service, or form of delivery you do not presently have on your contract, it gives you the opportunity to show the customer you are capable of delivering what they will be looking for in the next contract. They may be under the impression that, because you are not presently delivering, you are not able to.

- Introducing a product, service, or way of working which clearly interests the customer shows you are flexible and keen to continue to move the contract forward in line with the customer's needs.

- Putting the new service or methodology in place helps the customer better understand it and more clearly specify what they want (and in line with what you are now already delivering).

- The experience of putting in place and delivering the new service means you better understand the costs and processes involved and so can more accurately cost and describe it in your solution.

- You can use the fact that you are now delivering the new product or service as a reference in your recompete.

Section VII Prepare for the Recompete

- Already having the product or service in place reduces your cost, time, and risk of introducing it after the recompete is won—giving you a further advantage in the transformation/implementation element of your new solution in the recompete.

Of course you should also be careful to manage the potential challenges associated with making a change to the contract or introducing something new into the contract at this stage:

- You should be sure what you are introducing is indeed what the customer will be looking for.

- You need the customer's support for the change.

- The change must be carefully managed. You do not want to either impinge on the running of other aspects of the contract at this stage, or fail to effectively put the new initiative in place. Either would work against you with little time to recover before the recompete is in full progress.

List the potential changes the customer is looking for in the recompete and those in your solution (a useful exercise anyway to make sure your solution matches these needs). Then work through each—assessing the degree of importance to the customer; the difference from your present delivery; and the ease, speed, and cost of introducing:

Figure VII.14 Pre-recompete Change Priorities

Change	Importance to customer	Difference from existing delivery	Ease of introduction	Priority
	High/Med/Low	High/Med/Low	High/Med/Low	
Change 1	M	M	L	3
Change 2	H	L	M	2
Change 3	H	H	H	1

In the simple summary above, Change 3 has the highest importance to the customer, is significantly different from how you are presently delivering, and is easy to introduce. That should be your priority and, in this example, it is given priority 1 status. In reality, it might be the only change you make. Introducing a raft of changes to the contract at this late stage could cause confusion and problems in overall levels of delivery, so you should focus on those with the most impact and least effort. Often you will have a more nuanced decision to make. It is rare you will find a significant change that is easy to make; perhaps in this case you are already delivering on another contract, so you know how to make the change with little cost or risk. You can focus on one key change or a number of "easy wins" which might not be decisive individually, but add up to a set of changes showing the customer your ability to adapt.

Some examples of changes could be:

- Introducing a new way of measuring performance (output vs. input based for example).
- Introducing end user satisfaction surveys (be careful they don't initially have poor results!).
- Testing a new product, process, or technology that brings advantages to the customer by reducing cost or increasing performance.
- Testing a new shift pattern for staff in one region of the contract.
- Testing the cost/benefit of improved speed of delivery in an element of the contract.

If you don't have time to introduce a particular change to your contract, or the costs and risks are too high, look around the other contracts in your business: do they deliver in the way you are looking to move? If so, arrange a customer visit to the contract in question. Even though you are not able to directly show delivery on your contract, you will at least give the customer confidence you are experienced as a business in delivering in this way. If possible and appropriate, give your customer the opportunity to discuss with the other contract's customer the benefits of this different service or process. It may help inform their decision making process and (assuming your other customer is happy with your performance) reinforce your company's position as a capable supplier.

Finally, be sure that when you do make any changes, you can clearly show the outcome they deliver. Look at what measures of improvement or performance you can introduce to provide evidence the change has made a positive difference. This will help convince the customer in the months preceding the official recompete, and you can use the statistics as evidence in your recompete submission.

What aspects of incumbents' proposals have been particularly poor?

"Complacent on winning and so not addressing emerging needs; pricing high as cost of change makes moving hard; adding price escalation metrics which look good but cost more over time; not answering the basic specification."

Public Sector, UK

Section VIII

Run the Recompete

Figure VIII.1 The Contract Lifecycle Run the Recompete Stage

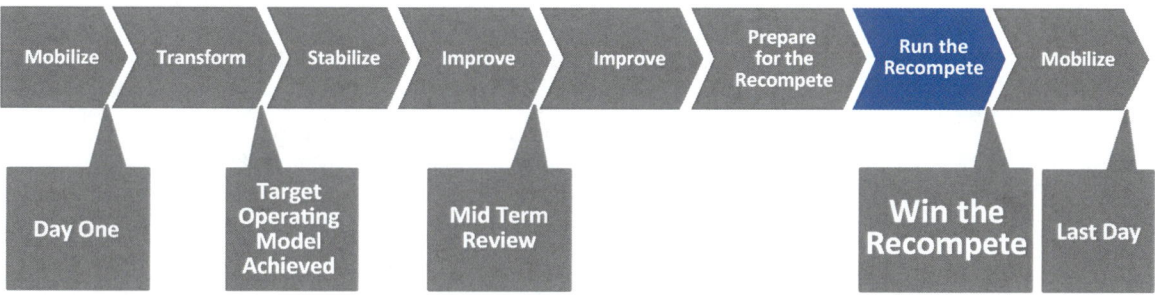

What is the Run the Recompete Stage?

"Run the Recompete" is the stage when the official customer solicitation is in progress. Typically, it covers the period from the customer first publishing their intention to recompete the contract through to the award of the new contract to the winning bidder and contract signature. During this stage, you will be writing your responses to the solicitation the customer is undertaking, presenting your solution, having discussions, and putting in your final pricing and solution. Depending on the extent of solution design you have completed during the previous "Prepare for the Recompete" stage, you may also be designing your solution during the "Run the Recompete" stage.

For your competitors, this is a bid for new business. For your customer, it is another solicitation. The processes involved are those used for a bid for new business. Most businesses have sales, capture, and bid teams experienced in bidding; clear governance processes for managing bids; and established best practice processes for winning. Indeed, to have won the contract in the first place, you will have followed these processes yourself. We don't intend to reinvent the well established bidding processes promoted by the many bid consultancies in operation around the world, or the best bidding practices established by organizations such as the Association of Proposal Management Professionals (APMP). At its most basic, your recompete is a bid and you should use the core processes you have established for bidding as the backbone to your recompeting efforts.

However, your position as the incumbent does mean your approach to a recompete will be different in a number of ways to how you bid for new business. As the incumbent, you have a number of advantages you should be making the most of. There are also a number of traps incumbents regularly fall into during their recompetes that you must avoid if you are to win.

The ideas in this section will help you make the most of the advantages, and avoid the pitfalls, of your position as the incumbent recompeting your existing contract and use your incumbency appropriately and intelligently. We have set out the ideas in this section to cover the key issues you are likely to face as the incumbent. Some of the detail and aspects of the advice we give is repeated across different ideas, and others might have organized the ideas on a different basis. However, we have organized the headings to make each idea as complete as possible in itself and cover a specific benefit or potential problem you, as the incumbent, should be taking account of in your recompete. So, as with the previous sections in the contract lifecycle, you can take all, some, or just one of the ideas and still get real benefit in improving your opportunity to win your recompete.

Ideas Included in This Section:

- **Idea 43: Approach the Recompete as if It Is a New Bid**
- **Idea 44: Review the Detail of the Published Requirements**
- **Idea 45: Don't Assume the Customer Knows You**
- **Idea 46: Use the Information You Have Gathered**
- **Idea 47: Write from the Customer's Perspective**
- **Idea 48: Be Future Oriented**
- **Idea 49: Admit Mistakes**
- **Idea 50: Discriminators, Differentiators, Benefits, and Win Themes**
- **Idea 51: Become the Benchmark Bid**
- **Idea 52: Price to Fit the Specification, Not What You Know**
- **Idea 53: Alternative Bids**
- **Idea 54: Use Risk Effectively**
- **Idea 55: Staff**

Section VIII   Run the Recompete

- Idea 56: Asking Questions
- Idea 57: Transition Plans

What aspects of incumbents' proposals have been particularly poor?

"An obvious lack of having read bid specifications, or responding to new specification sections, relying only on past business relationships and previous expectations (incomplete responses)."

State Government, USA

Idea 43: Approach the Recompete as if It Is a New Bid

Idea Summary:

What:

Put the same level of effort, creativity, attention to competitor threats, and focus on the customer's future needs into your recompete as you would for a bid for a new customer.

Why:

Incumbents often feel they are almost certain to win the recompete. Because of this, they tend to put less effort into the recompete and less effort into focusing on delivering a fresh new solution for the customer. This is one of the greatest issues customers have with incumbent bids. Taking the approach of the recompete being a new bid drives the level of effort and creativity required to win.

This might read as being inconsistent with what we have said previously about the recompete being different to a new bid. But one of the biggest issues customers have with failed incumbent recompetes is a lack of drive shown by some incumbents to put the same effort, creativity, and innovation into their recompetes as they would to a new bid. Some incumbents assume the win is "in the bag" because the customer already knows and likes them, there is too big a risk of change, and none of the competitors know how to deliver the contract as well as the incumbent team. The recompete is treated as a formality and it shows (in the eyes of the customer) in the lack of detail, the price, and the general lack of energy, focus, and innovation that goes into presenting the best possible solution to the customer for the future contract.

Internally, some of the symptoms (and warning signs) are:

- A lack of preparation for the recompete prior to the start of the official solicitation process.

- A more junior or smaller team allocated to the recompete than would be applied to a similar sized new bid.

- Less focus compared with a new bid on having a proper capture effort, run by an independent sales or capture professional, because there is the assumption that you already know the customer and the operational team already has all the right contacts.

- An assumption in financial forecasts that the full income from the contract will continue beyond the recompete into the next contract period and/or a very high "win probability" put against the recompete in sales or growth pipelines (or potentially not even including recompetes in sales pipelines).

- A lack of full governance processes being applied to recompetes, or more subtly, a lower level of involvement by senior management than would be the case for new bids.

- A lack of focus on fully and independently understanding the customer's future needs and drivers. Either based on an assumption that they are the same as they have been for the existing contract, or the contract team know these needs and can be a proxy source of information rather than fully researching the customer and having the capture or bid team talking directly with the key customer contacts.

- Not reading in detail the customer requirements set out in their specification, or a view these are flexible because, as the incumbent, you know how the contract really works, so can answer them in this way, rather than specifically addressing every aspect as the customer has requested.

- A solution based on the existing contract delivery model (perhaps with some changes added onto this core model) without a rigorous review of whether this is the best way to meet the new contract requirements.

- A lack of strong challenge to the solutions put forward to ensure they are the best possible in the market.

- A pricing level or structure based on the existing contract cost levels without a full investigation or challenge of whether they are the lowest possible available in the market or the most cost effective to meet the specification—or a presumption the customer will bear these higher costs as a trade off for the experience and quality levels they deliver (staffing levels and salaries are an area where this can particularly apply).

Section VIII   Run the Recompete

- An over reliance on the information gained from, and preferences of, the operational customer contacts (who are those the contract team know best) rather than a wider perspective of the needs and influence of other customer decision makers and influencers on the outcome of the recompete, such as the senior buyer or senior customer finance personnel.

- An assumption existing contract margins are acceptable for the new contract—or a reluctance to reduce these to a competitive market level as would be applied to a new bid. This can either be due to pressure to maintain the existing contract margins in the new contract, and so not have a negative impact on overall business or divisional margins, or an assumption the customer will again accept these margins for the higher quality and experience offered by the incumbent. Or even that the customer has accepted these margins to date, so will be okay with them in the next contract.

- Too much focus in the written submission on the past and how the existing contract has delivered rather than a focus on the future and how the new solution can best meet the changing needs of the customer over the coming contract period.

These assumptions can often be unconscious, rather than said out loud, and their acceptance and impact can, at first, be difficult to spot. But if you are already aware and alive to the potential for them to infect the recompete effort, and to the dangers they can represent, you will be in a better position to identify them and react. If you see any of these assumptions, actions, or omissions beginning to enter your recompete effort, you must challenge them immediately. Ask whether you would be taking this approach for a bid for new business with a new customer and make sure you drive out any presumption you are the favored bidder for the new contract. The team should be as motivated and energized (and have the same levels of adrenaline and nerves) as they would for a new bid where you are the underdog looking to overturn an entrenched and well organized competitor.

> ***What is the most important thing an incumbent can do to improve their chances of winning?***
>
> *"Read and respond to the document as though it was a new business opportunity that they were keen to grasp—this is often why they won the business the first time round!"*
>
> *Local Government, UK*

Idea 44: Review the Detail of the Published Requirements

> ### Idea Summary:
>
> **What:**
>
> Review the details of the customer's specification and instructions for the recompete. Ensure you don't assume you know better than the customer what is required. Complete all elements of the recompete as per the customer's instructions to all bidders.
>
> **Why:**
>
> A common complaint from customers is that incumbents do not follow the details of the instructions given in the procurement. This is often based on the incumbent feeling they know what the customer needs and that they can circumvent the requirements of the solicitation. However, most solicitations are evaluated as per the questions and instructions set. Not following the instructions and answering the question in full means you will lose marks in the evaluation—and potentially lose the recompete.

While this is standard practice for new bids, there can be a danger that, as the incumbent, you bring too much of your existing contract knowledge into your reading of the requirements the customer sets out in their documentation. This can happen at all stages of the process—from the initial RFI through to the detailed specifications and instructions at later stages.

Read all customer documentation with an objective mind. Don't simply put it into the context of your existing contract delivery or, if you have (as we recommended in *Idea 41*) already outlined your solution for the next contract, what you have previously put together as a solution.

While you will hopefully have had the opportunity to influence what the customer puts into their solicitation documentation earlier in the process (see *Idea 41*), they may not have taken all, or any, of your advice, so the recompete documentation may not be what you were expecting. It is unlikely to be the same as when you originally won the contract.

Answer the Specification and Questions Set by the Customer, Not the Specification You Think Is Best from Your Experience

In order to win, you must first and foremost be compliant with the instructions the customer has set out for submissions, answer the questions the customer asks during their solicitation, and meet the specification they have set out. The

Section VIII Run the Recompete

recompete team may be put under pressure from the contract team to ignore elements of the specification. The contract team might argue the customer solicitation team has not properly interpreted the needs that the "real" customer has (typically, this means in these arguments the operational customer contacts). This may or may not be true. However, the evaluation process and thus the winner of the recompete will be based on answering the questions and specifications as they are set in the solicitation documentation. These are the questions you will be marked on in the evaluation and therefore the ones you must answer.

If there is a genuine case where you believe the customer solicitation team has misinterpreted the reality of the contract, you still have some opportunity to challenge this through official questions to the customer during the process (see *Idea 56*). You might even consider putting in a variant bid alongside your compliant bid, if this is allowed (see *Idea 53*). However, your compliant bid should be just that: compliant with the specifications and questions set out in the customer's documentation.

Even if your contract is presently delivering well and you have produced a fantastic new solution for the next contract period, you now need to review this against the customer's written requirements in the recompete. If the customer's requirements are different, it's your delivery and solution that must change to fit what is being asked for in the procurement.

Understand the Changes the Customer Has Made for the Next Contract

It's rare for the customer to ask for exactly the same in the recompete as they did the last time they solicited the contract. The changes can be seemingly small, or they could be very significant. In *Idea 19: Keep Your Contract Up to Date*, we spoke about keeping track during the contract of changes in the customer's environment, strategy and needs, and wherever possible, anticipating or reacting to these in how you deliver your contract to keep pace with these changes. In *Idea 33: Understand the Customer's Next Contract*, we set out how, during the recompete preparation stage, you should thoroughly review the likely changes the customer would make to the next contract in the recompete and how to prepare for these changes. And in *Idea 42: Prepare the Contract*, we advised you to spend time, before the official recompete start, to make appropriate changes to the contract delivery to better align and prepare yourself and the customer for some of the changes you anticipate being asked for in the recompete.

We set out how the changes the customer could make to fit with their future needs might be dramatic, for instance:

- Combining different contracts into one.
- Expanding the geographical spread of the contract to cover significantly wider areas regionally, nationally, or even internationally.

- Broadening the scope of the contract to include a range of disciplines not previously included.

All of these could mean you may need to partner with other companies to be able to address the wider scope of the new contract. It could also mean you will face a completely new set of competitors in the recompete—from different geographical regions, from different core disciplines or sectors, or much larger competitors attracted by the increased size and breadth of the new contract. Some of these could already be incumbents with the customer in the wider areas now added to "your" contract.

Alternatively (or additionally), the customer could change the specification of the services they want, how the contract is measured, the basis on which you are paid, or the evaluation weighting of different aspects of the service (price, for instance, becoming more important than quality). Any and all of these could completely change the solution that is required to deliver the new contract—and to win the recompete.

Hopefully, your preparations will have alerted you to what these changes will be (and perhaps enabled you to influence them). But only once the solicitation documents have been published can you be sure of the changes the customer is actually seeking.

As you read through the requirements, list out each of the changes being asked for so you are clear on each of them individually as well as seeing the total set of changes. This will be a useful checklist later when you are reviewing your response to make sure you have addressed all the changes. It will also, by collating the total set of changes, give you a sense of the direction the customer is driving towards in their solicitation.

Remember though, we are not implying that by drawing up this list of changes, you should be putting in a bid that is essentially the same as your existing delivery plus the changes you have identified in the recompete specification and documents. Even where the customer's requirement has not changed, you should still be looking at new, innovative, best value, and lower cost ways of delivering all elements of the contract.

What do you expect of an incumbent that is different to new bidders?

"Since the incumbents have what is effectively 'insider' information, I expect a very precise and accurate bid on exactly what has been requested. In addition I expect value added additions and deletions to the job specifications."

Private Sector, USA

Idea 45: Don't Assume the Customer Knows You

> **Idea Summary:**
>
> **What:**
>
> Always answer all questions in full. Never assume the customer's existing knowledge of you will be taken into account in marking the recompete or that the customer will use their knowledge to fill in gaps in your written proposal
>
> **Why:**
>
> Even if your direct customer contacts know you and your capabilities in depth, other people will also be evaluating the recompete. Most evaluation processes only allow customers to give marks for what is written in the proposal—not use their existing knowledge to supplement these answers and marks. In addition, making assumptions about the customer's knowledge of you gives the impression of arrogance or complacency, which will also work against you in the recompete decision.

One of the common mistakes incumbents make in their recompetes is to assume the customer knows them and will "fill in the gaps" of their submission if they do not fully explain their solution. This can take a number of forms:

- In the early stages of the process (such as the RFI), or when the customer asks for evidence of experience in the type of work being procured in the recompete, not telling the customer all the details of how you have delivered the contract and your achievements.

- Assuming the customer already knows your staff and their capabilities, and therefore not including resumés, etc., in the submission because "the customer already has them."

- Not describing in sufficient detail the methods, management team structure, or other processes that will form part of your solution because "the customer already knows these things, as it is how we are delivering already."

The same applies to all other elements of the contract or specification the customer has requested. Even if you know the customer has a copy of one of your quality accreditations on the wall of the office where the recompete is being evaluated, if you don't include a copy in your official submission, they won't be able to give you the marks for it.

> **Example:**
>
> *The U.S. Government Accountability Office (GAO) reviews and adjudicates on bid protests by contractors unhappy with contract award decisions made by federal and some other U.S. government organizations.*
>
> *Case 1: In June 2007, the GAO denied a protest by HealthStar VA, PLLC regarding the loss of their contract at recompete to provide primary health care for assigned veteran patients.*
>
> *In summary, HealthStar protested against two areas of their bid that had been marked as having significant weaknesses by the customer evaluation team: a failure to adequately address the services to be provided for patient-focused care and a failure to provide proof of licensing of nursing staff and competency of support staff.*
>
> *HealthStar claimed that its proposal "was not evaluated in a reasonable manner because the agency should have considered its knowledge of its incumbent contract performance in evaluating these areas."*
>
> *The GAO stated in their denial of the protest that: "An offeror's technical evaluation is dependent upon the information furnished; there is no legal basis for favoring a firm with presumptions on the basis of its incumbent status. It is the offeror's burden to submit an adequately written proposal; an offeror, including an incumbent contractor, must furnish, within its proposal, all information that was requested or necessary to demonstrate its capabilities in response to the solicitation."*
>
> *This type of protest isn't an isolated case:*
>
> *Case 2: In May 2012, the GAO published their decision regarding a protest by ASPEC Engineering regarding the loss of their contract at recompete to another supplier. The company protested the rejection of its proposal as technically unacceptable. The GAO, in their write up of the decision, go into some detail of the specifics of what was written in the proposal, but a note towards the end of the paper is telling:*
>
> *"ASPEC generally responds to its unacceptable evaluation by suggesting that the agency should have known it had the necessary capability to perform the contract based on its incumbent performance of the waste water treatment plant contract. ASPEC's view that the agency was required to recognize ASPEC's incumbency as providing an adequate substitute for including required information in its proposal is unpersuasive; an offeror must submit an initial proposal that is adequately written and affirmatively states its merits, or run the risk of having its proposal rejected…where the proposal omits or provides inadequate information addressing fundamental factors."*
>
> *The GAO denied ASPEC's protest.*

Get an Independent Review

When you are writing your submission, always make sure you have included all the detail asked for by the customer and don't make any assumptions of the customer's knowledge of you as a business, or particularly your capabilities and performance, or the infrastructure or staff you already have in place on the contract.

Include a bidder or capture expert who is experienced in answering bid questions and specifications in the reviews of your written submissions, but who does not know your contract. Make sure they read the answers you have given with an objective mind and with a particular focus on checking that you have fully answered all the questions set as you would for a new business bid.

Be Professional in Presentations

The assumption of familiarity can also take other forms. If the customer asks for formal presentations as part of the solicitation process, don't assume you can be informal because you know the customer participants in the presentation. Take the presentation as seriously as you would with a customer you did not know.

Act professionally at all times during the presentation. Even if you have just had an informal meeting with the customer on a matter to do with the existing contract and are on very good terms with them, you should not take this informality into the presentation. In-jokes or informal asides should be avoided, even if all those present know each other well. Particularly if some of the customer representatives do not know you well, being overly familiar with the customer representatives you do know could embarrass them in front of their colleagues and give the impression they are not going to be objective in their evaluation and decision of the best supplier for their organization.

While this might make the presentation feel slightly stilted, the customer will usually appreciate that you are making no presumptions and are taking the process and the recompete as a whole seriously rather than as a foregone conclusion you will win.

What aspects of incumbents' proposals have been particularly poor?

"Often they assume we know all about them and put in a rather poor response."

State Government

Idea 46: Use the Information You Have Gathered

> **Idea Summary:**
>
> **What:**
>
> Collate and analyze all the information you have gathered during the contract and recompete preparation phases to use in your proposal. Format the information to enable its best use and review the information for ways you can use it to answer customer questions and confirm your solution.
>
> **Why:**
>
> As the incumbent, you should have the most relevant and detailed information about the contract and the customer. Taking time to collate, analyze, format, and decide where best to use this information in your recompete will ensure you can make the most of it to show you understand the contract and the customer's needs. Focusing your information to best support your solution gives it credence and substantiates the benefits you are pushing.

Throughout the earlier sections of the contract lifecycle, we have emphasized the need to gather relevant information ready for your recompete. Now you can put this information to use. There will be different types of information you will (or should) have:

- Information about how you have run the existing contract:

  - How the original contract was won and the transition process you undertook to implement your solution (see *Idea 2*).

  - Information on your performance over the whole period of the existing contract (see *Ideas 11, 12,* and *13*).

  - Information on improvements you have made, added value you have delivered, innovations you have implemented, and the positive impact of these on the customer's own organization and performance (see *Ideas 15, 16,* and *17*).

  - Customer, end user, and other stakeholder satisfaction data for the previous contract period (see *Idea 14*).

  - Monthly, quarterly, or annual reports to the customer on how the contract has progressed (see *Idea 18*).

- Customer commendations and positive quotes from end users or other stakeholders.
- Any issues you have had and how you have resolved them (see *Idea 20*).

▪ The processes you have put in place on the contract, for instance:
- Risk management process (see *Idea 9* and *10*).
- Continuous improvement process (see *Idea 16*).
- Reporting process (see *Idea 18*).
- Customer satisfaction process (see *Ideas 14* and *32*).
- Change process (see *Idea 21*).

And how you have used all these processes to deliver benefits to the customer.

▪ Information about the contract:
- The original contract.
- Volumes of work.
- Variations in volumes of work.
- Numbers and types of end users.
- KPIs.

▪ Information about the customer to date (which you should have captured during your contract):
- Their economic, political, and legal environment and the drivers this has placed on them.
- Their changing goals and strategies over the contract period.
- Their needs and how these have changed.
- The key contacts and decision makers within the customer.
- Their views on you and the contract.

▪ Information about the customer moving forward (which you should have captured during your recompete preparation stage):
- The future drivers the customer faces.
- Their goals, strategies, and priorities going forward.

- Their needs for the next contract.
- The key decision makers and influencers in the customer organization and their needs and preferences.
- How all these impact the procurement and specification of the recompete.

■ Information about your competitors.

Review the list to see if there are any significant gaps in the information you have. If there are gaps, you now have little time to fill them, but you should still make the attempt.

Using Information about Your Performance on the Existing Contract

Once you have gathered together the data of how you have performed on the contract and the other good things you have delivered (such as added value, alignment with customer processes, etc.), decide on the best ways to use this data in your recompete effort.

Hopefully, you will have made your customer (at least the operational customer) aware, through regular reporting and through annual contract reports, of all the positive work you have delivered as the information has become available during the contract. Ideally, you do not want to be presenting this sort of information to your customer for the first time in your recompete. Not only will you have wasted the opportunity during the contract to use the information to build a positive view of you during the contract, there is a danger that if you present previously unknown information to the customer at the recompete, they could be skeptical as to its accuracy.

Your main tasks now are to:

■ Turn your data into the best format to present it to the customer during the recompete—in such a way that it is most impactful, clear, and positive.

■ Decide how and where you will use the information to best effect.

Formatting Your Information from the Existing Contract

The two tasks are, of course, related. But it is worth formatting the data you have first; you can always reformat it again later if you need to illustrate a particular point. There are potentially a lot of advantages and learning you can gain from focusing some effort on this early, for instance:

Pull data together for the whole contract period.

The customer may only have seen monthly or quarterly information. If you can show, in one place, information for the whole of the contract (say, four years), the trends (hopefully improvements) can become much more obvious. You can also look at the data for the whole contract and pull out more impactful facts from it. For instance:

- What is the total improvement in performance? You may have improved performance by 3% per year on the contract, but this could add up to over 12% over a four-year contract.

- Even if performance was high to start, are there ways of presenting it that give a more impactful view? For instance if performance started at 92% and went up to 96%, does this mean you improved performance by 4%—or that you halved your failure rate (from 8% to 4%)? Which is the more impactful and relevant message for the customer? **NB** Don't get too tricky with the statistics or your information may lose credibility; but taking a different perspective can often bring the information to life in a positive way.

- What is the total volume of work, or number of end users, etc., to whom you have delivered over the contract? Totaling up these numbers can give impressive figures.

Put the information into different formats.

If you have numerical information, put it into various chart formats and see which best illustrate the information. Turning a set of data in a spreadsheet into a graph, histogram, or pie chart can make it much more accessible to the customer, save space, and draw out key trends more clearly than a set of numbers. Alternatively, taking numbers from different charts and putting them together in numerical format can also help you analyze the data in more ways.

Similarly, if you have information on processes in written format (for instance, a continuous improvement process or the workflow for a part of your contract delivery, which may have been developed over the period of the contract), turning this into a diagram can also help make it clearer to the customer, again save space and, if done professionally, give it a greater sense of credibility, order, or premeditated design.

Compare different sets of information for links.

As you explore the data you have gathered, look for potential links and trends between different sets of information. For instance, is there a cyclical trend to volume demand that has changed over time? You would expect the contract team to have spotted this during the contract, but in the day-to-day rush to deliver, these longer term trends can be lost. If there are trends, what are the causes? Are there other sets of information that suggest a cause or at least a link? It might be that the data itself doesn't tell you. But you now have the opportunity to ask the contract team to test what the reasons might be and understand what the implications could be for your solution for the next contract period.

Compare data on volumes, costs, and performance. Have volumes risen faster than costs (and particularly price to the customer)? If so, does this illustrate improved efficiency and value to the customer? Have you managed to maintain performance even when volumes have increased significantly or have been increasingly variable? Again, does this illustrate improving value for money and flexibility?

If you find dips in performance over the period of the contract, can you find information showing the causes of these dips? Perhaps, again, they relate to periods of exceptionally high volumes or demand variation. Can this be used to illustrate the reasons for these dips? More importantly, if the variations or peaks can be predicted and are likely to continue into the next contract, can you redesign your solution to ensure performance is maintained during these peaks (particularly if you can do so without increasing costs) in the future—and use the past information to show why this redesign has been done and the benefits it will deliver?

Alternatively, if the information shows your costs do not drop off in periods of low demand, does this mean you have been wasting money? Again, could you redesign your processes or staffing to make your costs more flexible to these dips and so reduce your cost and price? Hopefully, much of this analysis will already have been done during the solution design in the recompete preparation stage (see *Idea 40*), but if this wasn't done, it's not too late to react now.

Using Your Information from the Existing Contract to Best Effect

As you explore and reformat your data into usable information, you should always be looking at how you can use it to best effect:

- Which customer questions does the information help answer?

- How best to use the information to illustrate your role as an excellent partner to the customer over the previous contract period?

- How does the information explain the reasoning behind aspects of your new solution and why it is the best solution for the customer?

- What aspects of the customer's requirements or contract does the information illustrate that competitors may not have taken into account?

As you progress through the different stages of the procurement, you should use the information you have in different ways.

At the early stages, for instance the RFI, the customer is seeking to find a short-list of bidders with the qualifications, experience, and capabilities they need, but are not asking about the final solution you are proposing. Here you can use the information you have gathered about your performance on the contract to illustrate your superior experience, and it can be oriented toward showing how you have performed over the past contract.

However, as you reach the latter stages of the procurement process, the customer will be more focused on the solution you are proposing for the next contract period. Now your use of information about your performance on the existing contract needs to change. Only use information about the existing contract and your past performance to illustrate your new solution and the changed requirements of the next contract. The customer is interested in how you will deliver for them in the next contract; simply telling them how well you have delivered in the last contract will not gain you marks and could work against you, as the customer may feel you are simply repeating your existing contract rather than putting in place a new solution for the future. We will go into more detail about this in *Idea 48*.

Using Information about Your Customer's Future Needs

One of the benefits you have as the incumbent is your detailed knowledge about the customer: their environment, drivers, strategies, and needs. Over the period of the existing contract, you should have been using this information to focus your delivery, improvements, added value, and innovation on the areas that are strategically most important to the customer (see, for instance, *Ideas 15, 16, and 17*) and will have been adapting your contract to keep pace with these needs as they have changed (see *Ideas 19 and 23*). During your recompete preparation, you should have focused on understanding the customer's future drivers and strategies (see *Idea 33*) and how these will impact their needs for the contract. The solution you prepared (see *Idea 40*) should reflect these future needs, rather than simply assuming that the customer's past requirements will continue through the next contract. Now you can use this information in your submission to show the customer you understand their business: how your solution is designed to deliver in line with these future needs, and the benefits this will bring in helping the customer meet their wider strategies.

Make sure you link each element of your solution to the customer's future strategies and needs. Show how your solution is the best route to achieving these needs. The customer expects you, as the incumbent, to understand them better than the competition—don't disappoint them.

What are the primary reasons incumbents lose recompetes?

"*They do not provide a compelling service offer. They lack innovation and ideas. They do not demonstrate adequate desire to work for the client.*"

Private Sector, UK

Idea 47: Write from the Customer's Perspective

> **Idea Summary:**
>
> **What:**
>
> Make sure you focus your proposal, and how you write, on the customer and their needs rather than yourself and your business.
>
> **Why:**
>
> As the incumbent, you should have the best information and insight into the customer and their strategic and specific needs. Making the most of this advantage by constantly focusing your writing on the customer's perspective will show you are the most customer-focused of those bidding.

This is a standard requirement for any bid, but as the incumbent, it is particularly important for you to be very focused on writing your recompete submission with the customer's perspective at the very core of everything. The knowledge you have built up over the contract and during the recompete preparation period should shine through in your solution (operationally, financially, and commercially) but also in all aspects of how you present and explain your proposal. For instance:

- How you prove the solution fits with the customer's strategic needs.

- The examples you use to illustrate how each aspect of your solution is deliverable to the customer.

- The appropriateness of the benefits your solution has to your customer's key needs.

- Your writing style.

To ensure this is the case, make sure you focus on the customer at every stage of your bid development and review process. For example:

Win Themes and Discriminators

We will cover these in more detail in *Idea 50*, but in summary: as the incumbent, your win themes and discriminators should be more tightly aligned to the customer's real needs than will those of your competitors, because you should understand these needs better. Your win themes and discriminators should not just be variations on "we've done this for a long time, so know what we are doing." They should be real benefits the customer can identify from your solution and how you show it fits with their needs—and which are demonstrably able to be put into operation.

Storyboards

If you use storyboards as part of your proposal writing process, make sure they focus on the customer and their needs first, not on your history of performance or the fact you are already delivering the contract. Your experience should be used to help prove how and why your solution best meets the customer's needs. Simply stating that you have been delivering the service is not, in itself, evidence. Pick out real links between the solution you are proposing and examples of how your experience proves its appropriateness to best meeting the customer's requirement and your future ability to deliver. And don't rely only on your experience as evidence. Seek out and use appropriate evidence from other contracts, industry best practice, research reports, product performance data, etc. (always related to the customer's needs); your competitors will be using this type of information, just as you would on a new bid. Your experience with the customer should be additional to all these types of evidence, not used instead of them.

Executive Summary

Your executive summary should focus particularly on the customer's perspective and their needs. Bidders are always advised not to start their executive summaries with a description of their company, but with a description of the customer's key needs and how your solution meets these needs. The same applies to you, as the incumbent. If your executive summary starts with a statement of your excellent delivery of the contract to date or your experience of working with the customer, change it. Start with your understanding of the customer's needs. While you can say this understanding is enhanced by your knowledge of the customer from your long association with them through the existing contract, do so subtly.

Ultimately, if you have truly used your experience and understanding from your work and relationships with the customer, the accuracy and insight this brings to your description of their needs should make them so powerful, they stand above the competitor's equivalent statements by themselves without having to use your incumbency as an explanation for your insight.

As you work through your executive summary, you should keep this in mind: are you touting your incumbency anywhere as a benefit in itself? If so, start rewriting. The benefits you use should be specific aspects of your solution that fit a key customer requirement. Your incumbency, if you use it, should be relegated to the basis of a specific piece of evidence from your delivery or experience that is used to validate the benefit of your solution.

Reviews

As you review your proposal, ensure you have focused on the customer more than your business or your incumbency. Some simple tests will help:

- How many times have you mentioned your company compared with the customer? If you haven't mentioned the customer more often than your business, you are in danger of writing from your perspective rather than the customer's.

- How many sections or paragraphs start with an explanation or mention of your incumbency or experience from the existing contract? Go through each you identify and reword or reorganize it to start with the customer. Then use specific aspects of your incumbency as evidence of how your solution will meet their needs.

- Each time you mention your incumbency or experience, is this used as a benefit in itself? If so, rewrite. Find a specific aspect of your incumbency or experience that is actually the benefit (e.g. a particular performance level from a KPI, a process you have used such as continuous improvement, a piece of infrastructure you already have in place) and use this instead. If you can't find one, question whether the customer will see just the fact of your incumbency, without deeper evidence, as relevant to the point you are trying to make.

- For every time you mention your incumbency, is that mention linked to a specific customer requirement or need? If not, see if you can link it; if you can't, look carefully at what referring to your incumbency actually adds to the point you are making.

What do you expect of an incumbent that is different from new bidders?

"Understand the new requirement and not assume 'Business as Usual.'"

UK

Idea 48: Be Future Oriented

> **Idea Summary:**
>
> **What:**
>
> As you design your solution and write your proposal, always focus on the future, the customer's future needs, and the next contract period. Don't get drawn into too much focus on the present and the past.
>
> **Why:**
>
> Incumbents can tend to focus on the past and the existing contract, rather than the next contract period. By proactively focusing on the future and the next contract, you avoid this problem. It also means you focus past performance and achievements on how they will help the customer in the future and support your next contract's delivery—not just as evidence of how you have performed in the past.

There can be a great temptation, as the incumbent, to focus your proposal on the benefits you have delivered to the customer in the existing contract. This can take a number of forms, some of which we have mentioned in other ideas, but are worth revisiting in this context:

- Your solution is overly based on your existing contract delivery model, or on the last customer procurement, not this one.

- Your reading of the customer's requirements are influenced by your experience of, and thinking about, the existing contract.

- You overuse your incumbency in your proposal (or internally overestimate your incumbent advantage) as a reason the customer should choose you as the winner of the recompete.

- You base your solution, thinking about the customer's needs, and writing of the proposal on the customer's needs now or in the past rather than their needs in the future.

- You underestimate the changes the customer has asked for, or faces in the next period, in thinking about how you will change your ways of working and in rethinking your solution.

One of the biggest criticisms of incumbents made by procurement staff is that they tend to treat the recompete and proposal simply as "Business as Usual"—the incumbent is seen as not putting in the effort to properly focus on the changes the customer faces over the next contract period and simply repeats in their bid the solution that was appropriate for the past contract period.

Don't make this mistake in your recompete. Make sure every aspect of your recompete is focused on the future contract, not on the existing one or the last procurement. Throughout your proposal process, always check and recheck that:

- Your solution is based on meeting the strategic needs of the customer in the next contract period, not those they had in the last one—e.g., it is innovative, based on a ground up reassessment of the customer's needs for the future (see *Idea 38: Create a Green Field Solution*), and is not simply an adaptation or repeat of your existing contract model or delivery.

- You are putting your solution and answers together to meet the requirements and specifications set out in this procurement, not how you delivered the existing contract.

- The examples and evidence you use to illustrate your solution, and why it is the best way to meet your customer's needs, are relevant to the new solution and not simply evidence of how you have been delivering in the past.

- How you write your solution is focused on the future and not the present or the past. A simple check here is to review each mention of your existing or past contract in your solution—is it being used to effectively illustrate a future oriented part of your solution? If not, question why it is being used at all.

Let's take contrasting examples of use of past contract delivery:

Past performance.

Quoting past performance levels, no matter how good these levels were, will have limited benefit in illustrating your future performance. Unless you can show how you achieved these performance levels, the relevance of this particular type of performance to the customer's key future needs and your new contract, and how the methods you used to achieve this performance are to be continued or adapted to fit your new solution, they will continue to be about the past, not the future.

Key processes.

The processes you used to deliver aspects of your contract can have more impact if they are again related to the new contract, and therefore the future. For instance, if you used a continuous improvement process in your last contract and propose to do so in the next contract, this may give the customer some confidence. However only if:

- You can clearly describe how your continuous improvement process worked.

- You can show several quantified examples of the improvements delivered using this process.

Section VIII   Run the Recompete

- The examples you use are relevant to the customer's future needs.

- You can describe clearly how you will adapt the process, if needed, to better fit with future requirements.

As we have said in other ideas (for example *Idea 43*: *Approach the Bid As if it is a New Bid* and *Idea 47: Write from the Customer's Perspective),* the customer may be making significant changes to their requirements in the recompete, or they may appear to be making very few changes. Even if the customer appears to be making few changes to their specification at the recompete compared to the existing contract, it doesn't mean you should automatically repeat the solution for the existing contract or focus only on your existing delivery in how you write your proposal. Even in the least dynamic of marketplaces, things will have changed over the period of the last contract and will change more over the next contract timeframe.

Your competitors will not be putting in their bids the same solution they put in the last time around. They will be adding new approaches, innovations, more efficient processes, and lower costs (and you may also be facing new competitors, too). If your solution is the same as you proposed in your last bid (even though it was successful then), you will have fallen behind the market. Base your new solution on the next contract and how you can deliver that in the best way possible, and focus your proposal writing on that benefits you will deliver in the future (see more in *Idea 50*). Use your incumbency intelligently to illustrate how you will deliver well in the future, but innovate and improve to be the best solution for your customer in the future. If your solution is focused on what has worked in the past and not what will work best in the future, you risk losing the opportunity to deliver for your customer in the future.

> **Example:**
>
> *The following decision by the U.S. Government Accountability Office (GAO) illustrates the dangers of not putting forward an innovative solution:*
>
> *In October 2012, the GAO published its decision regarding a protest by Integrated Science Solutions Inc. (ISSi) relating to their loss of a recompete for safety, environmental and medical support services to NASA.*
>
> *Amongst a number of challenges to the customer decision, ISSi protested that NASA did not award it the highest evaluation score for its answer to a case study forming part of the RFP, but scored it at the same level as the eventual recompete winner. The GAO states "ISSi contends that the technical requirements in the statement of work were nearly identical to the technical requirements of the contract ISSi has been performing, so that its proposal of its incumbent approach demonstrated its proven ability to comply with the applicable regulations and demonstrated a clear understanding of the technical requirements."*

However the GAO notes that, while the eventual winner had in its answer proposed cost effective and innovative approaches, "In contrast, the agency notes that, although ISSi's response to the case study was appropriate, reasonable, and effective for all of the required elements, it did not propose anything unique or innovative that warranted a finding of a strength... Further, the agency states that its evaluation was based on its review of the offerors' proposals, and not upon an offeror's performance as the incumbent contractor."

Based on this and the GAOs rejection of ISSi's other complaints, the protest was rejected.

What are the primary reasons incumbents lose recompetes?
"Lazy. Attitudes that reflect arrogance and a misbelief that the client is never going to change because it is too much of a hassle."

Private Sector, Australia

Idea 49: Admit Mistakes

Idea Summary:

What:

If you have had issues on the contract, don't try to cover them up in the proposal. Show that they were resolved and what you have learned from them and present evidence of this learning in your new solution and proposal.

Why:

Your customer will know of any performance problems or issues you have had on the contract. They will expect you to be honest about these in your proposal. By showing you resolved these issues, what you learned, and how this has informed your solution, you illustrate your flexibility, responsiveness, and understanding of the risks involved in the contract—and how your solution takes these into account when your competitors' may not.

Not everything on your existing contract will have gone totally to plan. There may have been performance levels you failed to meet at times during the contract. There may have been an issue or event that interrupted service at some point. You may have had to change certain members of staff. In more extreme cases, you may have misunderstood the requirements of the customer in your original bid, failed to properly implement the contract, or generally performed poorly in the early period of the contract. You may have mispriced the contract and spent the first months or even years of the contract "getting well," renegotiating with the customer to get back into profit.

You might think the customer has forgotten about these problems. They haven't. You also have to assume your competitors will have done enough research to know all about any issues you have faced and are preparing to exploit them in their own bids.

If you brazenly ignore any issues you have had on the contract—pretending they have not happened and not mentioning them in your recompete—then your proposal will come across either as arrogant, misinformed, or even deluded. Any good words or examples you use of excellent performance will potentially be seen as selective and your solution and promises for the next contract will lose credibility. You will put yourself open to the attacks of your competitors, who will point out the issues you faced, the impacts these had on the customer, and how they (your competitors) will ensure these are not repeated.

We covered resolving problems quickly and completely during your delivery of the contract in *Idea 20*. And during your recompete preparations, you will hopefully have gained a clear and honest understanding of the views your stakeholders have of you (*Idea 32*) and resolved any outstanding contract issues (*Idea 36*).

Hopefully, you will have been able to fix any issues during the contract. If you have, you can turn what might seem a negative to be avoided into an advantage.

Ensure You Have Collected Information about Mistakes

As part of your recompete preparations, you should have collected from the contract team and customer contacts information about any past (or present) issues on the contract. Make sure you have gone through this effort thoroughly, as there will be a natural reluctance to talk about negative aspects of the contract from the team. Some problems may have happened earlier in the contract, and if the contract team has changed over time, these may not have been recalled by the existing team (though they may be by the customer).

As you enter the recompete management and writing phase, review these issues and check again that there are none unaccounted for, as these might leave you open to attack from competitors or embarrassment in front of the customer.

The advice given in the ideas mentioned above has been to make sure any issues are quickly resolved and a thorough lessons-learned process undertaken and recorded. Review these and, if necessary, collate them into summaries that allow you to use them in the recompete.

Your summary should include:

- What the issue was.

- The impact on the operation of the contract and on the customer.

- Any quantitative data that supports this (reduction in performance levels over what time period, etc.).

- The cause of the issue. Again, be honest with yourself here; the cause may have been an external event or even the customer, but if it was your own delivery at fault, be open about this.

- How you resolved the issue (again, if available, include quantitative data—for instance investment in the resolution, recovery of performance levels).

- The lessons learned from the issue and its resolution.

- The activities or safeguards put in place to prevent the issue from happening or impacting the contract performance again.

You should now have a useful set of case studies you can use appropriately in your recompete.

Make Sure Your New Solution Takes Account of Previous Issues

If your solution is designed without an understanding of the potential pitfalls from the last contract, it may not take into account the lessons you have learned and could be susceptible to repeating the problems of the past. Make sure your solution takes these previous issues into account, so you can be confident they won't be repeated; or if they are unavoidable, that your risk management processes have mitigation actions in place to reduce their impact.

Decide How Best to Use the Lessons You Have Learned in Your Recompete

Almost no contract runs its full course without any issues at all. Customers are fully aware of this; they face their own internal issues as well. Most customers will want to know the contractor they choose has the approach and flexibility to react to and solve problems quickly, openly and effectively. With your lessons-learned profiles, you have real examples you can use to show you are that type of organization. This is another positive reason for not ignoring any mistakes you have made. Work through your proposal and decide where you can best use the evidence you have in hand to show the customer you have used your experience to design a better solution, and where you can prove, through evidence, that in the next contract, you are able and willing to solve problems and learn from them if (when) they occur.

Section VIII Run the Recompete

Use the Lessons You Have Leaned to "Ghost" Your Competition

We said earlier that you should assume your competitors know of any issues you have had on the contract and will be using them to attack you. Use the lessons you have learned about the problems that can occur on the contract and your success in resolving and preventing them to turn this attack back onto your competition. While your competitors may have gained some insight into your previous problems, only you are likely to be in a position to understand them thoroughly. Use these lessons to point out the potential issues and risks the contract and its environment present and the impact these could have on contract delivery and the customer—and how you have taken these into account in your solution. The question this should raise in the customer's mind will be whether your competitors' solutions have also taken these potential pitfalls into account. If they haven't, the credibility of their solutions will suffer (and potentially the credibility of their price, if it is not seen to take account of the risks you have pointed out). We will cover in more detail how to emphasize this benefit in *Idea 51: Become the Benchmark Proposal*). For now, two points are most relevant:

- Be more subtle than simply asking in your proposal whether the competition has taken this into account. As with most aspects of your proposal, show is more effective than tell. Rather than simply telling the customer you have taken account of previous issues on the contract in your solution, show the customer through proven case studies what the problems could be, how they have occurred in the previous contract, how you resolved them, and how your new solution reduces (or prevents) their likelihood and impact in the future.

- Focus on issues that are relevant to the next contract period (the future) rather than the existing one (the past). While problems relevant to the existing contract could be used to show your flexibility (although even here, those relevant to the next contract are preferable), only those that are relevant to what the customer is asking for and the circumstances of the next contract are of use to ghost your competitors.

What do you expect of an incumbent that is different from new bidders?

"*Insider knowledge, no steep learning curve, lessons learned, suggestions for improvement.*"

Private Sector, Australia

Idea 50: Discriminators, Differentiators, Benefits, and Win Themes

> ### Idea Summary:
>
> **What:**
>
> Understand the difference between discriminators, differentiators, benefits, and win themes. Use them carefully in your recompete. As the incumbent, avoid the mistakes of having too much emphasis on your past performance as evidence of future performance or using your incumbency as a benefit or discriminator in itself. Check you have enough new discriminators rather than relying on your existing or past performance or solution.
>
> **Why:**
>
> Clearly understanding the customer's needs and how your solution meets these better than the competition is vital to being able to write a compelling proposal. There can be a tendency for incumbents to focus too much on past performance and the existing contract in deciding and pushing what discriminators and benefits they deliver to the customer. Focusing clearly on what your discriminators are, testing them against your customer's future needs, and ensuring you are not leaning on benefits of the past will avoid this dangerous tendency.

The use of Discriminators, Differentiators, Benefits, and Win Themes are standard practice for most bids for new business and just as relevant for recompetes. The processes recommended in the wider bid development literature for identifying, prioritizing, and writing your discriminators, win themes, etc., also apply equally to recompetes.

However, there are a number of checks incumbents should add to these processes when running a recompete. For clarity, let's outline what each of these terms means. The exact definitions vary in detail, depending on which book or consultancy you are dealing with, and if you have your own definitions, do use these. However, in general (and how we will use them in this idea), the meanings usually equate to the following:

Discriminators: Elements of your solution or overall offering that meet a key customer requirement or need differently (preferably better) than any of your competitors.'

Section VIII Run the Recompete

Differentiators: For our purposes, we will describe a differentiator as a part of your solution that is different from the competition. However, it is not necessarily related to an important need of the customer—if it is, it becomes a discriminator.

Benefit: The delivery of a key customer need. The benefit an aspect of your solution delivers and how it does so should ideally be quantified. However, a benefit is not necessarily unique to your solution—your competitors could be delivering the same benefit to the customer (albeit, perhaps through a different route or method).

Feature: An aspect of your solution or your business. However, it may not deliver a key benefit to the customer and equally may not be unique to your solution.

Win Themes: Win themes are broader. They are the route you use to link your discriminators to the relevant customer need and describe and show evidence of how they will deliver the relevant important customer requirement. Your proposal most likely only has a few key win themes. Your task in the proposal is to ensure that your win themes are clear to the customer and written (as well as presented and discussed with key customer contacts) consistently throughout your submission, so each section of your proposal or interaction with the customer reinforces the message, rather than confuses with inconsistent interpretations what your main win themes are and why they are relevant to the customer. In addition to your main overarching win themes, you may have sub or section win themes (sometimes just called themes) which apply to particular parts of your proposal and would be used to give clarity of how each part of your solution meets the relevant customer need. These might just be used in a particular answer to one customer question.

We sometimes represent these in a matrix format:

Figure VIII.2   Discriminator Matrix

Delivers a key customer requirement	Benefit	Discriminator
Does not necessarily deliver a key customer requirement	Feature	Differentiator
	Is not necessarily different to competitors' offerings	Is different from (preferably better than) competitors' offerings

The most powerful and decisive in helping you win your recompete is the discriminator. If you can develop discriminators for your solution, you will be delivering to your customer's most important needs better than your competitors. Benefits, of course, should not be ignored; even if your competitors are also offering the same benefit, not to emphasize that you, too, offer this would lose you marks in any evaluation.

We should, of course, emphasize that all of the above depend entirely on your customer's perception. What, in your view, may be a discriminator because you believe it meets an important customer need may merely be, to the customer, a differentiator if they do not, in fact, see the need as important—or you have not persuaded them how the aspect of your solution in question meets their need.

The key in developing your solution and in writing your proposal is to clearly understand what the most important needs are for the customer. Your experience of delivering the existing contract, the relationships you have built with your customer, your recompete preparation, and capture effort should have given you a strong understanding of these needs and the relative priorities between them (see also *Idea 41*).

Your analysis of the competition (and the customer's perception of them and their offerings) should help you understand what their own offerings are and whether they meet the customer's key needs in different (or perhaps even superior) ways to your own.

Dangers for You as the Incumbent

When we have worked with recompete teams, particularly in the early stages of their recompete preparation, we often see perceptions of discriminators, etc., which, if they follow through to the final recompete, could cause real problems. While these perceptions are all related, they typically take three forms:

1. A misperception of what the customer's most important needs are.

2. A tendency to focus on the building the new solution and on writing the proposal on needs (and therefore benefits and discriminators) from the existing contract, rather than those going forward.

3. A tendency to use (or more accurately, misuse) incumbency as a general discriminator without specifying what aspects of the incumbency are relevant and why they benefit the customer, when, in fact, they are sometimes neither relevant nor of benefit going forward—in short, not using their incumbency intelligently.

A good recompete preparation phase will often help reduce these dangers. However, if the independent members of the recompete team are brought into the recompete effort too late, or if the contract lead is particularly dominant (especially compared to the capture lead—or even more so if no independent capture lead is used), the necessary challenge to early assumptions is often not made, is too weak, and/or is overruled. This can lead to these flawed or distorted views flowing through into the final recompete submission and a subsequent loss of the contract.

Let's briefly look at these potential traps:

Misperception of the customer's most important needs.

Because the contract team has been fully absorbed in running and delivering the contract for the past few years, building relationships with the direct (usually operational) managers within the customer they deal with on a regular basis, there can be a natural urge to focus on a specific set of elements as key to the customer:

- *The views, opinions, and perspective of the operational customer contacts in understanding what is most important to the customer as a whole.* This can mean the perspective and needs of others in the customer organization—with whom the contract team has less or no regular contact—are not fully taken into account in their thinking of what is most important to "the customer." While perhaps having less day-to-day impact on the running and delivery of the existing contract, these people can become dominant during the recompete. They often include the solicitation team, finance teams, and senior executives whose needs and views can take precedence over those of the customer's operational team in thinking about the future form and priorities for the next contract and deciding who will run it.

- *A belief that performance, reputation, and picking a known contractor with strong existing relationships are key priorities to the customer in the recompete.* The contract team have worked hard to deliver excellent performance, build strong relationships with the customer, and gain an excellent reputation within the customer organization. These have been vital factors in the success of the contract operations to date. Surely the customer must value these highly in the recompete? Maybe, but maybe not. Other factors could be equally or more important to the customer in the recompete: the customer may be changing the breadth and specification of the contract to such a degree that performance in existing disciplines or existing relationships are only a small part of the overall requirements going forward; your competitors may have equally strong reputations built in the marketplace and be able to demonstrate equal or even better performance in equivalent disciplines and environments; your reputation within the customer may not be as widespread or as strong as you think. The customer may be willing to risk having to build new relationships if a competitor offers a compelling solution.

Before you take the assumptions of the contract team in these circumstances as true, you must fully research the customer and challenge the relative importance of what initially may seem to be the customer's priorities:

- Do you know who all the relevant customer stakeholders are, their relative impact on the recompete, and what their priorities are? (See *Idea 35*.)

- Where on the list of relative importance to the customer do the needs for things such as reputation, existing relationships, and existing/past performance lie?

- Are you sure the customer has the same perception of your performance and reputation as you do? (See *Idea 32*.)

Tendency to focus on needs, benefits, and discriminators from the existing contract rather than those going forward.

Even if your team has built up a broad and accurate understanding of the needs and priorities of the existing contract in the perception of all relevant customer influencers and decision makers (which will have been a distinct advantage in delivering the existing contract—see, for instance, *Ideas 14, 15, 16, 17,* and *19*) and have successfully delivered to these needs during the contract, these may not be the same going forward into the next contract.

There can be reluctance in the team to believe the priorities of the customer, which have been so clear during the contract, can suddenly change at the recompete. Unfortunately, this doesn't take into account the fact that the recompete, and the prospect of thinking forward for the next three, five, or more years is a catalyst for the customer to rethink. The sometimes extensive work and preparation the customer goes through in their own preparation for the recompete can bring about a radical change in their priorities for the contract and how they wish to see them met.

This reluctance to accept the changes to customer priorities can lead to overemphasis in the solution and in the proposal on priorities from the existing contract rather than the new (see *Ideas 47* and *48*). It can mean new priorities are ignored and not catered for in the new solution. It can also mean what are seen as discriminators by the recompete team are only differentiators (or worse features) by the customer when evaluating your submission.

Make sure your capture lead and the members of the recompete team who have not been involved in the contract build an objective view through their analysis of the customer's needs for the new contract and their interactions and questioning of customer contacts during the recompete preparation stage and through the whole recompete period. And from this, build an understanding of the new needs and priorities the customer has going forward. Challenge the relative importance

Section VIII Run the Recompete

of existing priorities and be prepared to move them down the priority list you are working to, or even discard them.

Another symptom of this potential problem can be using a preponderance of, or inappropriate, examples from the existing contract in the recompete proposal to prove benefits or discriminators for the new solution (again, see *Idea 48*).

Use the two related tests below to check your own balance of new versus existing in your proposal:

First list the discriminators, benefits, and differentiators you are using in your proposal in the appropriate boxes in the matrix below:

Figure VIII.3 **Balance of Discriminators, Benefits, and Differentiators Between the Past and Future**

	From the existing contract	New
Discriminators		
Benefits		
Differentiators		

If you have significantly more items in the "existing contract" column than the "new" column, you should rethink whether your solution is addressing the customer's new needs sufficiently. Even if the customer has not significantly changed their requirements and you are confident their needs have not changed radically, a proposal reliant on discriminators from the existing contract solution is unlikely to be as innovative and forward thinking as your customer would want. Are you falling into the trap of being the incumbent who offers "Business as Usual" in their recompete (see *Ideas 38* and *43*)?

As an aside, this is also an opportunity to check whether your proposal has enough discriminators and offers enough substantial customer benefits to be confident you will win. Be brutal and challenge each item; you may find you are relying on a lot of differentiators rather than having enough decisive discriminators and benefits.

Second, look at the examples and evidence you are using to support your discriminators and benefits. Again, list them in the boxes where they best fit in the matrix below:

Figure VIII.4   Balance of Evidence from the Existing Contract vs. New Evidence

	Examples and evidence taken from the existing contract	New evidence and examples
Used to support Discriminators		
Used to support Benefits		

As with the previous matrix, look at the mix of evidence you are using. While you would expect to have a strong set of evidence and examples from your existing contract, are you also using a strong set of new evidence? If not, look carefully at:

- Your solution. Is it truly bringing new thinking and innovation to the customer, or is it fundamentally the same as your existing delivery?

- New ways to document your solution. Are there examples you can use from elsewhere in your wider business, or other sources which will bring a fresh and broader feel to your solution? You do not want the customer to feel you are only relying on your existing contract experience.

Also, look carefully at the appropriateness of the evidence you are using to illustrate your solution. Just because you have a wide range of examples from your existing contract, are you attempting to use them in the wrong way or for inappropriate reasons? If so, take these inappropriate examples out of your submission and look for more focused evidence.

Tendency to use incumbency in itself as a discriminator

While your incumbency can be the source of a number of discriminators you use in your recompete and benefits you can deliver to the customer, incumbency in itself is not a discriminator. Simply assuming that their incumbency will be recognized by the customer leads some to be "lazy" in their thinking about, and writing of, their recompete document.

Section VIII   Run the Recompete

Your incumbency will have given you, among other things:

- Experience of the delivery of the existing services.
- An understanding of the customer and their requirements.
- An opportunity to reduce the risk of transition to the customer.

But it is how you use this knowledge and advantages in creating a solution that better meets the customer's needs; the clear and specific evidence you use to demonstrate how this solution fits these needs; and how you demonstrate you are the most suitable company to continue to work for the customer that should be your focus.

Bland statements, such as the examples in the table below and on the next page, will not work. All they are likely to do is make the evaluators ask about what benefit this brings to them. If you don't also clearly answer these questions, not only will you not get the marks in the recompete, you will give the customer the impression you have not put in the effort to create the best possible bid for them.

Figure VIII.5   Examples of Poor Use of Incumbency in Proposals

Example statement	What the customer will be thinking when they read this
"We have (X) years experience of delivering this service to the customer."	What has been learned in these years? What unique insights into our situation or needs have been presented in the recompete document as a result of this? How has this experience informed the solution presented—what relevant and compelling examples are shown in the recompete document? What will it mean in terms of delivering better and more robust performance than the competition over the coming period?
"Our staff are highly experienced in delivering to the customer."	Will these staff be used in the coming period? How has their experience increased their performance for us over other staff? What does this experience mean in terms of benefits for us in improved performance? Does this experience make them more expensive than the cost of staff who could do the work anyway?
"As the incumbent, we understand the customer's needs."	Have these needs been explained in the recompete document more clearly than the competitors? What has the incumbent done to meet these needs to date? How does the solution presented cater to these needs over the coming period better than the competition does?

Example statement	What the customer will be thinking when they read this
"Our solution has been successfully delivered for (X) years."	Show me how—where are the numbers or examples in the document that convince me it has been successful for us? Surely the solution has developed and improved over the past (X) years—tell me how and to what effect? But how will this solution meet the needs we have over the coming (X) years? Convince me how this success will continue to be delivered over the coming period.
"Our solution is based on the experience we have gained during the current contract."	What specific experience do you mean? How has your experience influenced the new solution? What examples can you show me of how this experience has made the solution better for us? But what about our next contract? Our needs are different, how is your experience of what you were delivering help with our new needs? Have you just repeated your present solution?

Your incumbency can be used as one of your win themes—or as part of others. But you need to be intelligent in how you use it; always use specific, relevant, and proven examples of exactly how an element of your incumbency has informed a better solution or illustrates you are a better suited supplier for the customer.

As we have said elsewhere, you must show the customer *how* your incumbency is of benefit, not just tell them that it is.

And never rely entirely on your incumbency—for the new contract, there should be other reasons why your solution is better than your competitors' and more suited to the customer's requirements.

As you plan your recompete strategy, create your storyboards, write your recompete submission, and run your reviews, always check any statement you make about your incumbency. Are you using it intelligently to clearly prove a point or benefit, or are you being lazy and simply stating it is an advantage without any evidence?

Use the Blind Proposal Test

Some customers use blind (or blinded) proposals. These stipulate that the bidders cannot use their company name anywhere in the bid. The goal is to prevent any bias the evaluators may have (positive or negative) toward or about the reputation of any of the bidders. The proposals should, in theory, then be marked entirely on the merits of the solution and price presented.

Section VIII Run the Recompete

One way to test whether you have used your incumbency intelligently is to use this test yourself in your reviews:

- Is your solution, and the evidence you have given to show why it is the best proposal, as powerful if you take out any specific reference to your company and the fact you are the present incumbent?

- Is your solution the best possible solution on its own merits?

- Do you clearly explain your understanding of the customer's strategic requirements?

- Do you show how your solution meets these requirements better than the competition?

- Does your evidence, and the examples you give to illustrate this, stand up on its own merits?

- Are your discriminators and the benefits you deliver still as clear and powerful?

If not, how can you improve the persuasiveness and clarity of your recompete and pass this test without resorting to using various versions of "because we are the incumbent?" Of course, you shouldn't erase all mention of yourself as the incumbent in your recompete (unless you are, in fact, being asked to submit a blind proposal). But this type of exercise will help you use your incumbency and all mention of it more intelligently.

> ***What is the most important thing an incumbent can do to improve their chances of winning?***
>
> *"If given the opportunity, this is what I would tell them: 'Don't assume you're going to win the recompete. Using the knowledge and experience you have acquired, respond to the bid as if it's brand new and the relationship doesn't exist, because that's how the bids will be evaluated.'"*
>
> *State Government, USA*

Idea 51: Become the Benchmark Bid

> **Idea Summary:**
>
> **What:**
>
> Use your knowledge of the customer's needs and the contract to make your proposal the benchmark the customer uses to test the validity of all other bidders' proposals against. Use real evidence from this knowledge to illustrate each of your points, and to prove why alternative solutions (i.e. your competitors') would not work as well.
>
> **Why:**
>
> By using your superior knowledge to prove your solution and becoming the benchmark bid, you ensure your customer can best understand how your proposal is the most realistic and viable. You also put doubt into the evaluators' mind about whether competitor proposals have taken the aspects you mention into account and whether they are viable solutions.

Your incumbency gives you many advantages in writing your recompete; only you have the detailed experience of:

- How the contract has worked in practice.
- All the specific quirks of the customer's requirements.
- Variations in volumes.
- The end users and their own needs and preferences.
- Customer staff and contacts and their needs and ways of working.
- Who the other stakeholders are, and the impact they have on delivery.
- The costs of the contract.
- The processes involved.
- The risks and issues the contract faces.

Your competitors will be attempting to convince the customer they also understand all these aspects of the contract and have taken them into account in their solution and pricing (and they may know more than you think). But they will never have as much detail to draw on, or examples and evidence specific to the customer and contract, to illustrate and prove their assumptions and assertions.

Use this disparity to your advantage. We have warned, in most of the ideas in this section, against overly relying on your incumbency to win the recompete, but this is an area where you can make full use of the knowledge your incumbency has given you.

Your goal should be, through using your knowledge of the customer and the contract, to show evidence of all the key aspects of why you are proposing your new solution with clear and relevant detail (always bearing in mind that you must respond to customer changes to the contract in their procurement). This will make your proposal the document the customer comes back to time and again to check whether competitors have taken these factors and details into account in their own solutions and proposals.

Ghosting or Knockdown of Your Competitors

Becoming the benchmark bid includes all the use of "ghosting" or "knocking down" your competitors' weaknesses and likely approaches and solutions that you would do on a new bid. As the incumbent, you have the benefit of knowledge built up over your existing contract to make this even more effective. Use the usual approaches you would to identify potential ghosting or knockdown opportunities in a new bid. Build on the knowledge you built up of your competitors from *Idea 39: Understand Your Competitors*. Use your knowledge advantage, not just to illustrate and verify why you have chosen your own solution in each area of the contract, but also to show why you rejected alternative solutions (i.e. those your competitors are likely to propose).

Approach this as you would win themes—linking customer key needs with elements of the solution you are knocking down—but reversing the link. You are creating "anti win themes" for competitor or alternative solutions, showing why the alternative solution would not best meet a customer requirement, strategic need, or aspect of contract delivery.

For instance, if you know there is a surge in demand on a Tuesday afternoon, this might not be clear to competitors (or even some of the evaluators marking the bids). To become the benchmark bid in this area:

1. Clearly show this surge exists using your volume knowledge from the existing contract (having checked that the circumstances of the new contract will not change the surge).

2. Show the consequences of not meeting this surge (e.g., lost sales for the customer, end user dissatisfaction, interruptions in customer production facilities, consequences for supply arrangements the following day—whatever is most important to the customer). Again, it will help if you can give quantified evidence and examples.

3. Show how your solution is designed to meet this surge in demand and how it achieves this.

4. Then show how an alternative solution (one your competitors may have put forward) was investigated by you and the apparent benefits this might have seemed to bring—for instance, lower cost.

5. Then to show why you rejected it, document how this solution would not have met the surge and the costs or consequences to the customer of this failure.

The consequences of this approach will be:

- The customer will see you have investigated a range of alternatives, not just gone directly to a particular solution, which should work in your favor in the minds of the customer by showing you have been proactive.

- As the customer evaluates competitors' solutions, they will have in mind the dangers you have confirmed regarding the alternative solutions they are proposing. They will be encouraged to question whether the competitor has thought of the issue you have illustrated. If the competitor has not adequately explained their understanding of the issue and given a strong explanation of how they will overcome it, doubt will be created in the mind of the evaluator. As a minimum, they will be asking the competitor to clarify their response; ideally they will mark this aspect of the solution down and question the realism of their price as a result.

- Your knockdowns will also clarify to the customer the risks they will be taking if they choose a competitor's solution (for more on using risk, see *Idea 54*). As each part of your solution is evaluated, these risks will add up and potentially cause those evaluators not familiar with the contract to refer to the operational customer more often to check these risks. This can give your operational customer (with whom we assume you will have a strong relationship) more influence in the decision making process, which will often be to your advantage—unless the customer is willing to take the now known risks of taking on a solution where you have clearly set out the negative consequences it entails.

Planning for Being the Benchmark Bid

There is another consequence for you of taking the benchmark bid approach—it makes your proposal longer than it would be if you were only to propose your own solution. Take this into account in storyboarding processes, timing given to writers, and in the overall proposal plan. As with many other aspects of the "Run the Recompete" stage, the better and more extensive your recompete preparations have been, the easier it will be to take this time now.

Section VIII Run the Recompete

As you plan your proposal, make sure you have in hand all the details and evidence which will help you with your arguments. Your recompete strategy (see *Idea 28*) should include the collation of these, and as you write your outline solution prior to the start of the official recompete process (see *Idea 40*), go through the alternatives and seek out the information you need to deliver compelling evidence that alternatives are inferior. Your Green Field exercise (see *Idea 38*) will also have helped test and challenge assumptions and tested alternative solutions. Your review of the information you have collated throughout the contract and during your preparations for recompete will also help you identify potential evidence for knockdowns (see *Idea 46*). Have your benchmark bid approach in mind when reviewing this information and how you can use it to best effect.

If you are still looking for the right detail, go back to the contract team and explain the arguments you are planning to put in the bid. They might be able to help if given a focus for their efforts—there will often be some aspects of the contract that, no matter how thorough your investigations, the team has not bought to your attention because they seemed insignificant without this focus.

If your customer has specified word limits to your answers you will not always be able to use this approach to its fullest extent. Pick out the two or three most impactful knockdowns and find space for these. Or if you are able, use the appendices or attachments you are often allowed with limited word responses to explain your knockdowns.

Be aware that customers may informally grumble when they first see your proposal—it will most likely be much bulkier than your competitors' (or be more megabytes in size, if submitted electronically) and they may initially see their evaluation task as now being more difficult. We have seen this in a number of post recompete customer reviews. However, this complaint is usually followed by the admission that as the evaluators read the proposal, they came to appreciate the detail and comprehensive nature of what was written, and did indeed end up using it as the benchmark against which the competitors' proposals were (albeit informally) measured.

There is one final point to make here. As you are going through the exercise of identifying the potential alternatives to your solution you will be ghosting/knocking down, are working through the apparent key customer benefits these might be argued to bring by your competitors, and are documenting the problems and risks the alternative would actually present, have an open and objective mind. If, as you work through the exercise, you identify an alternative that you find a number of apparently compelling benefits for, but are struggling to prove why it won't work, ask yourself why you aren't proposing this alternative yourself as part of your own solution.

It may be late to make the change now, but if you can see more key customer benefits to the alternative than problems, challenge yourself: why would you reject it? If you can't answer the question, then why would you expect the customer to reject it in favor of your solution?

> ***What is the most important thing an incumbent can do to improve their chances of winning?***
>
> *"Approach the bid as if it was a new client whom you really wanted to work for, because you have true value to add to the client's operation."*
>
> *Private Sector, Australia*

Idea 52: Price to Fit the Specification, Not What You Know

Idea Summary:

What:

Always price against the specification the customer has set out. Do not add in elements to your solution, or costs, because your knowledge of the contract as the incumbent indicates they will be required. If the customer does exclude vital elements, influence the customer to include them—but if this fails, do not include them in your own pricing.

Why:

As the incumbent, you have more knowledge of the contract than your competitors. However, this knowledge can work against you if you include things you "know" are needed but are not included in the customer specification. Competitors will not price for these and the customer may well pick the competitor's cheaper offer.

Your knowledge of the contract as the incumbent gives you a lot of advantages for the recompete. But it also presents some dangers. One of these is that you know too much about what it costs to deliver the contract. This might seem to be a strange statement—surely more knowledge of costs is an advantage?

Unfortunately, we have seen many recompete losses where the incumbent's knowledge of the real costs of the contract has worked against them. This usually occurs when the customer doesn't specify the requirements of the contract in their procurement to include elements the incumbent believes are necessary to deliver

Section VIII   Run the Recompete

it (effectively, safely, or to the KPI levels set). The incumbent team prices in the costs of delivering to the levels they "know" are required to meet these levels, then lose to a competitor who has not included these costs, but has stuck to the specification set by the customer.

While the losing incumbent may have the satisfaction of seeing the competitor fail or lose money as the new contract progresses, this is usually little real compensation—the contract has still been lost. Sometimes the losing incumbent sees the customer renegotiate with the winner to take into account the unspecified requirement, which only adds insult to injury. Often, however, the now previous incumbent sees neither of these things; the customer accepted the solution being delivered by the new contractor because they didn't actually need the element the contract team "knew" was required; or they knowingly accepted a lower level of delivery for the saving in cost; or the winning competitor found in their solution a way to deliver the contract without incurring the "necessary" cost.

There are rare occasions when the customer will come back to other bidders once negotiations with the preferred contractor break down due to the missing costs/delivery element, terminate the new contract early due to the failings of the winning contractor, or come back to the market next time around with a greater emphasis on quality due to poor experience during their latest contract experience. However, none of these eventualities are worth basing your pricing strategy on.

Always cost and price your solution on the specifications and instructions the customer has set in the procurement. Never include additional costs because you "know" they are required to deliver the contract.

If you believe the customer is likely to exclude from their specification elements required to deliver the contract effectively, the best time to act is during your recompete preparation stage. In the best situation, the customer will be asking you for help in drawing up some or even all of the specification for the recompete, in which case you can ensure all the elements you believe are required are included. Even if you are not directly involved, you can spend time influencing the customer (see *Idea 41*) to help them understand which elements need to be included in the procurement if they are to get the "right" level of service in the next contract.

If you still find the specification doesn't include cost elements you believe are required to deliver to the customer's needs and expectations, you still have some opportunity during the "Run the Recompete" stage to get the customer to make changes:

- You can use your coaches (see *Idea 56*), pointing out to them the consequences of the exclusions and seeing if they can influence a change in the specification. Or try to find out from them if the customer already knows the potential issues and has still excluded the element in question, accepting that they will receive a reduced service in the next contract as a result.

- You can, if the procurement process allows it, ask official questions (Clarification Questions or CQs—see *Idea 56* again). This way, you will at least have raised the question with the customer officially, and get an official response from them. There will, in many customer processes, be opportunities to ask questions "in public," where the question and customer answer will be made visible to all competitors. In these cases, your question, written correctly, will alert your competitors to the potential dangers faced and may (though this isn't guaranteed) influence them to also take these costs into account.

You can, of course, also decide to take on the test the customer has (perhaps deliberately) set: Challenge yourself to find a way of delivering the service without incurring the cost you believe initially is required. Look at alternative ways of delivering the service, perhaps going back to your Green Field exercise (see *Idea 38*) for ideas. Challenge your initial assumptions: are they based on a desire to repeat your existing contract model rather than thinking the solution through innovatively or from scratch? Often, you will eventually find a way.

Ultimately, if you don't find a better way of delivering the contract without the cost you believe is required, and you have not succeeded in influencing the customer to add to or change their specification to account for it (either through including the cost element or reducing the KPI requirements to compensate, if this is the issue), you have a choice:

- Put in a compliant bid that meets the specification set and cost and price to that specification. You may be able to put in a number of commercial caveats to protect yourself from the consequences of the poor performance you believe will result, or put in place opportunities to negotiate changes later in the process to adjust the service and price to compensate—but be clear whether these may themselves reduce your score or even make you non compliant.

- Put in a compliant bid as above, together with a "non compliant" variant bid (see *Idea 53*), which strongly argues through win themes and knockdowns with as much evidence as you can muster why this will deliver a better service for the customer. Be aware though, that customers rarely choose non compliant bids that are more expensive than the compliant versions available to them.

- Put in a bid which includes the cost elements you believe are required and, as with the variant above, put as strong a set of arguments together as possible to persuade the customer that this is necessary and the best solution for them. As you will have seen from our advice above in this idea, we don't recommend this choice; you are putting your recompete at a significant risk no matter how much you feel the improved quality or safety of your solution will compensate for the increased cost over your competitors. If you do take this chance, be sure you have exhausted all the alternatives above, have been clear in all your

Section VIII   Run the Recompete 309

recompete reviews that this is the choice you are taking, and ensure all your team (recompete, contract, and management) are aware of, and agree with, the risk you are taking.

What is the most important thing an incumbent can do to improve their chances of winning?

"*Bid against defined scope. Not what you think is wanted.*"

Federal/Central Government

Idea 53: Alternative Bids

Idea Summary:

What:

If you have the opportunity to put in an alternative bid which offers the customer more or different benefits to those required in the specification, look seriously at doing so.

Why:

As the incumbent, you should have ideas for how you could offer more variations which meet specific customer advantages. Offering these in an alternative bid gives you an opportunity to outflank your competitors.

We have already said in a number of other ideas that, as the incumbent, you should know the customer and details of the contract better than your competitors. This should mean you can identify a range of opportunities for the customer to save money, get improved performance, or otherwise have the contract delivered in a more effective way.

While, in most cases, you will include all these ideas in your main proposal, there may be situations where this is not possible. For instance, in some solicitations, the customer sets a specification or requires a particular way of answering their questions which does not allow you to offer a very different type of solution and still be compliant.

An Alternative Bid Is Additional to Your Compliant Bid

If you are convinced you can offer a better solution than the customer is asking for, don't fall into the trap some incumbents do of ignoring the customer's specification or prescriptions for answering the RFP. This could be seen by the customer as arrogant and complacent. In many situations where the evaluation of bids is tightly controlled, it could also mean your proposal is rejected as non compliant or marked down to such an extent you lose.

Even if you are convinced you can offer a better solution than you are able to describe in the core documentation, always put in a compliant bid and then, if you are able, put in an alternative bid as well.

Find Out Whether You Are Able to Put in an Alternative Bid

Some customers will state in their solicitation that you are able (sometimes even encouraged) to offer alternatives to the specified bid. Others, however, don't specifically make this clear. Some even state they won't countenance an alternative bid. If you feel you will be able to put in an alternative bid, start communicating early with the customer, preferably before the official recompete process starts. Ideally, you will want to ensure the core solicitation enables you to put in a winning and profitable proposal; but you also have the option to put in alternatives which will leverage your understanding of the customer and their needs and put in an offer giving the customer a more compelling offer that outflanks the competition if they only answer the questions and specification set in the core bid.

The customer may want you to tell them what improvements you think can be made to the solicitation to enable them to get all bidders to put in a more advantageous solution. In this case, balance the benefits you will gain from having your ideas included in the core specification (you will have influenced the specification to fit your solution, for instance) versus the disadvantage of having some of your good ideas opened up to the competition prior to the bid. In most cases, it will be better not to hold back on the customer; if you do, and then put in a better alternative offer, they will (with some justification) feel you have not been open and honest with them, which can only work against you.

What Makes a Good Alternative Bid?

An alternative bid might only offer a difference to the customer in one specific area of the contract or specification, in several, or it might be a completely different way of delivering the customer's needs. Whichever elements of the alternative bid are different, these differences must offer the customer real, specific, and quantifiable benefits which are relevant to key customer needs. An alternative bid which is just different will gain you little or no advantage.

Section VIII   Run the Recompete

Your first task, therefore, is to identify what the customer's key needs really are. If you have been keeping close to your customer over the previous contract, you will have a strong insight to their key needs and how they have changed (see, for instance, *Idea 8: Create a Contract Plan*, *Ideas 15, 16,* and *17,* and *Idea 19: Keep Your Contract Up to Date*). You should also have completed this exercise as an early part of your recompete preparations (see *Idea 33*) to understand your customer's needs over the next contract period.

Your next task is to devise and decide on what alternative offerings will meet these needs better than the customer is allowing for in their core solicitation instructions. Ideas for these may have come from earlier in your contract via ideas for added value and innovation (*Ideas 15* and *17*) you were not able to put in place during the existing contract, or perhaps from your Green Field exercise (see *Idea 38*) or other ideas you generated while putting together your solution (*Idea 40*), but were not compliant with the customer's stated bid requirements. The specifics will depend on your contract, the services, or products you deliver and the marketplace within which both you and the customer work.

Don't restrict yourself to operational or service delivery ideas within your solution:

- Commercial or financial changes to your offering might make a significant difference to the value for your customer. For instance, you may be able to:

  - Offer a significant price reduction if the customer accepts a particular risk rather than pass the burden (and therefore cost of managing or covering the potential cost of dealing with the risk if it occurs).

  - Provide better long-term value for the customer by offering a different pricing structure.

  - Reduce prices by offering a different payment mechanism—for instance, one with lower penalties for underperformance to certain levels.

  - Reduce your costs substantially if the customer is willing to accept a slightly lower level of performance (the final percentage of performance is usually the hardest and most expensive to guarantee achieving, especially as performance levels approach 100%).

  - Offer the customer a lower price for giving a longer-term contract (for instance, if this allows you to get a return on your initial investment over a longer period or gain improved terms from suppliers for longer-term commitments).

- You should also look at dependencies on customer actions which could improve the value you are able to offer them. For instance:
  - If the customer can guarantee a certain volume of demand, a reduction in peaks and troughs in demand, or more planned demand with more time to react, could you offer a lower cost or better level of service?
  - You might be able to suggest changes to customer processes which could offer both themselves and you a reduction in costs—for instance, simplifying the ordering or quality checking processes for work (see example below).
  - There may be "non-cashable" benefits you can offer the customer through your contract solution which would allow them to make substantial savings or improvements in their own organization (for instance, by reducing their own staff levels), but would require the customer to act on these benefits to get a real cash advantage (by choosing to act and reduce their staffing levels).

Submitting Your Alternative Bid

As we have said above, your alternative bid must be submitted in addition to your compliant bid, not instead. While this requires you to do additional work to complete both offers, it means you are still "covered" if your alternative is rejected with a compliant bid which will be scored. It also has an advantage, as it enables a comparison between the price and technical/quality levels offered in the compliant bid with the improved offer in the alternative bid.

Ensure the customer has clearly indicated (even if you have had to influence this preferably prior to the bid stage, or at worst, through clarification questions) that they will accept an alternative bid.

State clearly in your introduction to your compliant bid whether this is a cover letter, executive summary, or other communication (without overstating the fact or denigrating your compliant bid as inferior), that you are also submitting an alternative bid.

Clearly state at the start of your alternative bid why you are submitting it and the benefits it offers the customer over your compliant bid, where your alternative bid is non compliant to the core specification, and why this is necessary to deliver the benefits offered.

Throughout your alternative bid, ensure that you are focused on the key quantified benefits the alternatives offer the customer. If you are offering a number of options within your alternative bid, be clear whether they are all interdependent or which of the alternatives you are offering can be chosen by the customer independent of others, and which areas of the alternative could be combined in favor of areas of the compliant bid (if any). This might take the form of a matrix of

Section VIII Run the Recompete

alternatives the customer could choose. With all of these alternatives, ensure you clearly show the individual and cumulative benefits the options offer.

> **Example:**
>
> *A customer for a housing maintenance contract required in their bid contractors to follow the process below for completing work:*
>
> 1. *Housing tenant phones customer call center to register an issue.*
>
> 2. *Customer sends person to the house to see if there is an issue requiring work.*
>
> 3. *Customer informs contractor call center work is required.*
>
> 4. *Contractor sends assessor to house check work required and send a price to the customer.*
>
> 5. *Customer approves price and the work to be done.*
>
> 6. *Contractor sends worker to complete the work.*
>
> 7. *Contractor required to send assessor to check work has been completed and report to customer.*
>
> 8. *Customer sends person to the house to check work has been completed satisfactorily and contractor can therefore invoice.*
>
> *As well as being onerous on the contractor, the process took a significant amount of time to get any repair or work completed, was unsatisfactory for the tenant (five people visiting, only one of whom actually fixed the issue), and involved unneeded costs for the customer.*
>
> *The incumbent had attempted to get the process changed during the previous contract period, but as the local operational team had tight control over changes to the contract (and some vested interest in retaining the existing processes), had been unable to do so.*
>
> *In the alternative bid put forward, the incumbent suggested a significantly simplified system:*
>
> 1. *Tenant reports issue to the contractor.*
>
> 2. *Contractor sends worker to fix the problem, taking before and after photos and getting signature of tenant on satisfaction form (a complaint line was also offered for tenants, as well as a follow up satisfaction call from the contractor).*
>
> 3. *Contractor sends assessor to check 30% of calls completed.*
>
> 4. *Customer sends their own assessor to check 10% of calls completed.*

The contractor also offered an increased penalty for any work not completed to the satisfaction of the tenant and where assessors found issues with the level of work completed (i.e. too much work invoiced or quality not to standard). They also offered set prices for particular types of work—based on their knowledge of costs and typical workload mix from the previous contract.

The alternative solution offered significantly reduced time and disruption from reporting of an issue to it being fixed (increasing tenant satisfaction), reduced cost from the contractor for the work (as they needed fewer assessors) and offered the customer the opportunity to cut their operational costs (by not doubling up on a call center with the contractor, requiring fewer of their own assessors to pre and post check work). While the operational customer was unhappy with the proposed change, the senior customer decision makers (who were more financially focused and also beginning to be measured on tenant satisfaction) backed the alternative solution and the incumbent was awarded the recompete.

Idea 54: Use Risk Effectively

Idea Summary:

What:

Use your understanding of the risks of the contract and the risks of changing contractors carefully in your recompete. Analyze your customer's view of important risks and reflect this understanding in how you respond to them in your proposal. Be specific about particular, verified risks, not general about the risk to the customer of choosing a different supplier.

Why:

Customers do understand they face certain risks in choosing a new supplier. They also understand that as the incumbent, you are, in certain ways, the lowest risk choice for them in the recompete. However, you should not overplay this general advantage. Showing your detailed understanding of the risks in the contract and confirming how you will specifically reduce these risks makes the most of your advantage—and by being specific, puts potential doubt in the mind of evaluators as to whether competitors have addressed these risks.

As the incumbent, you should be the bidder presenting the lowest risk to your customer. But before we look at how best to use this in your recompete, let's look at what your customer's perception of risk is likely to be.

Your customer will see risks in the recompete. Indeed, they will see risks in outsourcing and using suppliers or contractors. Most likely, these risks will be well understood within the customer organization and they will have their own risk registers and risk management processes to ensure these risks (together with the other risks they face) are reduced and mitigated. Every customer will be different in how they perceive risk, what risks they face, those they see as important, and how they choose to deal with them. But there are likely to be some relatively common factors regarding a recompete which you should understand and react to in your proposal.

Understand the Variables

The more risk your customer sees in the recompete solicitation, and the decision they have to make as to who will be their chosen contractor, the greater your advantage is likely to be. But there are some variables you need to understand as part of your recompete planning, solution design, and presentation:

- *The customer will see less risk in a product or service they see as a commodity.* If the customer believes that your product or service is the same as many other suppliers can deliver to them and there is little relevant variation between suppliers in what the service is or how it is delivered, they will see less (if any) risk in changing supplier. But if there are few suppliers in the market and their products or services vary significantly, and they deliver in very different ways, the customer will see a greater risk in choosing the wrong option.

- *The customer will see less risk in a simple service or product versus a more complex one.* If your contract is a relatively simple one (for instance, a single service) the customer will feel they have a greater understanding of that service and will most likely see less risk involved in it than a more complex contract that, for instance, involves a range of services or products, or perhaps one involving more complex technology.

- *The customer will see less risk in a contract that is not vital to their own business.* The consequences to the customer of a contract (or contractor) not performing will lessen if it is in an area which is not vital to their own core business success and the consequences of failure on the contract are not going to be high profile for the customer. For instance, delivery of warehousing and delivery of components vital to the functioning of a manufacturer's production of its own products, where delay could stop their delivery of these products to their own customers and jeopardize their own income and reputation, would be seen as more vital than a contract to clean those same warehouses. However, a contract to clean a hospital would be seen as more vital than a cleaning contract for a warehouse, as the hospital would see greater risks in infection of patients if the contract is not delivered effectively. It isn't just the work that is done on the contract; it is the context of and for the customer that will also be important in determining the level of risk they see.

- *The customer's perception of risk will vary, depending on how much they are changing the contract.* If the customer is making few changes to the contract at the recompete, their perception of the risk on that contract will be lower. However, if they are making significant changes, for instance changing the specification, number of services, geography, measurement, payment mechanism, or use of new technology, they will see a bigger risk. At the same time you as the incumbent will potentially suffer, as your experience with the existing contract (if the new contract is very different) may not be seen as relevant to the changed new contract.

- *The customer's perception of risk will vary with their own experience.* If the customer feels they have a lot of experience in managing a contract for a service or product, the level of risk they see will be reduced. A different point also fits under this heading; if the customer has had a very bad experience with a contract for this or a related service, their perception of risk will be increased.

- *The customer's perception of risks will vary with how well they believe they have been able to mitigate them.* If the customer believes, through how they have specified or otherwise organized the contract, they have mitigated the risks they have, their perception of the risk in which supplier they choose will be reduced. For instance, if the customer feels they have specified every aspect of the contract well, they may feel their risk is reduced. Or if they have put in significant penalties for non delivery, they may feel their risk has been reduced, as the contractor will be more motivated to deliver. Alternatively, the customer may feel they can reduce their risk by creating a framework contract or one with a number of similar Lots so they have a number of suppliers for the service—if one fails or fails to perform, the customer has backup suppliers they can use.

- *The customer's appetite for risk will vary, depending on the importance or level of other benefits they feel they will receive.* If one bidder offers the customer a significant advantage over and above all the other competitors, this might impact their attitude toward the other risks they are evaluating. What and how much this significant advantage offers will vary from customer to customer and contract to contract. But a customer may accept a number of risks from a bidder offering a major advantage to them in an important area which they would not do if that advantage was not offered. Sometimes (but by no means always), this advantage is a significantly reduced price—however, a very low price can be seen as a risk in itself by the customer. They will need to be assured the price is realistic and the bidder will really be able to deliver the service for that price (and will not either go bankrupt, withdraw from the contract, or negotiate the price up later) if they are to accept a particularly low price bid.

Section VIII Run the Recompete

> ■ *Different people in the customer organization will perceive risks differently.* While the customer as a whole may have set out the risks of the contract and recompete decision in a single risk register and all the key decision makers and influencers will be aware of these risks, different people or groups may perceive each risk in a different way. For instance, operational staff will most likely be more impacted by a contractor delivering lower levels of quality and will have to manage the impact more directly—so will perhaps see any risks of quality services not being delivered as more important than the customer finance team do.

Know Which Risks Are Important to the Customer

The variables above are general. You also need to understand all the specific risks the customer sees in your contract and in the decision they will be making at the recompete. You should already have a good idea from your experience of the risks involved in the contract and the general risks the customer has in their organization and business (see, for instance, *Idea 9: Help the Customer Manage Risk*). But don't take this accumulated knowledge for granted. The customer is now looking at the next contract; you need to understand the risks they see going forward. Gaining this understanding should be part of your capture effort during your recompete preparations. Set out the risks in a simple table. Remember, it is the customer's perception of the risk that is important, not yours.

Figure VIII.6   Customer Perception of Risk Table

Risk	Impact/Detail	Level of risk			Customer contact risk most important
		Low	Medium	High	
Risk 1					
Risk 2					
Risk 3					
etc.					

Once you have an understanding of the customer's perceptions of the risks involved in the contract and recompete decision, check these against your own strengths and weaknesses and your planned solution. If there are risks you feel the customer has missed or are underestimating (or if relevant, overestimating), influencing this perception becomes part of your capture plan (see *Idea 41*). You can now focus on building into your solution and proposal ways you will be able to show the customer you are the bidder who will best reduce or eliminate these risks.

Demonstrating You Are the Lowest Risk Option

Even if you know the customer sees you as the lowest risk option, you must still prove this to them in your proposal. Some of your advantages will be:

- You understand the risks of the contract (bearing in mind, as we have said, that the new contract may be different in places) and can show, with specific examples, how you have managed these over the previous contract period.

- You should generally be able to show that your risk management methodology and approach has worked on the existing contract. Even if the risks for the new contract change, being able to demonstrate you have used your risk management processes successfully on the existing contract will give the customer confidence you take risk seriously, have a robust process that works, and therefore can use this proven methodology for the next contract to address the new risks it presents.

- The customer knows your culture and approach to delivery. Assuming they approve of this, they will be keen to keep this for the next contract rather than risk a new supplier who may not have a compatible approach. This could also apply to your contract leadership team and your staff, assuming you will be keeping these the same for the next contract.

- You will have learned the problems and issues the contract (and, potentially, the customer) presents (see *Idea 49*) and should be able to demonstrate you have learned from these. This learning should be reflected in your new solution and you should show clearly in your proposal where and how this is the case.

- As you already have an infrastructure delivering the existing contract, you don't need to start from scratch for the new contract. If they won, any other contractor would need to set this infrastructure up, mobilize ready for Day One of the new contract, and get a handover from you as the incumbent in order to do so. The risk of choosing you is therefore less—as the incumbent, you face fewer risks in transitioning to the new contract delivery solution (see *Idea 57: Transition Plan*).

- You may also have embedded infrastructure in the contract or with the customer. This could be "soft" infrastructure, such as shared processes for risk management or other areas (see *Idea 10: Aligning to the Customer*), or it could be "hard" assets such as a software system developed specifically for the contract which the customer uses, a database of end user activity you have developed which is integral to the delivery of the contract, existing offices (possibly shared with the customer), machinery or equipment already in use on the contract and paid for that could still be used on the new contract, or a range of other assets. Make sure you have identified all of these and can use their presence as part of your recompete.

Some customers include sections in bids that specifically ask bidders to identify the risks they see for the future contract and transition. Some will even list specific risks and ask bidders to show how they will manage and minimize or eradicate the risks listed. This is an ideal opportunity for you to go into detail as to how you will be able to do so. Always give evidence and examples in these sections of how you have, and will, reduce the risks. As with other aspects of your bid, your incumbency itself is not a sufficient reason for risk to be reduced; you need to show the customer how with specifics.

If the customer doesn't ask specifically about risk, we don't recommend you create your own section. Instead, place specific aspects where you will reduce risk within other relevant parts of your bid; for instance, within each delivery section. Your goal is to demonstrate (again through showing, not just telling) how you are the bidder who will be the lowest risk option (particularly regarding those risks you have identified as the customer's main worries). Unless you are ghosting or knocking down specific aspects of competitor solutions where you can demonstrate the specific risks of these alternative approaches, your emphasis should be on how you will reduce risk rather than simple attacks on competitors as generally being riskier options.

Finally, while reduced risk may form one (or the specifics of particular ways you will reduce risk may form some) of the discriminators and benefits you will provide the customer in the next contract, don't lean too heavily on this aspect of your proposal. Focus mainly on the positive benefits of your new solution and delivery. If the main thrust of your proposal is to tell the customer that it is too risky to choose an alternative supplier, but are not offering a compelling and innovative solution informed by your experience and focused on meeting their needs over the next contract at the best price, you may find they are willing to take the risk of choosing a supplier that does.

> ***What do you expect of an incumbent that is different from new bidders?***
>
> *"Three things: 1. More innovation and ideas for improvement to the organizations core services by simple improvement in service provision. 2. A value for money counter specification where the incumbent feels the client has over specified and can therefore save money. 3. On a like for like basis a reduced cost from previous contract because all lessons have been learned."*
>
> *Private Sector, Australia*

Idea 55: Staff

> **Idea Summary:**
>
> **What:**
>
> Be aware of the regulations regarding transfer of staff to the winning bidder. Use these regulations to your advantage. Where transfer regulations do not apply, be aware that your staff costs may have increased during the contract and be higher than the market and competitors' staff costs. Understand how you can reduce your staff costs to these levels.
>
> **Why:**
>
> Where staff transfer to the winning bidder, showing how you are the best employer who can get the most from your staff will be the differentiating factor between you and your competition, rather than the skills of the staff themselves. Using this advantage will help you win. However, when staff do not transfer and competitors can bring in their own staff, if you do not take action to reduce potentially higher staff costs which have built up during the contract, you will be more expensive than your competitors and risk losing the contract.

As the incumbent, your staff should be a strength for you as you write your proposal. But be aware of the issues you can face based on the rules and regulations in place in different countries and how these impact what your approach should be to staff in your recompete.

In the United States, your competitors are not obliged to use your staff, or offer staff the same level of terms and conditions you are presently paying. In this situation, your incumbency can be a cost disadvantage. Over the period of the contract, staff will have become more experienced and are likely to have had pay increases. This could mean they are more experienced than the customer's specification requires. Their salaries may also be higher than the prevailing labor market conditions. Your competitors will offer the customer staff with the specified skills and experience, not more. They will also offer staff the present going rates for that level of experience. This could mean, unless you objectively review your staff capabilities and costs against the specification, you are costing in staff with too high a level of experience, who are too highly paid in comparison. For any contract where staff constitute a significant percent of the overall costs, this will potentially cost you the contract.

Section VIII   Run the Recompete

In your recompete preparations, identify the relevant level of capabilities the customer requires, and the present (and likely future) market rate for staff with this capability and experience. If you find the experience levels the customer will be asking for are lower than your staff, you could try to influence the customer to increase the levels they specify. Alternatively, you may need to start cycling through, or "greening," your present staff over the period before the recompete, bringing in staff with lower experience and skill levels—and lower costs—akin to what will be required on the new contract. Or make it clear to your staff that their salary levels will be an issue in winning the new contract and seeking to get them to accept terms at market levels for the new contract.

As with all other aspects of your present delivery (see *Idea 45*), don't assume the customer already knows your staff and their backgrounds, skills, and capabilities—even if they do. Make sure you write about your staff in your proposal as if the customer has never met them and you are a new bidder. Describe their resumés fully, update and include them (even if the customer already has them on file) if the customer asks for them. Describe in detail your proposed management structure and working methods, even if they are not changing.

However, if you hold contracts you are recompeting in other countries, be aware that the regulations, and therefore your approach, can be very different. For instance, if you are recompeting a contract in countries across Europe where variations of the Acquired Rights Directive are in place—such as in the UK where Transfer of Undertaking Protection of Employment (TUPE) regulations apply—staff will normally transfer to whoever wins the new contract, together with their historical terms and conditions. As the incumbent, you will be required to communicate to all bidders (usually, but not always, via the customer) how many staff would transfer, together with their salaries and other relevant terms and conditions (how long they have worked on the contract, holiday entitlement, etc.). Think carefully how you will respond to this. Of course, the information about staff must be accurate, but there are a number of questions to ask yourself:

- *Has the customer made it clear that TUPE does apply?* The customer may have some reason for believing that TUPE does not apply, or they may be working under a misunderstanding as to whether it does or doesn't. If you believe TUPE does apply, you must make sure you communicate this to the customer and get their acceptance (and official communication to yourself and all competitors) that TUPE will, in fact, apply. If this is not made clear, competitors may price without costing in for the full cost of the staff they will inherit, potentially putting in a low cost and winning based on this. You are then left with the contract staff but no contract, and either a legal wrangle after the event with the competitor and customer, or the cost of making these staff redundant—and the morale-sapping situation of a group of your staff in uncertain situations regarding their jobs, or no jobs at all.

- *Will we put all staff onto the list?* Usually, the answer will be yes. The TUPE list tells competitors how many staff they will be required to take on if they win, and at what cost. Even if they plan to reduce the number of staff used on the contract, they will still need to cost for staff redundancy entitlements. Even though it may seem to be giving the competitor an advantage in giving them an understanding of your present staffing numbers and costs, you want the competition to price in the full cost of this. If you don't put in the full staff numbers and costs, competitors may price lower than they otherwise would—and potentially win because of this. It will be little compensation for you that they may then lose money as they have to take on greater costs than budgeted for—because you will have lost the contract.

- *Are there staff we want to retain even if we lose?* You may have some specialist staff or managers you want to retain in the business even if you lose the contract. If so, think carefully how you will communicate this in the bid and through TUPE. If these staff are on the contract, not including them in TUPE data could mean their posts are not costed for by competitors. If you intend to use them on the next contract, you would be costing their posts in—giving you a price disadvantage. However, if they are staff the customer see as particularly vital to the contract and you will not transfer them across if you lose, you must be clear in your proposal that any competitor would not have these staff working for them—only you would be able to offer their services.

    Of course, you also need to make sure the staff you want to keep stay with you. If your competitors realize these particular staff members are important to the customer, they may well already be offering them jobs on better terms and conditions in an attempt to take them away from you!

Always involve your company's HR or Personnel team in TUPE decisions and information. The regulations can be strict in terms of what is and isn't allowed. Don't fall foul of these and find you end up either with a challenge from a competitor after the recompete or staff putting in claims if they feel the process has not been followed.

The fact that your staff would transfer to whoever wins the contract means your proposal should not include bland statements such as "Our staff are highly experienced in delivering quality work on the existing contract" or variations on this theme. For a start, the next contract might have different requirements. But more importantly, with TUPE, these experienced staff will transfer to any of your competitors who win, so the customer will retain this experience and high quality delivery no matter who they choose as the winner. Instead focus on what you have done (and will continue to do) to build this experience and quality delivery:

Section VIII   Run the Recompete

- Do you regularly train staff to enhance their skills or build and maintain relevant qualifications or accreditations?

- Do you develop your staff so they have opportunities for progression either within the contract or across the business?

- Do your management culture and processes involve and motivate staff in bringing forward new ideas for improvements in delivery and successfully implementing them?

- Do your company management style and HR processes mean you have motivated staff and a low turnover so staff stay with you longer and build experience (and your recruitment costs are lower)?

- Do you use staff satisfaction surveys or other methods to test how staff are feeling about their work and your company—and do you act on the results?

- Does the way you arrange staff terms and conditions (for instance, giving options for how staff members organize their overall package to pick between levels of holiday, pension, healthcare, etc.) enable you to attract excellent staff in the first place?

- Do your recruitment processes mean you employ the best possible staff for the job?

If you do any of these, or other activities which you can claim and verify have led to benefits for the customer—and will continue to do so for the next contract; use these as evidence of why your staff are delivering high quality work for the customer and how this high quality will continue to improve over the coming contract if the customer picks you as the winner. Staff testimonials or case studies of how members of staff have progressed while working on the contract add color to this type of win theme. Training Needs Analysis matrices, lists of courses staff have attended, accreditations they have received, churn figures, etc., can also add evidence showing you are the reason for staff capabilities and performance—which could all be lost if the customer picks a competitor not offering these methods of staff motivation, involvement, and improvement.

Don't create a solution that takes the existing staff levels as fixed without challenging this assumption. You may be able to deliver the contract with fewer staff, and you should take an objective view about the number of staff you need. If you need to cut staff, ensure you include redundancy costs into your pricing.

The flip side to this is keeping your staff motivated during the recompete period. It will be a time of uncertainty for them, and you need to ensure they maintain their productivity during the run up to the recompete. Assure them you are taking the recompete seriously and have prepared well for the work. It is likely they will have seen the recompete team around the contract and perhaps have been involved in some of the contract review sessions. Keep staff informed that you are working hard on the recompete, but maintain information security about the details of your recompete solution and win themes, etc.; you never know to whom the competition may be talking.

What is the most important thing an incumbent can do to improve their chances of winning?

> *"Assume nothing—act as if we do not know anything about them and provide all information: tailor the response to capture their experience of working with us."*
>
> Local Government

Idea 56: Asking Questions

Idea Summary:

What:

Use the official routes for asking the customer questions about the procurement to your advantage during the recompete to ensure your competitors are aware of all the costs and risks inherent in the contract.

Why:

If competitors are not aware of the costs and risks inherent in the contract, they may under cost and under price their bids and win against you even if they subsequently cannot profitably deliver against their price. By asking questions with a clear purpose in mind, you level the playing field to ensure all your competitors price the contract fully.

While you will hopefully have the opportunity for informal conversations with customer contacts during the recompete process (see *Idea 41*), this may, in some circumstances, be restricted. Particularly in government solicitations, there are rules the customer is required to follow to ensure there is a level playing field between the incumbent and all competitors in the amount of information and access they have to the customer and information and feedback about the process.

Most customers will have a formal process to allow bidders to put questions to the customer regarding the procurement process, instructions given in the documentation, and specification set. These clarification questions asked by each bidder, and the answers given, will be made available to all bidders—again to ensure equality of information between competitors. In the private sector, processes can vary, but there are usually opportunities to ask questions to clarify the terms, specification, etc., being published.

As the incumbent, you can use this process beyond simply finding out what you need to know.

Informing the Competition of Costs and Risks Not in the Procurement Documentation

Hopefully, you will have been able to influence the customer prior to the recompete documentation being published (see *Idea 41*) to include information about all the costs bidders need to take into account when pricing for the contract, as well as those risks requiring further costs or price increases to cover the potential consequences.

As the incumbent, you have unique insight into these details and there is a real danger you cost in for elements of delivery, costs, or risks not included in the customer's specification or information passed to your competitors. Your competitors will be bidding strictly against the published requirements. By adding in costs not included in the published requirement (even if you know they are required to deliver the contract), you will be higher priced than the competition and run the real risk of losing (see *Idea 53*).

You will want to keep knowledge of some contract details and risks to yourself, to differentiate your bid from the competition, showing the customer your unique insight into their needs (see *Ideas 50, 51* and *54*). But anything which could cause you to increase your costs where the competition will not is a disadvantage and a danger.

Use the customer's clarification questions process to highlight these costs and risks by asking the customer whether they need be taken into account in bidders' solutions. As you read through the documentation (see *Idea 44*), make a note of any areas where the customer has not exposed costs or risks, or not specified necessary tasks you feel will incur costs. List these out and decide how you will approach them. You may decide some are best asked early in the process, while others may be more effective if asked later. Carefully work out the wording of each question to make it clear what the potential issue is without putting the question in such a way as to annoy the customer. Even if the answer coming from the customer is unclear, the question itself may alert the competitors to an additional cost.

Ideally, the customer will clarify that the cost is indeed required. In the event they specifically say the cost is not required, you can either ask the question in a different way—perhaps pointing out the consequence of not including the item in question, or revise your own solution to not include the cost. Even if you know this would make the contract difficult to deliver as the customer requests, you have at least highlighted the issue and can potentially use this in negotiations later.

Using clarification questions is always a balance between getting changes made to the requirement and giving away information you have, exposing your plans, or indeed exposing your lack of knowledge. As the incumbent, you might feel you should avoid using the official questions route, as it exposes more than it helps you. But if there are elements of the future contract or procurement you are either unclear of, or feel the need to ensure all bidders are aware of, it can be a useful tool that you shouldn't ignore.

What aspects of incumbents' proposals have been particularly good?
"Ability to price due to practical knowledge of requirements."

Public Sector, UK

Idea 57: Transition Plans

Idea Summary:

What:

Put in as full a transition plan for how you will move to the new contract solution as you would for a new contract.

Why:

There is a danger that, as the incumbent, you assume the benefits you have in the transition (lower risk, less cost, and faster to transition) are obvious to the customer. Even if they are, you must still clearly show how you will make the transition in order to illustrate these advantages.

As the incumbent, you should be in the best position to transition to the delivery of the new contract. You are already running the contract and will not need to hand over to a third party to take on the contract delivery. You will be in a position to potentially start moving toward the new way of working before the start of the new contract (you may already have done so prior to the recompete—see *Idea 42: Prepare the Contract*).

Section VIII Run the Recompete

Your transition should offer the customer:

- Lower risk than competitors' transitions.
- Faster transition to the new solution.
- Lower cost than the competition.

However, this doesn't mean you should take the transition for granted, either internally or in your proposal. If you do, you will lose many of the advantages in the customer's evaluation of the proposal. Even if they believe you will offer the lowest risk, lowest cost, and fastest transition, you still need to show exactly how you will achieve this; to show the customer you are taking the recompete seriously, that you have robust plans in place, and to get the marks allocated to this element of the evaluation. Your competitors will be well aware of the benefit you have in transition and will be putting forward their own plans and assurances they will be able to provide the customer with a seamless, risk free transition to their own solution. You do have an advantage, but don't take it for granted.

As with all other aspects of your proposal, you won't get the marks from evaluators unless you write into your bid the detail of what you will do, why this is the best way to do things, and the benefits this gives the customer—to the specifications and instructions given in the procurement documents—just as you would for a new bid.

Put as much effort into your transition planning as you would for a new bid, and ensure you identify all the specific advantages of this plan for the customer matched against their key needs.

You already have an example of your ability to successfully mobilize and transform a contract for the customer—you did it when you first started the contract. Look back at your last implementation process (see the section on Day One, Mobilize, and Transform). What went well? What lessons did you learn? Which of these can you show have influenced your transition plan this time?

Don't assume the transition will be simple. How much has the customer changed the specification of the contract and how much have you changed your solution? Even if the changes are minor (and as you will have picked up from the ideas earlier in the guide, there should be changes in your solution, otherwise you risk losing the contract), ensure you have a clear and detailed plan in your proposal to show how you will deliver these changes.

Identify the resources and people you will need for the transition to your new solution. While you have the advantage of having the existing contract team in place, don't rely on them to make the transition alone. They might be able to take a significant role in the transition, but show the customer you will take the transition seriously by bringing in the additional staff to support the team, as you would for a new contract (keeping a clear eye on the costs of this). After all, the contract team will still need to maintain a high level of contract delivery throughout the change.

What do you expect of an incumbent that is different from new bidders?

"The incumbent should have the inside track on the positives and, if any, the negatives regarding the contract, as well as knowing that if successful, less mobilization period is required so a sensible adjustment to the contract price will be expected."

Private Sector, UK

Section IX

Win the Recompete

Figure IX.1 The Contract Lifecycle Win the Recompete Stage

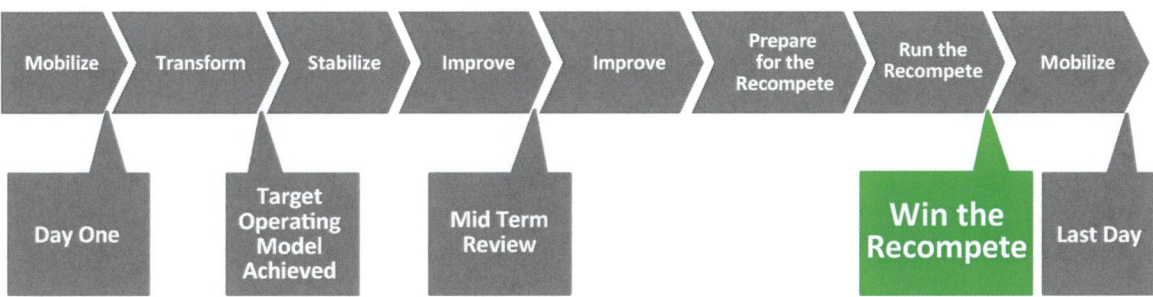

This is not so much a stage in your contract lifecycle as an event. You have won your recompete—congratulations!

But this isn't the end of a process; it is another step in a continuation of your business relationship with your customer. You now have the opportunity to keep building your relationship with your customer and enjoy the turnover and profits from their business for another contract period.

We have a small number of final ideas in this and the following sections to ensure you maintain the focus on your customer you have shown to date.

What aspects of incumbents' proposals have been particularly good?

"I've seen incumbents take advantage of their existing position to put in a tender specifically focused around our needs taking into account geographic, political, cultural, and operational factors. Where incumbents put in the same effort as they did to win the business first time round, they tend to be able to put together a better submission than non-incumbents."

Local Government, UK

Idea 58: Celebrate

> **Idea Summary:**
>
> **What:**
>
> Celebrate your recompete win as you would a new contract win.
>
> **Why:**
>
> Properly celebrating your recompete win sends a message to your customer, and internally, that you take the recompete seriously and were not taking the win for granted. The celebration also indicates the change from the old contract to the new and the changes about to take place to transition to the new solution.

When most businesses win a new contract, they celebrate. The form this celebration takes varies from business to business, but typically all those involved in the bid get some congratulations (and possibly a bonus) from senior management, there is an announcement in internal company newsletters or other staff communications, and the win is publicized in news releases or even investor communications.

Often, this doesn't happen to the same extent with recompete wins. Unlike with new business wins where the sense is often of excitement, with a recompete, the sense is either one of relief or simply a confirmation of expectations—of course the contract was going to be retained!

This is a wasted opportunity and can send the wrong message. As much effort should have gone into a recompete win as a new win. And the benefit you gain from retaining business is just as great in terms of future profit, turnover, and cash as a new win. We would argue that retaining existing business is, in some ways, even more valuable than new contract wins. It maintains a solid base on which to add new business, promotes a sense in the business that you have long-term prospects, and shows your staff, customers, and investors you can deliver what you promise on contracts and build long-term relationships with customers.

So make sure you celebrate and publicize your recompete win just as you would a new contract win. Ask your customer to add their quotes to your publicity about why they chose you and how they are happy to be continuing to do business with you—just as you would for a new contract win. Not only will this help build a culture in your business where retention of business is as important as winning new business, getting your customer involved and aware of your celebrations of the recompete win will confirm to them you appreciate their custom. (Yes, you are already starting to think ahead to your next recompete by showing you don't take their decision for granted!)

Section X

Mobilize and Last Day

Figure X.1   The Contract Lifecycle Mobilize Stage

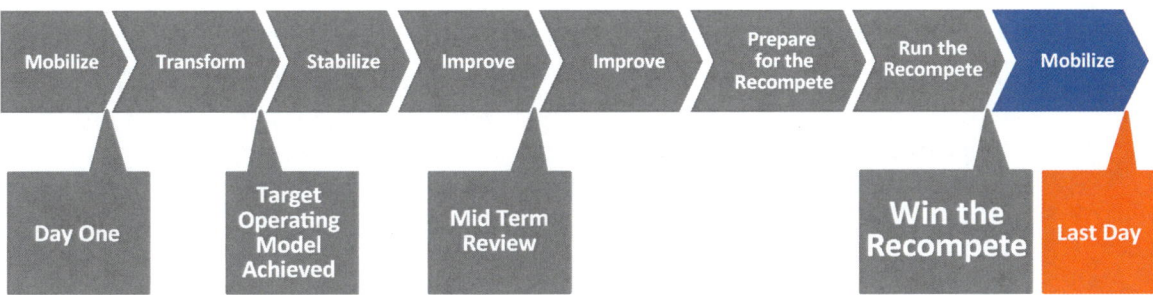

The final stage of the contract lifecycle (before you start the process again) is to mobilize the changed contract to put your new solution in place.

Idea 59: Take the Transition to Your New Solution Seriously

Idea Summary:

What:

Take the transition to the new contract seriously by following proper governance processes and resourcing the change properly, rather than relying entirely on the contract team to make the change.

Why:

By taking the transition seriously, you will make the changes to the new solution successfully and on time, starting the new contract on a positive note—this will count when you get to your next recompete.

As we said in *Idea 57: Transition Plan,* you should have created a full plan for your transition to your new solution and put in place a team to make the transition happen. Now that you have won the recompete, there can be a tendency to fall back into a comfort zone—your existing contract is working well, you have cleared the hurdle of the recompete, and there is less pressure to make all the changes you promised in your recompete at the pace you may have promised. If your solution involved cutting staff, this can be more difficult for the contract team than when you first won the contract. These are, after all, people who have worked with you for the previous contract period and have perhaps contributed significantly to the contract delivery over that time.

However, you are now starting a new contract cycle and will again face a recompete in the future. What you do now will continue to have an impression on the customer when you get to that recompete.

Put in the effort and resources to mobilize your new contract solution to the time, budget, and specification set, just as you would for a new contract. In your proposal, you should have set out the advantages you have as the incumbent in completing this faster, at less cost, and with less risk than you competitors. Show the customer this was indeed the case. Use the advantages of already being in place to start the new way of delivering as soon as you can, so the customer sees the benefits as early as possible and feel justified in, and happy with, the decision they made to retain you as their chosen supplier. Make sure you have everything in place for Day One of the new contract.

And on the last day of the existing contract, mark the change from the old to the new with your staff. Even if you have had to release some of the existing staff as part of the change in solution, thank everyone for their efforts over the previous contract and make it clear the new contract is just that—new.

Make sure everyone understands the changes you are putting in place—why these were needed to win the recompete and are required to keep the contract relevant and delivering the best possible service for the customer into the future. Explain what the changes mean to staff and what your expectations are moving forward; they should all see the new contract as being different from the last one and be ready and willing to make these changes.

What aspects of incumbents' proposals have been particularly good?

"*A willingness to be flexible to our needs and priorities, to their business, to our strategic directions that may diverge from previous or current business relationship.*"

State Government, USA

Idea 60: Start Planning for the Next Recompete

Idea Summary:

What:

As you prepare for your new contract, start the whole process of preparing for your next recompete again.

Why:

You have won this recompete, but there is no certainty you will win the next one if you don't take all the positive actions from the start of this contract period as you did for the last.

We said in the introduction to the guide that one of the common pieces of advice given to incumbents is to start planning for the recompete on Day One of the contract. As you approach Day One of your new contract, that advice is just as true and relevant.

Even though you have been the incumbent for the previous contract, go back to the start of the guide and put into action all the ideas from the first section. Make sure you ask the customer why you won, capture all the information you collated over the previous contract, and make sure you have it filed safely, ready to use for your next recompete. Set up a new Recompete File for the new contract period, and get ready to put in place Day One Impact Measures to build on the work from *Idea 59* to show to your key stakeholders that things are changing and will be different and even better over the next contract period.

Good luck with your next contract and with your next recompete—you should be in a great position to win it and continue expanding your relationship and business with your customer for even longer.

What aspects of incumbents' proposals have been particularly good?

"They treat the bid as if it were the first time bidding for the organization and put the effort to show they are the best fit."

State Government, USA

Index

Bold page numbers refer to definitions.

A

achievement review, 178
Acquired Rights Directives, 321
action map, 78–79
added value, 97, **105,** 105–112, 109fV.6
ad hoc added value, 107–108
alternative bid use, 309–314
annual contract published review, **120,** 120–124
Association of Proposal Management Professionals (APMP), 265

B

benchmark bid, **302,** 302–306
benchmarking performance, 85–87, 87fV.2
benefits. *See* key customer benefits
Best Value contract approach, 257, 258
blind proposal test use, 300–301
bottom up added value, **106,** 106–107
budget expectations, customer, 218

C

CAI/SISCo, x, xii
capture expert role, 166
change
    changes made review, 175
    contract incorporation of, 124–132
    customer changes and future needs, 124–132, 134–138, 200–201, 271–272

change *(continued)*
    customer involvement in, 124–132, 134–138, 271–272
    customer specifications and questions, 15–16
    existing contract, 261–264, 263fVII.14
    formalizing, 136–137
    impacts of, 130
    mechanisms for, 134–138
    process delivery of, 137–138
    recording, 137
    response to, 130–131, 132
    reviews, 129–130, 175
    routes use, 134–138
    See also customer changing needs review
clarification question use, 15–16, 93–95, 270–271, 324–326
competition "ghosting," 291, **303,** 303–304, 305
competitor analysis, 188–189, 218–219, **234,** 234–238, 244
complacency, 234, 267–269, 273–275, 331–332
    See also incumbency
continuous improvement, 97, **113,** 113–116
contract
    best value approach, 257, 258
    capabilities, 111–112
    change incorporation into, 124–132
    change routes use, 134–138
    contract team preparation, 168–170
    customer changes and future needs, 124–132, 134–138, 200–201, 271–272

contract *(continued)*
  customer specifications and questions, 15–16, 93–95, 270–271, 324–325
  data analysis use, 278–281
  existing contract changes, 261–264, 263fVII.14
  extensions management, 160–163, 251
  measurement, 36–38, 71–74, 176–177, 278
  mid term review, **145,** 145–152, 145fVI.1
  performance information use, **23,** 23–26, 25fII.3, 73, 278
  performance review, 149, 176–177
  performance session timing, 186–187
  price reductions, 162–163
  profitability, 18, 148–149
  published annual review of, **120,** 120–124
  recompete review preparation, 173–180
  renegotiations management, 161–162
  update, 124–132
  vulnerability analysis, 205–209, 207–208fVII.8
  workability issues of, 259–260
contract, measurement, 176–177
contract capabilities added value, **105,** 109fV.6, 111–112
contract issues resolution, 36–38, 132–134, 177–178, 214–216, 288–291
Contract Lifecycle, **3,** 3–10, 5fI.1, 6–8fI.2
contract management team, 151, 168–170, 179, 181, 247
Contract Plan, **42,** 42–57
  contents of, 45–46
  creation of, 42–44
  key steps in, 50–57, 55fIV.2
  limitations and potential objections to, 46–50
  use, 257–258
Contract Review, **173,** 173–180
  achievement review, 178
  added value, **105,** 108–112, 109fV.6
  changes made review, 175
  information sources and use, 179–180

Contract Review *(continued)*
  issue resolution review, 36–38, 132–134, 177–178, 214–216, 288–291
  key processes review, 178–179, 286–287
  original implementation review, 174–175
  original procurement and bid review, 174
  performance review, 149, 176–177
  published, **120,** 120–124
  work volumes review, 175–176
contract team preparation, 169
contract update, 124–132
contract vulnerability analysis, 205–209, 207–208fVII.8
Corporate Responsibility (CR) initiatives, 66–68
cost reduction, staff, 168, 320–324, 332
CRM (Customer Relationship Management) software, 142–143
customer
  added value, **105,** 105–112, 109fV.6
  annual review involvement of, 123
  budget expectations, 218
  changing needs review, 126, 131–132, 134–138, 197–204, 202fVII.5, 203fVII.6, 204fVII.7, 271–272
  contract change routes, 134–138
  contract specifications and questions, 15–16, 93–95, 270–271, 324–326
  decision makers, 209–214, 212fVII.9, 213fVII.10, 261
  drivers and pressures on, 99–105, 100fV.3, 103fV.4, 104fV.5
  flexibility, 17
  future needs, 187–188, 240–241, 241VII.11, 271–272, 285–288, 333
  innovation introduction and, 119–120
  involvement in change of, 124–132, 134–138, 271–272
  mid term review involvement of, 149, 152
  needs misperceptions, 234–235, 294–300
  perception of change goals, 251–255, 253fVII.12, 255fVII.13

customer *(continued)*
   perception of risk by, 317, 317fVIII.6
   performance measurement discussions with, 76, 82
   performance problem resolution and, 36–38, 132–134, 177–178, 214–216, 288–291
   perspective focus of, 282–284
   priorities review, 74–83
   procurement timetable and recompete preparation timing, 156–160, 157fVII.2
   published requirements review, 270–272
   recompete decision makers' preferences and priorities, 209–214, 212fVII.9, 213fVII.10
   relationship and trust building, 138–144, **192**, 192–195, 215–216, 329
   risk perceptions, 59, 277–278, 281, 317, 317fVIII.6
   risk vs. reward allocation, 222–224
   specifications and questions, 15–16, 93–95, 270–271, 324–326
   status and needs information use, 277–278, 281
   value adding for, **105**, 105–112, 109fV.6
   view of your winning bid, 13–18
customer, influencing, **249**, 249–261
   benefits alignment, 260–261, 292–301, **293**, 296–297, 297fVIII.3, 298fVIII.4
   contract extension goal, 160–163, 251
   contract workability and, 259–260
   customer's perception change goal, 251–255, 253fVII.12, 255fVII.13
   decision makers involvement, 209–214, 212fVII.9, 213fVII.10, 261
   outcome goals, 73, 250–260
   recompete avoidance goal, 250–251
   recompete composition influence goal, 255–258
customer changing needs review
   contract changes and future needs, 124–132, 134–138, 200–201, 271–272

customer changing needs review *(continued)*
   customer contacts interview, 201, 204
   findings collation, 197–204, 202, 202fVII.5, 203fVII.6
   internal changes and drivers review, 126, 200–201
   likely changes list use, 203–204, 204fVII.7
   market change review, 126–128, 199
   social change review, 126–128
   solution building, 204, **238–239**, 238–248
   supply side market review, 126, 199–200
customer recompete team review session, 184–185
Customer Relationship Management (CRM) software, 142–143
customer's process alignment, 66–68, **68**
customer's procurement timetable and, 156–160, 157fVII.2
customer's risks, understanding, 59, 277–278, 281
customer team session, 184–185

D

data analysis use, 278–281
Day One Impact Measures, 11–12, 11fII.1, **29**, 29–32, 31fII.5
debtors and creditors, 149
decision makers, customer, 209–214, 212fVII.9, 213fVII.10, 261
   See also key stakeholders
Dependency Register, 64–65
Discriminators, Differentiators, Benefits, and Win Themes, **292**, 292–301
   benefits, 260–261, 292–301, **293**, 296–297, 297fVIII.3, 298fVIII.4
   blind proposal test use, 300–301
   customer's needs misperceptions, 234–235, 294–300, 299–300fVIII.5
   differentiators, 292–301, **293**, 297fVIII.3
   discriminators, 282, **292**, 292–301, 297fVIII.3, 298fVIII.4

Discriminators, Differentiators, Benefits, and Win Themes *(continued)*
  existing contract focus, 296–297, 297fVIII.3, 298fVIII.4
  feature, **293**, 293–294, 296–297
  matrix, 293, 293fVIII.2
  win themes, 189–190, 190fVII.4, 282, 292–301, **293**
drivers and pressures, customer, 99–105, 100fV.3, 103fV.4, 104fV.5, 126, 200–201

E

end user satisfaction measurement, **88**, 88–105
  action plan creation, 96
  added value, 97
  common themes in, 98–99
  continuous improvement, 97
  innovation, 98
  input measures, 72, 91–93
  key user identification, **88**, 89–91
  process testing, 95–96
  results analysis and presentation, 96
  survey, 93–95, 97
  targeting improvement, 99–105, 100fV.3, 103fV.4, 104fV.5
  See also key stakeholders
end users' perspective in solution creation, 244–245
error acknowledgment and resolution, 36–38, 132–134, 177–178, 214–216, 288–291
executive summary use, 283
existing contract
  changes, 261–264, 263fVII.14, 296–297, 297fVIII.3, 298fVIII.4
  existing performance measures review, 76
  experience consideration, 246
  focus of, 261–264, 263fVII.14, 296–297, 297fVIII.3, 298fVIII.4
  information use, **276**, 276–277
  issues resolution, 36–38, 132–134, 177–178, 214–216, 288–291
  process information use, 277
  See also incumbency
extensions management, 160–163, 251

F

false assumptions hazard, 273–275
financial and commercial options in solution creation, 247–248
formalizing change, 136–137
future planning, 187–188, 240–241, 241VII.11, 271–272, 285–288, 333

G

"ghosting" your competition, 291, **303**, 303–304, 305
Green Field solution, **226**, 226–233
  development, 231–232
  ground up creation of, 228
  incorporation in solution creation, 243
  information collation, 229–230
  key steps in, 226–228
  recompete team and, 230–231, 233

H

Historical Register, 64

I

impact measurement and demonstration, 80–81
impacts of change, 130
importance vs. cost matrix, 104, 104fV.5
improvement, continuous, 97, **113**, 113–116
improvement targeting, 99–105, 100fV.3, 103fV.4, 104fV.5
Improve Stage, **69–71**, 69–144, 69fV.1
  annual review publication, **120**, 120–124
  continuous improvement, 97, **113**, 113–116
  contract change routes use, 134–138
  contract update, 124–132
  customer added value, **105**, 105–112, 109fV.6
  customer priorities review, 74–83
  customer relationship and trust building, 138–144, **192**, 192–195, 215–216, 329

Index

Improve Stage *(continued)*
  end user satisfaction measurement, **88,** 88–105
  importance vs. cost matrix, 104, 104fV.5
  innovation, 98, **116–117,** 116–120, 245
  measurement balance, 83–85
  measurement benchmarks, 85–87, 87fV.2
  problem resolution, 36–38, 132–134, 177–178, 214–216, 288–291
  See also performance measurement
incumbency
  advantages of, 266, 301, 314–315, 318–319
  cost disadvantages of, 168, 320–324, 332
  misperceptions of, 234–235, 294–300, 299–300fVIII.5
  use and misuse of, 283–284, 286, 287, 292, 298–300, 299–300fVIII.5
  See also complacency
independent review use, 275
information capture, 11–12, 11fII.1, **13,** 13–18, 23–26, 25fII.3, 179–180
information collating and formatting, 229–230, **276,** 276–281
initial aiming point, 50
innovation, 98, **116–117,** 116–120, 245
input performance measurement, 72, 91–93
Issues Register, 64
issues resolution, 36–38, 132–134, 177–178, 214–216, 288–291

K

key customer benefits, 260–261, 292–301, **293,** 296–297, 297fVIII.3, 298fVIII.4
Key Performance Indicators (KPI), 24–25, 36, 74
key processes connection and review, 178–179, 286–287
key risk factors, contract, 205–209, 207–208fVII.8

key stakeholders, 74–83, **88,** 89–91, 195–197, 201, 204, 261
  See also decision makers, customer
knockdown of your competition, 291, **303,** 303–304, 305

L

lessons learned profile use, 289–290
LPTA (Lowest Price Technically Available) approach, 220, 256–257, 258

M

management and staff mid term review, 149–150
management team, contract, 151, 168–170, 179, 181, 247
market changes, 126–128, 199
measurement, contract, 36–38, 71–74, 278
measurement balance, 83–85
measurement benchmarks, 85–87, 87fV.2
measuring performance. *See* performance measurement
mechanisms for change, 134–138
meetings, relationships building through, 142, 143–144
Mid Term Review, **145,** 145–152, 145fVI.1, 147
misperceptions, customer needs, 234–235, 294–300, 299–300fVIII.5
Mobilization and Last Day Stage, 331–333, 331fX.1
Mobilize, Day One, and Transform Stages of the Contract Lifecycle, 11–32
  bid pricing, 14–15
  customer flexibility, 17
  day one impact measures, 11–12, 11fII.1, **29,** 29–32, 31fII.5
  importance of, 12
  previous performance information capture, **23,** 23–26, 25fII.3, 73, 278
  profitability management, 18, 148–149
  promises register, 11–12, 11fII.1, **19,** 19–23, 20fII.2

Mobilize, Day One, and Transform Stages of the Contract Lifecycle *(continued)*
    recompete file creation, **26,** 26–28, 27–28fII.4
    winning bid information capture, 13–18
    See also questions and specifications, customer

N

needs information use, 187–188, 277–278, 281, 285–288, 333
needs misperceptions, customer, 234–235, 294–300
new bid approach to the recompete, 267–269

O

original implementation review, 174–175
original procurement and bid review, 174
outcome performance measurement, 73, 250–260
output performance measurement, 72

P

partners and supply chain review solution creation, 247
past performance levels use, 286
perception of change goals, customer, 251–255, 253fVII.12, 255fVII.13
perception of risk, customer, 317, 317fVIII.6
performance
    previous performance information capture, **23,** 23–26, 25fII.3, 73, 278
    problem resolution, 36–38, 132–134, 177–178, 214–216, 288–291
performance improvement. *See* Improve Stage
performance measurement
    action map, 78–79
    balance, 83–85
    benchmarks, 85–87, 87fV.2

performance measurement *(continued)*
    continuous improvement link, 97, **113,** 113–116
    contract measurement, 36–38, 71–74, 176–177, 278
    discussions, 76, 82
    existing performance measures review, 76
    impact measurement and demonstration, 80–81
    importance of, 71–72
    input, 72
    key steps in, 75–82
    outcome measures, 73
    output, 72
    priorities review, 74–83
    See also Improve Stage
performance review, contract, 149, 176–177
performance session timing, contract, 186–187
presentation professionalism, 275
previous performance information, **23,** 23–26, 25fII.3, 73, 278
price reductions, 162–163
pricing to win
    competitors, understanding your, 188–189, 218–219, **234,** 234–238, 244
    contract price reductions, 162–163
    customer budget expectations, 218
    customer's risk vs. reward allocation, 222–224
    price factor weighting, 219–220
    the Price To Win approach, **217,** 217–225
    pricing against the specification, **306,** 306–309
    pricing options review, 220–222
    summary, 225
    won contracts pricing review, 14–15
Priorities Matrix, 54–55, 55fIV.2
priorities review, customer, 74–83
problem resolution, 36–38, 132–134, 177–178, 214–216, 288–291
process alignment, **66,** 66–68
process delivery of change, 137–138

Index

processes and systems mid term review, 149
process testing, 95–96
procurement timetable and recompete preparation timing, 156–160, 157fVII.2
professionalism, presentation, 275
profitability, contract, 18, 148–149
Promises Register, 11–12, 11fII.1, **19,** 19–23, 20fII.2
publicity, 330
published contract review, **120,** 120–124
published requirements review, 270–272

Q

questions and specifications, customer, 15–16, 93–95, 270–271, 324–326

R

RAID (Risks, Assumptions, Issues, and Dependencies) registers, 37, 58–59, 62–65
Rebid Centre, ix
Rebidding Solutions Ltd., ix
recompete, running. *See* Run the Recompete Stage
recompete avoidance goal, 250–251
recompete composition influence goal, 255–258
recompete decision makers' preferences and priorities, 209–214, 212fVII.9, 213fVII.10
Recompete File, 11–12, 11fII.1, **26,** 26–28, 27–28fII.4, 150
The Recompete Guide, 1–4
recompete preparation, **153–155,** 153–264
    competitor analysis, 188–189, 218–219, **234,** 234–238, 244
    contract extensions management, 160–163, 251
    contract price reductions and, 162–163
    contract renegotiations management and, 161–162
    contract team preparation, 168–170

recompete preparation *(continued)*
    contract vulnerability analysis, 205–209, 207–208fVII.8
    customer, influencing, **249,** 249–261, 253fVII.12, 255fVII.13
    customer changing needs review, 126, 131–132, 197–204, 202fVII.5, 203fVII.6, 204fVII.7
    customer recompete decision makers, 209–214, 212fVII.9, 213fVII.10, 261
    customer relationship reinvigoration, 138–144, **192,** 192–195, 215–216, 329
    customer's procurement timetable and, 156–160, 157fVII.2
    existing contract change priorities, 261–264, 263fVII.14, 296–297, 297fVIII.3, 298fVIII.4
    existing contract issues resolution, 36–38, 132–134, 177–178, 214–216, 288–291
    green field solution, **226,** 226–233
    recompete strategy preparation and implementation, 170–172
    stakeholder relationship research, 195–197
    timing of, 155–160, 161
    workshop, **180,** 180–191
    See also Mid Term Review; pricing to win; solution creation
Recompete Preparation Workshop, **180,** 180–191
    agenda, 181–191
    competitors session, 188–189
    contract performance session, 186–187
    customer future needs session, 187–188
    customer team session, 184–185
    introduction, 182
    key actions, 191
    output and actions, 191
    recompete timetable, 182–184, 183fVII.3
    SWOT session, 189, 234–238
    win themes session, 189–190, 190fVII.4
recompete review preparation, 173–180

recompete strategy, **170,** 170–172
  See also recompete preparation; Run the Recompete Stage
recompete team, 163–170, 230–231, 233
recompete timetable, 182–184, 183fVII.3
recompete victory celebration, 329–330, 329fIX.1
recompete workshop, contract team role in, 169
recording change, 137
redundancy, staff, 168, 320–324, 332
regulations, staff transfer, 320–324
relationship building, 138–144, **192,** 192–195, 215–216, 329
renegotiations management, 161–162
response to change, 130–131, 132
results analysis and presentation, 96
risk management, **58,** 58–66, 314–319
  advantage of incumbency in, 266, 301, 314–315, 318–319
  caveats, 61
  customer perception of risk, 317, 317fVIII.6
  key steps in, 60–61
  RAID register use, 37, 58–59, 62–65
  risk *versus* reward allocation, 222–224
  understanding the customer's risks, 59, 277–278, 281
  variables, understanding the effect of, 315–317
Risk Register, 37, 58–59, 62–65
Roadmap to BD Success Series, x–xii
Run the Recompete Stage, **265–267,** 265–328, 265fVIII.1
  alternative bid use, 309–314
  becoming the benchmark bid, **302,** 302–306
  clarification question use, 324–326
  complacency, warning signs of, 267–269
  contract data analysis use, 278–281
  contract performance information use, **23,** 23–26, 25fII.3, 73, 278
  customer changes and future needs, 126, 131–132, 134–138, 197–204, 202fVII.5, 203fVII.6, 204fVII.7, 271–272

Run the Recompete Stage *(continued)*
  customer specifications and questions, 15–16, 93–95, 270–271, 324–326
  customer's perspective focus of, 282–284
  effective risk use, 314–319
  error acknowledgment and resolution, 36–38, 132–134, 177–178, 214–216, 288–291
  executive summary use, 283
  existing contract information use, **276,** 276–277
  false assumptions hazard, 273–275
  future orientation of, 285–288, 333
  "ghosting" your competition, 291, **303,** 303–304, 305
  independent review use, 275
  information collating and formatting, 229–230, **276,** 276–281
  key processes connection use, 178–179, 286–287
  needs information use, 187–188, 277–278, 281, 285–288, 333
  new bid approach to, 267–269
  past performance levels quotations, 286
  presentation professionalism, 275
  pricing to fit the specification, **306,** 306–309
  published requirements review, 270–272
  review use, 284
  staff cost reduction, 168, 320–324, 332
  storyboard use, 283
  transition planning, 320–324, 326–328, 331–332
  See also Discriminators, Differentiators, Benefits, and Win Themes

S

senior management, mid term review involvement of, 151
social changes, 126–128
solution creation, 204, **238–239,** 238–248
  competitor's approach considerations in, 188–189, 218–219, **234,** 234–238, 244
  contract staff ideas in, 247

Index

solution creation *(continued)*
   customer needs consideration in, 187–188, 240–241, 241VII.11, 271–272, 285–288, 333
   end users' perspective in, 244–245
   existing contract experience consideration in, 246
   existing contract focus, 261–264, 263fVII.14, 296–297, 297fVIII.3, 298fVIII.4
   financial and commercial options in, 247–248
   green field solution incorporation in, 243
   innovations and process changes in, 98, **116–117,** 116–120, 245
   partners and supply chain review, 247
   transformation and implementation, 248
   work specifications changes in, 241–243
specifications and questions, customer, 15–16, 93–95, 270–271, 324–326
Stabilize Stage, **41–42,** 41–68, 41fIV.1
   contract plan, **42,** 42–57
   customer process alignment, **66,** 66–68
   priorities matrix, 54–55, 55fIV.2
   risk management, **58,** 58–66
staff
   mid term review involvement of, 151, 152
   redundancy, 168, 320–324, 332
   transfer regulations, 320–324
stakeholders, key, **88**
   priorities and performance measurement, 74–83, 89–91, 195–197, 201, 204, 261
   relationship research, 195–197
   See also decision makers, customer
status and needs information use, 277–278
storyboard use, 283
Strengths, Weaknesses, Opportunities, and Threats (SWOT), 189, 234–238
supply side changes, 126, 199–200

T

Target Operating Model (TOM) review, 33–40, 33fII.1, **34**
Thacker, Nigel, ix
transfer of staff regulations, 320–324
Transfer of Undertaking Protection of Employment (TUPE), 321–322
Transform. *See* Mobilize, Day One, and Transform Stages of the Contract Lifecycle
transformation and implementation in solution creation, 248
transition planning, 320–324, 326–328, 331–332
trust building, 138–144, **192,** 192–195, 215–216, 329
TUPE (Transfer of Undertaking Protection of Employment), 321–322

U

under performance, analysis and correction of, 36–38, 132–134, 177–178, 188–291, 214–216

V

value adding, **105,** 105–112, 109fV.6
variables, understanding the effect of, 315–317
victory celebration, 329–330
vulnerability analysis, contract, 205–209, 207–208fVII.8

W

winning bid information capture, 13–18
win themes, 189–190, 190fVII.4, 282, 292–301, **293**
Win the Recompete Stage, 329–330, 329fIX.1
won contracts pricing review, 14–15
workability issues, 259–260
work specifications changes in solution creation, 241–243
work volumes review, 175–176

Made in United States
Orlando, FL
06 March 2024

44443772R00201